THE PHENOMENOLOGY OF MORAL EXPERIENCE

Maurice Mandelbaum

THE PHENOMENOLOGY OF MORAL EXPERIENCE

The Johns Hopkins Press
Baltimore and London

TO

WOLFGANG KÖHLER

MANUFACTURED IN THE UNITED STATES OF AMERICA

THE JOHNS HOPKINS PRESS, BALTIMORE, MARYLAND 21218
THE JOHNS HOPKINS PRESS LTD., LONDON

STANDARD BOOK NUMBER 8018-1095-7

Originally published, 1955
Johns Hopkins Paperbacks edition, 1969

PREFACE TO THE PAPERBACK EDITION

The present work stands apart from many of the issues which, during the past two decades, have engrossed those who have written the books most widely known in recent Anglo-American ethical theory. It does so because it did not arise out of concern with moral discourse and the logic of moral argumentation but out of an interest in the characteristic nature of moral experience. In seeking to analyze the structure of that experience, and the types of judgment to which it gives rise, my analysis took as its point of departure an attempt to sift the claims of three different traditions: that of British moral philosophy from the eighteenth century through the first third of the present century; that of the phenomenological movement in Germany; and, in addition, the naturalistic, psychologically oriented theories of value which, on the whole, were characteristic of American philosophy in the first half of this century. My attempt to find a way through the conflicting claims of these traditions met with some measure of gratifying response. However, the tenets which I attempted to establish may perhaps meet with greater approval now.

That there is some reason to expect that they may, follows from these considerations. First, there is a growing acquaintance in this country with the phenomenological movement; furthermore, the points of contact between that movement and what has come to be called "philosophical psychology" should by now have become obvious. Second, there would seem to be affinities between the principles concerning the validity of moral judgments which are here suggested and more recent, influential discussions of "the moral point of view" and of the role of the principle of generalization in ethics. Third, it may be the case that ethical theories need no longer present epistemological credentials, and be judged noncontagious, before the analyses which they offer are considered in terms of the problems with which these analyses are actually concerned.

The point of greatest divergence between my own approach and that which has recently come to dominate Anglo-American ethical theory may be stated as follows. I do not find it plausible to assume that the problems of meta-ethics can be adequately discussed without first examining with considerable care, and with reference to a wide variety of data, the characteristic features of those judgments on conduct and character which are generally recognized to be instances of moral judgment. In the current literature, however, this has not appeared to be a matter of great concern. In the various attempts to formulate noncognitivist theories, for example, one generally finds few references to the actual situations in which moral judgments are made, and little or no effort is expended on showing that there is a good fit between the data of moral experience and the models chosen to elucidate those data. This study, on the other hand, seeks to analyze moral experience; it is hoped that, because of this fact, some of its conclusions may not be irrelevant to more recent discussions of meta-ethical issues.

M. M.

PREFACE

THE FOLLOWING STUDIES may appear to constitute an anomaly among present discussions of the problems of ethics. During the past decades most philosophers have been prone to approach the issues of ethical theory through logical and epistemological analyses. On the other hand, there have been a few philosophers, and a considerable number of social scientists, who have attempted to derive an ethical theory from their interpretations of psychological or sociological facts. Because of prior commitments, neither group has, I believe, examined the full range of moral experience with sufficient care.

In the first of the studies which follows I have attempted to show the necessity for grounding any ethical theory upon a phenomenological analysis of moral experience. In the remaining five studies I have attempted to analyze the nature of that experience and of the moral controversies to which it gives rise. In making these analyses I have consciously sought to avoid prejudging any of the issues of ethical theory by the introduction of epistemological, psychological, or sociological hypotheses. What I have sought to render is a faithful description of the most significant features of various types of moral experience, and of that which all possess in common.

The results of these analyses are not, in my opinion, devoid of import for ethical theory. Not only can they serve as a basis for testing the adequacy of alternative theories, but they also directly suggest certain significant conclusions. The conclusions to which I believe them to give rise are such as to lend very powerful support to the basic contention of those recent moralists who have attacked the utilitarian tradition. However, unlike the majority of these moralists, I should be unwilling to hold that the data of moral experience suggest that rightness is a "non-natural" property of actions, or that judgments of rightness and wrongness are apriori in character. In the language of current technical distinctions, I believe that the ethical theory which is most consonant with the facts of moral experience would be classifiable as a naturalistic and (in Sidgwick's sense) a perceptional form of deontological theory. To those acquainted with both the rationalists and the empiricists among the British moral theorists of the eighteenth century, and who find some degree of force and subtlety in the arguments of both schools, such a view should not appear too implausible to merit consideration. However, its defense against alternative theories would demand broadening the scope of the present inquiry to include certain strictly epistemological and psychological topics. To an examination of these problems I hope soon to return.

Among the writers on ethics who have perhaps influenced me more than others I should mention Butler, Sidgwick, Scheler, and Ross. But I have also received invaluable aid from the following friends who have discussed the problems of ethics with me, and who have been kind enough to examine my manuscript at various stages in its history: Richard B. Brandt, Roderick Firth, William Frankena, Herbert Spiegelberg, Charles L. Stevenson, and (at a time long past) the late Karl F. Duncker.

I am deeply obligated to the John Simon Guggenheim Memorial Foundation for a fellowship which was granted me to pursue these studies. I wish also to express my debt to the administrations and to my colleagues of the faculties of Dartmouth College and Swarthmore College for their friendship and for the assistance which they have given me in many ways.

To my wife I wish to express my heartfelt thanks for all of her help, without which I should almost surely have failed to complete these studies. And to Wolfgang Köhler I am indebted not only for many ideas (which the reader will easily discern), but for his friendship, and what it has meant to me, over many years.

M. M.

CONTENTS

CHAPTER

1

THE PROBLEM OF METHOD

In spite of the admirable clarity and rigor of many contemporary British and American studies in ethical theory one cannot easily escape the conviction that they have been confined to a narrow enclave within what was once thought to be the province of ethics. In my opinion, such a narrowing dates from the turn of the present century.

Perhaps the most significant factor which has led to this limitation of the scope of ethics has been the attempt to draw a sharp distinction between normative and descriptive disciplines. Among most contemporary philosophers it now passes for an obvious truth that ethics is not to be regarded as having a descriptive or explanatory function; it is held that its task, being normative, is to deal not with "what is" but with "what ought to be." However, it has been insufficiently noted that this distinction between normative and descriptive disciplines has been espoused only in the last decades; in its present form it can scarcely be said to have been current before Sidgwick.[1]

To be sure, the distinction between descriptive and normative *statements* is by no means new. For example, in the eighteenth century, Hume was not alone in noting it. However, neither Hume nor his contemporaries held that a distinction between these two types of statements in any way precluded ethical inquiry from investigating problems which concerned matters of fact. For them such matters of fact were not merely of peripheral interest: Butler and Price, no less than Hume and Smith, apparently believed that some of the central problems of ethics could only be solved on the basis of adequate descriptive and explanatory inquiries. If these moralists (and many others) are not to be considered as hopelessly confused, the distinction between normative and descriptive statements, and the existence of "normative problems," does not entail that one should attempt to define the province of ethics by means of a distinction between normative and descriptive *disciplines.*

What, then, has led to the current assumption that ethics must be defined in such a way as to exclude descriptive and explanatory inquiries from the field of its competence? Doubtless, the cruder mistakes of certain "scientific" theories of morals have played their part. In addition, however, there have been two powerful tendencies in recent philosophic thought which have supported the belief that ethical inquiry can be freed of the obligation to investigate matters of fact. The first (which is the one of lesser importance so far as British and American philosophy are concerned) was the general revolt against "scientism" in the closing years of the last century. The attempt to draw a distinction between scientific explanation and other modes of knowing made it plausible to hold that the proper method for ethical inquiry was a method different from that which the sciences followed. From this conviction it was but a short step to the further and more radical assumption that it was possible to divorce normative questions from whatever answers to factual problems were proposed by the sciences.

The second tendency was the growth of "analytic philosophy." There were two points at which this movement lent plausibility to the dichotomy between descriptive and normative disciplines. In the first place, once the dominant problem for philosophy became the clarifying analysis of meanings and of controversies concerning meanings, the distinction between normative and descriptive *statements* led to the view that the discipline of ethics had for its primary task the analysis of the meanings and implications of normative statements. In the second place, since a philosophic analysis of meanings was believed to be independent of any causal, explanatory inquiries, the analysis of normative statements was believed to constitute a self-contained and self-sufficient discipline. The upshot of the analytic method was, then, to confine attention to *what* moral judgments assert, and interest was focussed upon the basic normative terms contained in these assertions. Thus, for a time, ethical theories tended to concentrate upon the tasks of discussing the meanings of various normative terms, of analyzing the connections between these terms, and of applying the implications of these findings to the question of whether there is a universally valid standard for conduct. This program (even when it dealt with the more specific content of moral assertions, and did not confine itself to discussions of the most general normative terms) limited ethical inquiry. Excluded from ethics "proper" was any consideration of the conditions under which moral judgments were made, or of the characteristics of man which were responsible for such judgments.[2] In brief, the primary problems of ethics came to be regarded as problems which concerned the language used in describing moral experiences, rather than problems arising out of the need to analyze that experience itself. It was this willingness to deal with moral experience through its reflection in language which made it possible to utilize the distinction between normative and non-normative statements for the purpose of segregating those problems which are normative from those which are "merely" descriptive.[3]

Strangely enough, despite the widespread acceptance of the thesis that ethics is a normative discipline, and that the solution of its problems can proceed independently of investigations of matters of fact, little has been said concerning the question of what constitutes an adequate method for such a discipline. Objection has been raised to past attempts to make ethics dependent upon metaphysics, upon sociology, or upon psychology, for such attempts would of course break down the distinction between normative and descriptive disciplines. However, those who have been most insistent and most thorough in their objections have often failed to provide any positive statement concerning the method which a self-contained normative ethics can follow. Where we find such statements, they are not as carefully formulated nor as systematically defended as one would presumably have a right to expect them to be.

I shall not attempt to make up for this deficiency. Instead, I wish to examine the problem of method in a form which is applicable to all ethical theories, and not merely to those theories which have antecedently restricted the scope of ethics by accepting the current dichotomy of normative and descriptive disciplines. In the wider context of the history of ethical thought it is possible to distinguish at least five general types of approach. These I shall characterize as the metaphysical, the psychological, the sociological, and two forms of a phenomenological approach. It is with the first three, and with one form of the phenomenological, that Section *i* of this chapter will be concerned.

i.

OF THE FIVE APPROACHES to ethical theory which I find it useful to distinguish, no two need be mutually exclusive. In fact, every ethical theory naturally tends to use first one and then another in obtaining a solution to its problems. Yet, what constitute its problems will in some measure depend upon which of these approaches, or orientations, it originally adopts. It is therefore of importance to consider the advantages and disadvantages which each holds when taken as a basic method for ethics.

1. The metaphysical approach to ethics seeks to discover the nature of a *summum bonum* or of a standard for moral obligation through recourse to a consideration of the ultimate nature of reality. In this it has often been allied with a system of moral beliefs which claim divine sanction. However, a system of moral beliefs is not an ethical *theory*: what is called "theological ethics" is, in the terminology here used, merely one relatively pure type of metaphysical theory of ethics. Like other instances of the metaphysical approach, a system of morals founded on divine sanction, and guaranteed validity by it, seeks to derive the standard of value and of human obligation from the ultimate nature of reality.

The temper of contemporary thought in the western world has tended to obliterate most traces of the metaphysical approach, but the examples of Plato and later Christian thought, and the names of Spinoza, Clarke, Hegel, Bradley, and Green testify to the influence which it has had. And if we examine the thought of others, for example, of Aristotle, or the Epicureans, or Kant, we find that at critical points in their systems they too have been influenced in their manner of posing ethical problems by the use of a metaphysical approach.

What underlies this approach is the belief that if we are fully to understand the nature and significance of any of man's characteristics we must first understand the nature of man, and that such an understanding necessarily involves a consideration of the ultimate order of which man is a part. Not being content to assert that moral phenomena have their metaphysical implications, those who follow the metaphysical approach believe that the sole means by which an ethical theory may be validated is to start from the whole and deduce from its nature what the standard of moral action must be.[4]

All such attempts have of late been attacked on strictly theoretical grounds. It has been argued that to derive a standard of value or obligation from any facts of existence, however unique, is to confuse "what is" with "what ought to be." Let ultimate reality be what it will (so the argument runs), we may still meaningfully ask "Is it really good?" To this attack there is, I believe, an adequate answer. No matter where we start, we must in the end reconcile our conceptions of value and of obligation with what we conceive to be true of the world. In specific instances our normative judgments may unhappily come into conflict with actuality, but we inveterately believe (as the normative senses of the term "nature" constantly recall) that what is good and what is morally obligatory have their foundations in the underlying properties of being. Only the most violent diremption enables us even to suppose that reality and value are antagonistically related. This common belief may spring from the fact that our conception of "reality" is itself normatively determined, or (as I think) from the fact that we prize that which strikes us as being real—not sham, illusion, mere artifice, or appearance—*because* it is real. In either case it is fallacious to argue that the metaphysical approach to ethics is guilty of error in coupling what is ultimately real with what is ultimately valuable.

The error in the metaphysical approach is, in my opinion, a quite different one.

No system of ethics can be validated merely by showing that it is entailed by the nature of ultimate reality. If the system which the metaphysician deduces is not consonant with the judgments of value and obligation which men actually make, no amount of argument will convince us that the system is valid and its metaphysical basis true. Of course, some judgments of value and obligation may be claimed to be false, but the falsity of these will be connected with the truth of others which, independently of the system, we are willing to accept. Thus, it is possible to claim that the metaphysical approach to ethical theory is not self-sufficient: the validity of a metaphysical ethics must be tested through an appeal to what one is willing to acknowledge to be an enlightened moral consciousness. Every such system therefore also involves one form of what I shall term the phenomenological approach.

If it is possible to unite a careful, unbiased investigation of the data of man's moral consciousness with a metaphysical approach, some advantages may accrue to those who follow the metaphysical method. I do not seek to deny that such a possibility exists; however, it has rarely, if ever, been actualized. Those who adopt the metaphysical approach are concerned to deduce, and thus validate, only those judgments of value and obligation which they find to be ultimately justifiable. Consequently, their examination of men's moral judgments is permeated by an initial distinction between the enlightened and the unenlightened moral consciousness. To draw such a distinction at the outset of inquiry is, as I shall later show,[5] to commit a methodological error. It is for this reason that (whatever its other advantages may be) I find it imprudent to adopt the metaphysical approach.

2. The psychological approach, considered merely as method, has something in common with the metaphysical approach: both seek to ground their interpretations of judgments of value and obligation in a more general theory than could be provided by an examination of these judgments themselves. In the one case the more general theory which is employed is an empirical psychology, in the other it is a metaphysics. However, the fundamental aims of the two approaches are different. The metaphysical approach is concerned to deduce a standard for conduct from the metaphysical truths which it accepts. The psychological approach does not focus its primary attention upon whether there is or is not such a standard, but seeks to understand moral phenomena in psychological terms. The questions which it raises relate to either or both of the following problems: (a) why men make the moral judgments which they do, and (b) what light is thrown on what is called "moral conduct"

by a knowledge of the general nature of human motivation. Some theories which have used a psychological approach have placed more emphasis upon one of these questions than upon the other,[6] but it is characteristic of a psychological approach that it should assume that when these questions have been answered one need merely follow out the implications of the answers in order to have solved the basic problems of ethics. At the heart of these basic problems is the problem of whether there is a universally valid standard for conduct, and (if there is) what its nature may be.[7] Thus, the psychological approach, unlike the metaphysical approach, does not usually define the task of an ethical theory in terms of the discovery of a standard for conduct; it deals with this problem indirectly, through the conclusions it has drawn regarding the psychological basis of moral judgments and of moral conduct.

In weighing the advantages and the disadvantages of the psychological approach, it will be well first to examine the assumption that if one were to give both a psychological explanation of moral judgments and an account of the springs of what is denominated as "moral conduct," one would be in a position to solve the main problems of ethics. After examining this question—which reduces to the question of the relevance of a psychological inquiry to a solution of questions which concern normative issues—we shall be in a better position to assess the promise which a psychological approach may hold.

The attack on the view that a psychological inquiry may solve the problems of ethics can come from either of two sources. There will be those who would admit that a knowledge of the nature of man is the basis on which these problems must be solved, but who would deny that empirical psychology can ever ascertain his true nature. Such an attack, which is characteristic of most who today incline toward the metaphysical approach, raises issues which can not possibly be treated within the scope of this study.[8] However, the second source of attack raises what has already appeared as the central methodological question posed by recent discussions of ethics: to what extent, if at all, can descriptive and explanatory studies solve problems in ethical theory? This second attack on the psychological approach would deny that either a psychological explanation of moral judgments or a psychological inquiry into motivation would entail any conclusions for ethics, since the latter is a normative, and not a descriptive or explanatory discipline.

I think it possible to show, within a very brief compass, that such a charge is not consistent with modes of argument frequently employed by those recent moralists who seek to uphold the dichotomy between normative and descriptive disciplines. In the first place, they have in fact often considered the question of the springs of "moral conduct" to be a question relevant to normative inquiry. If they had not done so they could not claim (as they almost universally do) that if the doctrine of psychological hedonism were true, the term "ought" would lose all meaning; nor could they claim (as some do) that if any form of psychological determinism were true, the same conclusion would follow. Those who have made such claims, or who find any force in them, can scarcely at the same time hold that an investigation of the springs of what is termed "moral conduct" entails no conclusions for the traditional normative problems of ethics. In the second place, it is equally clear that they have not actually divorced the question of why men make moral judgments from the question of whether there is or is not a universally valid standard for conduct. If the psychology of these judgments were really irrelevant to a consideration of this normative question, those who attempt to deal with the latter would not have felt themselves forced to debate whether the source of moral judgments can be said to lie in "feelings" or in "reason." Furthermore, it is impossible to trace out all of the similarities (if such there be) between moral assertions and assertions which concern mathematical relationships (or which concern the "natural" properties of objects) unless one is willing to examine the sources of these various types of assertion; yet those who draw a sharp distinction between normative and descriptive problems are by no means unwilling to discuss the question of whether such similarities exist, nor are they unwilling to draw inferences on the basis of their findings. We may therefore say that, in practice, both the question of the springs of moral conduct and the question of the sources of moral judgments are tacitly acknowledged to be relevant to ethics even by those who seek to separate normative from descriptive disciplines.

Within the wider context of traditional ethical thought this recognition has often been more explicit, and it will be well to single out for attention at least three points at which moral inquiry is intimately connected with general psychological theory.

In the first place, the question of whether value or obligation are engendered by man, or whether in some sense they are independent of him, and he is merely responsive to them, is an important problem of ethics. However, this question is inextricably bound up with the question of what "faculty" in man is responsible for his moral judgments. It is, for example, often thought that if "feeling" is responsible, the first alternative must be true, and that if "reason" is responsible, the latter must be true. Such is not, of course, the case.[9] However, as the traditional discussions show, the question of what constitutes the faculty of moral judgment is not a question which is merely ancillary to the question of whether values and obligations are dependent upon man or are independent of him: one cannot *defend* either side of the latter question without committing oneself to a theory of moral "cognition." Such a theory is inescapably concerned with the problems of human psychology.

In the second place, all ethical theories will have to cope with the fact that there either are, or that there seem to be, errors among moral judgments. As is shown by the traditional discussions of the deleterious effects of self-interest and of the sentiments, the attempt to account for such errors is frequently couched in psychological terms. But if errors in moral judgments are to be accounted for psychologically, it can only be because those psychological forces which lead to error interfere with the "normal," or "proper," psychological factors through which obligation is cognized. Thus, those who hold that there are genuine errors in the sphere of moral judgments are forced to uphold some theory as to the psychological factors which are present in moral cognition. Similarly, those who deny that what appear to a person as "errors" in moral judgment are really to be denominated as errors, can only defend their position by showing that the same psychological factors which are held to be responsible for these "errors" are to be found (in precisely the same form) in all moral judgments. Thus, whatever one's view of what, if anything, constitutes an error in moral judgment, the attempt to defend the view which is held will involve a consideration of the psychological factors responsible for moral judgments.[10]

In the third place, moralists do not in general believe that man's moral judgments leave his conduct unaffected. If these judgments are not to be considered impotent, we must be ready to show how they are related to the other forces which move men. And if it be held that moral judgments do not in fact move men to action, but are themselves merely epiphenomenal representations of other forces, it still remains a problem of moral psychology to explain the sources of that conduct which is usually denominated "moral." As one can see from today's estimate of Kant's moral psychology and from the widespread acclaim given Hume's principle that only the passions, and not reason, can be a spring of conduct, the estimate of the truth of a moral system is not independent of the estimate of its psychology of moral conduct.

In sum, then, if one considers the history of ethical theory one does not find any support for the contemporary thesis that a solution of all of the traditional problems of ethics are separable from problems of moral psychology. Yet even if this were not the case, there would be no reason to exclude moral psychology from the province which it is proper for an ethical theory to investigate. There is, so far as I can see, no natural terminus for curiosity in merely knowing what men prize or what they feel obliged to do; why they prize these things, why they should feel obliged toward anything, or why when they prize or feel obliged they act in one way rather than another, are also questions which it would be well to answer, if we can.

Why, then, should recent ethical theory have often been so hostile to admitting the relevance of psychology to moral inquiry? There are, I believe, two factors which have been operative. The first of these, historically speaking, is to be found in Mill's famous error in his attempted proof of hedonism.

Mill said, it will be recalled, that "the sole evidence it is possible to produce that anything is desirable, is that people do actually desire it."[11] As has been pointed out time and again, this proof is fallacious in so far as it rests upon his explicit comparison of the desirable with the visible and the audible: the term desirable does not mean "what is capable of being desired," but "what should be, or is really to be, desired." Mill's confusion on this point has apparently led many recent moralists to the conclusion that an investigation of desire, or of any other matters of psychological fact, is not of direct relevance to the normative issues of ethics.

However, the critics of Mill, content with having disproved his "proof," have not been careful to understand what lay behind the obvious error. There is an element of truth in the "proof" which doubtless served to obscure from Mill the fallacy that has so frequently been singled out for attention. This lies in the connection between the "proof" and the sentence which immediately follows: "If the end which the utilitarian doctrine proposes to itself were not, in theory and in practice, acknowledged to be an end, nothing could ever convince any person that it was so." Taking these sentences conjointly, it becomes clear that Mill's real proof lies in the claim that man is so constituted as to desire happiness, and nothing save happiness, as the end of his actions, and that, this being so, nothing save happiness can be claimed to constitute the end of man. Thus, what Mill here really rests his case upon (and it is of more importance than his trifling confusion of the desirable with the visible and audible) is the fact that whatever appears to man as being valuable can only so appear because of its relation to human nature. Like the metaphysician (and with no less force) those who follow a psychological approach can claim that there is an infrangible bond between what can be said to be valuable or obligatory for man and what, because of his nature, man is capable of valuing or doing. No moralist, it may be pointed out, has ever contended that man has an obligation to do something which does not lie within his powers.[12] On the contrary, almost every moralist has sought to ground values and obligations upon the essential nature of man. However we may seek to apprehend this nature, whether through metaphysics as did Aristotle and Green, or whether through "philosophical anthropology" as did Butler and Scheler, we shall sooner or later be compelled to speak in psychological terms. Hence those who, like Mill, uphold the psychological method may, with some show of force, argue that one can best approach the problems of ethics through an empirical inquiry into man's nature.

In my opinion, the difficulty with this approach to the establishment of a norm for conduct is not that it confuses matters of fact with normative issues, but that it seems to me implausible to argue that all men do in fact find the same ends desirable. If they do, the argument is conclusive; if they do not, the attempt to show that among the ends that are found desirable there are some rather than others which *should* be desired would be a question-begging argument. If I am not mistaken, those who today attempt to ground an ethical theory in a psychological account of man's "essential nature" are guilty of precisely this begging of the question. Naturally those who wish to establish a self-contained normative ethics are never slow to point out their error.

The second reason recent ethical thought has been particularly hostile to admitting the relevance of psychology to ethics is a reason of an entirely different order. This reason lies in the fact that those who have recently been concerned with the relation of psychology to ethics have (in the main) uncritically utilized concepts borrowed from other areas of psychological investigation. Instead of attempting to establish the rudiments of what may be termed "moral psychology," they have sought to interpret moral judgments and moral conduct in terms of concepts which had antecedently been stripped of all connotations which have moral import. Thus, the praiseworthy attempt to construct a general psychology which would be capable of rendering intelligible both moral and non-moral aspects of experience, has led the psychologist to attempt to understand valuations and the recognition of obligations by means of concepts derived from a study of those forms of behavior in which the problem of human norms does not arise. To the extent to which this point of view has been consistently adhered to, psychology has given the moral inquirer a portrait of man which lacked all of those features in which he was primarily interested.[13] As a consequence, much (though not all) of current psychology appears to be irrelevant to moral inquiry.[14]

A psychological approach to ethics need not proceed in this manner. What might be termed "moral psychology" can investigate moral judgments and moral conduct as psychological phenomena, can note the conditions under which they arise and change, and can thereby become cognizant of their sources. Such knowledge, I have claimed, has never (until recently) been considered to be irrelevant to the normative problems of ethics; nor, as I have tried to indicate, can it now be so considered.

The real difficulty in the psychological approach is not at all that it is psychological, but that it is so often used as a first approach. If we are to concern ourselves with the psychology of moral judgments, a careful description and phenomenological analysis of the immediate data of the moral consciousness are the sole means of obtaining adequate material. To neglect this material (which we have reason to suppose is of a certain subtlety and complexity), and to proceed on the basis of inferences drawn from other materials, is to risk a complete misunderstanding of ethical data. In this respect the psychology of moral phenomena must follow a rule which is, I believe, applicable to all psychological investigations: phenomenological description is a necessary propaedeutic to causal explanation.

What then, in general, may we expect from a psychological consideration of moral judgments? It will certainly not provide us with new moral insights, nor will it be able to deduce from within itself a moral standard which we must then accept and apply; it will not, in short, directly change our moral experience at all. There is, for example, no more reason to suppose that an adequate psychology of the causal factors involved in moral judgments would eliminate praise and blame, than to suppose that an understanding of the causes of color-vision would alter the colors which we actually see. This is as it should be:

the purpose of psychology (and, I might add, of ethical inquiry) is to understand man, not to manufacture him. What psychology can contribute to ethics is a more comprehensive understanding of the sources of moral judgments than direct inspection by itself can reveal, and a clearer interpretation of the relation between moral judgments and conduct than can otherwise be attained. Such understanding would, I have argued, be of significance for a reasoned solution of at least some of the traditional issues of ethics. In addition, it would contribute to our knowledge of what relations obtain between moral judgments and other psychological phenomena. In this respect an adequate moral psychology has a contribution to make to general psychology, showing what place values and obligations occupy in the economy of our natures. To the extent to which such an attempt could succeed, it would have freed ethical thought from some of the burden placed upon it by recent bifurcations of "the ideal" and "the real." This, if I mistake not, is an end to be sought.

3. The psychological approach to ethics is not the only approach which attempts to arrive at a solution of normative problems through a causal understanding of moral phenomena; such an aim is also characteristic of what I shall term the sociological approach. This approach may assume a variety of forms, some of which are of relatively recent origin. What all have in common, however, is a combination of a descriptive inquiry into the moral norms of various societies and an analysis of the existence or changes of these norms in terms of the needs or structure of the society in which they appear.

In the past those who have followed the sociological approach have sometimes been insufficiently aware of the fact that if sociological inquiry is to be made the foundation for an ethical theory it must do more than merely describe variations in moral judgments at different times and in different places. As has often been pointed out, variability in norms does not of itself prove that all standards for conduct should be considered as equally valid. However, the fact that some who have followed the sociological approach have failed to recognize this error should not lead us to dismiss that approach as irrelevant to the traditional problems of ethics. Its relevance to these problems lies not in its descriptive inquiries, taken by themselves, but in the hypotheses which it attempts to establish by means of them. Such hypotheses concern the manner in which social needs or social structure determine the moral norms which are to be found in different societies. The attempt to show that these norms are socially determined, and to explain just how they are thus determined, is not an undertaking to be dismissed as irrelevant to the problems of ethics.

However, it has often been characteristic of those who follow a sociological approach to assume that if they can establish certain correlations between moral norms and social needs or social structure they will have established generalizations which are of ethical significance. However, not all such generalizations are equally relevant to the problems of ethical theory. For example, if it can be shown that every major shift in social organization is followed by a major shift in what is considered as being acceptable or proper conduct, it would by no means establish the fact that either the existence or the nature of moral norms is capable of adequate explanation in terms of social organization. As is readily seen, it *might* (but need not) be the case that there were certain basic norms which remained unaltered, and that the shift in standards of conduct reflected a change in the manner in which these norms were best realizable under the new conditions. The fact that many of those who have followed the sociological approach have identified variations in moral practices with variations in moral standards, and have uncritically taken certain correlations to be evidence of a direct determining relationship between sociological facts and moral standards, is one of the reasons that the sociological approach has been so widely criticized.

Yet it should also be clear from the above example that the establishment of correlations between moral norms and social needs or social structure is by no means without interest for ethical theory. Even if such correlations do not of themselves establish how this relationship is to be conceived, they do point to some relationship which is of significance for an understanding of at least some of the facets of moral experience. In so far as ethical theory is broader in scope than the attempt to reach a decision concerning specifically normative issues, such investigations do properly belong within the province of ethics.

There is, however, one fundamental difficulty with the sociological approach, when this approach is taken to be the basic method for ethical inquiry. This difficulty lies in the fact that, taken by itself, it is not a self-contained method.

In the first place, the hypotheses by means of which the sociological approach goes beyond mere correlations of social structure and moral norms, showing in what ways sociological conditions determine these norms, are not (and can not be) hypotheses which are exclusively sociological in character. Since acts of prizing or despising, of praising or blaming, are acts which can only be performed (in any literal sense) by individuals, a sociological approach will be dependent upon psychological hypotheses concerning the springs of moral judgment and the relation between these judgments and the general principles of human motivation. Thus, a sociological approach to ethics is by no means independent of the psychological approach.[15]

In the second place, a sociological approach is not independent of what I shall term a phenomenological approach. As we have already noted, a correlation between certain social conditions and certain moral norms, or between their changes, does not prove that these conditions are responsible for the existence of these norms, nor for all aspects of their content. Before claiming that social conditions actually determine the norms, it is therefore necessary to examine the latter with care, attempting to analyze what constitutes the meaning of the judgments which are made. Such a direct inspection of actual moral judgments, initially proceeding independently of causal hypotheses, would constitute one form of the phenomenological approach to ethics, and would be a necessary propaedeutic to an adequate sociological study of ethical data.[16]

For these reasons I should claim that a sociological approach cannot be considered to be an independent method for ethical inquiry, and therefore that a genuine "*science des moeurs*" cannot be conceived in merely sociological terms.[17] There is, however, a further possible criticism of most examples of the sociological approach which I should like to call to the reader's attention. It is this defect which, in my opinion, lies at the root of much of the criticism which has been directed against one or another of these theories, although the precise nature of the defect has frequently been left undefined.

Many who follow the sociological approach fail to distinguish two distinct problems which it is essential that their hypotheses should cover; in fact, many fail to say anything, even by implication, concerning one or the other of these problems. The problems are: first, what is the precise relation between the sociological determinants and the content of the moral judgments which are either made or which are "effective" in a particular society; and, second, why is it that in all societies we find moral judgments? For example, the first of these questions receives little attention from Sumner, although he is much concerned with the second; the second receives little attention from Marx, though he has (by implication at least) much to say concerning the first. When either question is neglected the theory involved seems truncated; when the two questions are confused, the theory shows the effects of this confusion. To my knowledge there is no sociological theory which clearly distinguishes these two questions, nor one which gives a sufficient answer to either. If there were, it would (I suggest) be found to presuppose both psychological and phenomenological investigations, and would therefore not be an example of a purely sociological approach to moral phenomena.

Yet we cannot dismiss the attempt to follow a sociological approach without seeking to understand the reasons for its constant recurrence in forms which, however old, always bear the fashionable marks of modernity. These reasons are not to be found in what it accomplishes, but in the motives from which it springs and to which it appeals. Traditional ethical theory has sometimes based its standards upon moral judgments which betray a vested interest or an unwittingly biased principle of selection; at other times it has unfortunately failed to examine a sufficiently wide range of moral data. In either case it is natural that men should have noted the discrepancy between the moralist's principles and rival moral beliefs. Such a discrepancy is not, of course, fatal to a normative ethics: it may be the case that the moralist in question has truly delineated the norms on the basis of which all moral beliefs ought to be assessed, and that those who disagree are simply mistaken. But the fact that there is a conflict of authorities, each claiming his authority, arouses presumptive doubt regarding any single system of moral truth. And this doubt grows larger as the number of conflicting authorities increases. At such times the conviction that there is no moral truth, that there are only truths about a variety of sociologically determined moral beliefs, seizes upon thought with a violence out of all proportion to its intrinsic strength. There is, then, at least one lesson to be learned from a consideration of the sociological approach: we must exercise the greatest possible care to include in our purview not only those moral data which are by their nature congenial to us (or to those members of our society with whom we agree), but we must be ready to absorb as relevant to our inquiry *any* moral judgments, no matter how remote in time and place, nor how disturbing to our systematic equilibrium they may be. Of this I shall shortly have more to say. Here it suffices to note that while the purely sociological approach may not satisfactorily answer a single fundamental question in ethics, it has opened up rich veins of material which one cannot with impunity now neglect.

4. The phenomenological[18] approach to ethics starts from a point which all paths must eventually cross: a direct examination of the data of men's moral consciousness. However, it differs from the other approaches with respect to how these data are to be used. Those who follow a metaphysical approach seek to deduce a standard for conduct from metaphysical considerations, and merely use their examination of men's moral consciousness as a means of confirming the standard which they have deduced. Those who follow a psychological approach seek to interpret men's moral judgments and that form of conduct which is denominated as "moral conduct" in terms of an antecedently accepted and more comprehensive set of psychological hypotheses; from this interpretation they deduce solu-

tions to the questions which ethical inquiry has posed. Those who follow the sociological method also seek to deduce conclusions concerning the problems of ethics from hypotheses which are scientific in character. However, their hypotheses are ostensibly based upon and confirmed by historical and anthropological studies which show correlations between the social organization in different societies and the moral standards of those societies. The phenomenological approach utilizes moral experience in another way. Its method is eductive rather than deductive. Its essential methodological conviction is that a solution to any of the problems of ethics must be educed from, and verified by, a careful and direct examination of individual moral judgments. In other words, the phenomenological approach holds that the proper basis for any moral generalization, and for the confirmation which we rightfully demand for such a generalization, are to be found in an examination of the moral judgments which men make.

Now, it might be thought that the attempt to follow such an approach would make ethical inquiry a wholly self-contained discipline, severing all connections between it and metaphysical, psychological, or sociological issues. Such, however, is not necessarily the case. To hold that a solution to the problems of ethics is to be arrived at through an examination of the specific moral judgments which men make, and that the verification of any such solution is to be sought in its concordance with these judgments, is not to deny that the results of an ethical inquiry must also be consonant with metaphysical, psychological, and sociological theses. All that the phenomenological approach demands is that the solution to the problems of ethics must not be dictated by a prior acceptance of hypotheses drawn from these other fields. When an examination of men's moral judgments has led to an ethical generalization which receives adequate confirmation from a further examination of these judgments, then, and only then, does a phenomenological approach seek to relate its conclusions to metaphysical, psychological, and sociological theses which are derived from other data. Thus, the phenomenological approach demands only an initial, and not an ultimate severing of ethics from non-ethical inquiries. As the diverse examples of Aristotle, Butler, Hume, or Scheler clearly show, there is no ultimate opposition between a phenomenological approach and a willingness to connect the results of ethical inquiry with non-ethical hypotheses.

That which is really responsible for severing the connections between the phenomenological approach to ethics and a discussion of metaphysical, psychological, and historical issues is not inherent in that approach; it is the recent dichotomizing of normative and descriptive disciplines. In so far as such a dichotomy is consistently maintained, any consideration of these issues is not only initially to be avoided, but is also to be considered as ultimately irrelevant to a systematic ethical theory. So extreme a position has rarely been held, but that is only because the dichotomy has not been, and cannot be, strictly maintained.

Once it is recognized that a phenomenological approach to ethics does not commit one to a permanent exclusion of metaphysical, psychological, or sociological considerations, it becomes clear that most ethical theories have actually utilized this approach. However, most have not consistently adhered to it. At crucial points, moralists introduce into their theories considerations which have not been derived from, and are not confirmed by, the data provided by the actual moral judgments which men make. In my opinion, the reason for this inconsistency is not primarily to be found in the difficulty of meticulously following a phenomenological approach, suppressing one's theoretical predilections, but in the fact that most moralists have conceived it to be the task of ethics to establish a universally valid standard for conduct. If one defines the nature of ethical inquiry as the determination of what constitutes such a standard,[19] a strictly phenomenological approach encounters formidable obstacles. It will be useful to show precisely what these obstacles are.

Those who have assumed that there must be a single universally valid standard for conduct and who have sought to establish the nature of this standard by examining men's moral judgments have concerned themselves with the *content* of these judgments. They have sought to educe a set of moral truths from the common moral opinions of mankind. It is here that difficulties arise. It is no easy matter to maintain that the content of all moral judgments adumbrates a single standard for conduct. Where inconsistencies arise, the phenomenological approach is sometimes hastily abandoned; metaphysical, psychological, or sociological theses are introduced as a means of upholding a standard which is affirmed by one set of judgments, even though it is denied by another. Thus, for example, a metaphysical or historical thesis concerning social evolution is made to serve as warrant for the dismissal of certain judgments which are claimed to represent a more primitive, undeveloped moral consciousness. Or, to take another example, when the task of educing a standard of conduct from the common opinions of mankind runs into the obstacle of inconsistent judgments, it is a temptation to abandon the phenomenological approach by introducing a special psychological thesis: those who fail to judge as do most men, represent "maladjusted" or "neurotic" personalities.

It cannot of course be said that all moralists so readily abandon the phenomenological approach, attempting to purchase a standard for conduct at this cheap a price. In their attempts to educe a standard from the common opinions of mankind, most moralists have painstakingly sought to remove ambiguities with a view to reducing apparent inconsistencies to consistency. However, where inconsistencies have remained, an appeal has usually been made to what are considered to be the more enlightened and acceptable of the opinions, and the core of moral opinion thus obtained has been systematized and then submitted for approval to the moral awareness of others. In so far as it has not been found wanting, it has been claimed to have been verified. A classical statement of this method is to be found in the *Nichomachean Ethics*: "We must . . . set the observed facts before us and, after first discussing the difficulties, go on to prove, if possible, the truth of all common opinions about these affections of the mind, or, failing this, of the greatest number and the most authoritative; for if we both refute the objections and leave the common opinions undisturbed, we shall have proved the case sufficiently."[20]

This concern with the every-day moral judgments of mankind

ought not to be disparaged. Nor should it be lightly assumed that one cannot educe a universal standard of conduct from them. Nonetheless, as this quotation suggests, there are formidable methodological difficulties in the way of justifying whatever conclusions one reaches through examining the content of individual moral judgments. The temptation to oversimplify this content, paying special attention only to those moral judgments which bear an affinity to our own, is always exceedingly strong. And if it is the case that one cannot find a universally accepted norm, which of the various conflicting judgments should one accept? When faced by this question it is of no use to appeal to either the opinions of "*the greater number*" or of "*the most authoritative*," as Aristotle would have us do. Those who follow this form of the phenomenological approach would not in any other instance decide a normative question by majority vote, and the question as to who *should be* "the most authoritative" is the very problem at issue. Thus, unless it can be shown—in a positive and convincing manner—that in *all* moral judgments there is implicit a single common norm, the attempt to educe a standard of conduct from the content of moral judgments is apt to lead the inquirer to identify the standard which he already accepts with the standard which it is his aim to discover.

That this is a real danger can be seen from the use which is sometimes made of concepts such as "value-blindness." To hold, at the outset of moral inquiry, that certain judgments show a lack of moral education or an insensibility to values is to prejudge the issue with which a normative system of ethics is concerned. Unless it can be demonstrated that the moral judgments found among people of other cultures, among socially ostracized individuals, and among those whose standards we abhor, are essentially different in character, and not merely in content, from the moral judgments which we ourselves make, we have no right to exclude them from consideration. So long as we follow a phenomenological approach, the fact that they conflict with what we take to be values and obligations provides no adequate ground for dismissing them. It may be that, in the end, one can show them to be in some sense "mistaken." At the outset of inquiry, however, no moral judgments may be dismissed as invalid; if they are, the moral system which we finally reach will probably be little more than a formal profession of antecedently held personal beliefs.

When this difficulty is grasped a phenomenological approach seems to lose much of its promise. The moral judgments which men make, and have made, apparently vary so widely in content that it would seem next to hopeless to attempt to educe a single valid standard from them.[21] Whether in fact this impression would survive a careful phenomenological analysis of the data is a point which could only be decided by carrying through the requisite inquiry. Such is not my purpose. For reasons which will become clearer as we proceed, I shall follow another method, a method which, while maintaining a phenomenological orientation, by-passes this particular problem.

ii.

IN THE PRESENT SECTION I shall attempt to show that a phenomenological approach to ethics need not follow the standard procedure of attempting to educe a valid standard for conduct from an examination of the *content* of moral judgments. As the examples of Smith and Hume illustrate, normative conclusions may also follow from what I shall term a "generic" approach to the nature of moral judgments.

It is perhaps linguistically awkward to contrast a "generic" with a "contentual" consideration of moral judgments, but this contrast calls attention to a real and characteristic difference between two methods of employing a phenomenological approach. The essential conviction of a phenomenological approach is, it will be recalled, the insistence that an adequate moral theory must be based upon, and remain faithful to, the facts of moral experience. But there are two different points of view from which this experience may be examined. On the one hand, the attempt can be made to educe a valid contentual standard for conduct from what is asserted in moral judgments. (However, we have already seen the methodological difficulty in this form of a phenomenological approach.) On the other hand, one can initially abstract from these judgments the specific content of their affirmations, and can aim to uncover that which—whatever they assert—all have in common. Such an approach, like the generic approach to value,[22] aims to discover the generic characteristics of all moral experience. Again, like the generic approach to value, this approach is not at the outset concerned with discriminating between those judgments which are well-founded or ill-founded, correct or incorrect, valid or invalid, nor between the spurious and the genuine, the merely apparent and the real. All such distinctions must be established later, at the conclusion of the generic inquiry, if they are to be established at all.

In order that there should be no mistake as to why such distinctions must only be drawn at the conclusion of a generic inquiry, let me recall my previous argument. It is, I have claimed, methodologically unsound to discount any moral judgments at the outset of an ethical inquiry merely because they assert what the moral judgments of others deny. To do so is to beg the question which those who are concerned to establish a single universally valid standard for conduct are attempting to prove. Until it can be shown that these deviant judgments differ from "normal," "correct," or "true" judgments with respect to characteristics other than that they deny what the latter affirm, there is a vicious circle in the argument that their testimony can be discounted. But if we are to establish that these deviant judgments *do* differ from uncriticized judgments in respects other than that they assert false moral propositions, we can only distinguish these differences by means of an inquiry designed to differentiate between the properties common to "genuine" moral judgments and those properties common to judgments which evince "moral blindness." If we can show that the latter lack some of the properties which the former possess, or that they possess additional properties, we can distinguish between the two classes by means of differences other than the disagreements in their assertions. But only in this way—*via* a discrimination of different classes of "moral judgments" which have erroneously been lumped together—can we utilize the concept of "moral blindness." It is for this reason that I should claim that if there really are ultimate conflicts between the moral assertions of different persons, any defensible attempt to distinguish between true and false moral propositions must rest upon a prior examination of the non-contentual generic properties of moral judgments.[23]

It appears to me that recent ethical studies have paid too little attention to the problem of what constitutes the generic nature of those moral judgments with which they attempt to deal. To be sure, every analytic treatment of the meaning of "right" and every consideration of what constitutes the "object" of moral judgment, is an example of the fact that ethical inquiry is unavoidably concerned with the generic nature of these judgments. However, even as basic a problem as that which we have just noted—the discrimination of "genuine" moral judgments from those erroneously classified as genuine—has rarely been explored.[24] Equally important, and more obvious, is the extent to which contemporary ethical theory has neglected the problem of the range of moral judgments. Traditional ethical theory recognized that judgments concerning the virtues and vices were no less moral phenomena than judgments concerning the rightness or wrongness of specific acts. Yet in England and America the former have recently received little consideration. For example, G. E. Moore, the most influential exponent of the method of analysis, has confined his attention to problems concerning the rightness or wrongness of specific acts. While he has made the suggestion that there may be different species of moral judgments,[25] he has failed to attempt to characterize the essential property of the genus to which these species presumably belong. And, on the other hand, when we find contemporary ethical theory dealing with the virtues and vices, as in Scheler and Hartmann, the equally important problems of analyzing the nature of the rightness or wrongness of specific choices is left almost wholly out of account. Thus, although no ethical theory can fail to consider *some* aspects of the generic nature of moral judgments, it is not infrequently the case that many fundamental problems, including the problem of the range of these judgments, are left unexplored.

It is, of course, by no means certain that all so-called moral judgments constitute a single class, even though common parlance in many cases suggests that they do. To determine whether they do constitute such a class is one of the most fundamental tasks of an ethical theory. And if it is held that they do, it is incumbent upon the theorist to show what constitutes their common generic property, and also to show what differentiates them into species.

It has become customary to assume that the common characteristic of all moral judgments is the fact that when verbalized they contain certain specific terms, such as "right," "wrong," "good," "bad," "ought," and "duty."[26] That these terms are in fact used in moral judgments cannot be denied. Nor can it be denied that, in the end, many of the traditional problems of ethical theory turn upon how these terms are to be construed. However, it by no means follows (as some would today have us believe) that the *first* task for ethical theory is to determine the meanings of each of these terms and thus establish their inter-relationships. Any such semantic and syntactical analysis actually presupposes a knowledge of the characteristics of moral judgments, rather than being the means through which such a knowledge can be obtained. This can be seen from the fact that it is impossible to determine the connotations of terms such as "good" or "right" or "ought" without first inquiring upon what occasions and in what different alternative ways these terms are used. Only after we have distinguished between their moral and their non-moral connotations (which is sometimes too readily assumed to be an obvious distinction)[27] are we in a position to state whether or not these terms, taken in their moral connotations, are definable or indefinable, whether or not they refer to natural or non-natural properties, or whether they are in fact referential at all.

If this be true it follows that the generic characteristics of moral judgments are not to be determined simply through a semantic and syntactical analysis of that which they assert. A more promising type of generic inquiry would seem to involve an inquiry into the occasions on which moral judgments are made, and into other aspects of moral judgments which will doubtless also be disparaged as being of merely psychological interest. Yet there is nothing in the logic of the situation (nor in the history of ethical thought) which suggests that it is less legitimate to inquire into the nature of the occasions which elicit acts of moral evaluation than it is to inquire into the nature of the objects which are valued or praised. Nor is it less legitimate to ask what characterizes the attitude of the person making a moral evaluation than it is to ask what predicates he asserts of the object evaluated. So long as our aim is that of understanding man's moral experience, an ethical inquiry must constantly cross and recross the boundary between what is asserted by a moral judgment and the psychological aspects of the judgmental act.

One reason why such a thesis is apt to be rejected and the boundary between the two aspects of moral judgments is likely to be held to be inviolable, is that ethics (as we have seen) has come to be defined as a "normative" study. From the contemporary definition of what constitutes such a study it has seemed to follow that an ethical theory should only be concerned with the content asserted by moral judgments, and not with the attitudes which are present when the judgments are made. On the other hand, those who have been concerned with the psychological aspects of acts of moral judgment have been inclined to assume that what a so-called moral judgment "asserts" is not in fact referential in character, and that an analysis of whatever attitudinal factor is present in moral judgments constitutes the major portion, or the whole, of an ethical theory. In this respect they have been no less one-sided in their approach than have been those who have refused to cross this boundary from the other direction.

Now, there are, I submit, good reasons to suspect that neither a purely attitudinal nor a purely contentual approach to the nature of moral judgments is likely to be adequate. On the one hand we have already noted a difficulty inherent in a purely contentual approach: there appears to be great diversity in the content of the moral judgments of different individuals, especially when one compares the moral judgments of individuals who belong to different cultural communities. A second and probably even more formidable difficulty with the contentual approach lies in the fact that among the moral judgments of any one individual there appear judgments so different in type that it is difficult to see what common content is asserted by them. When, for example, I hold that 'I ought not to have lied to him' and when I feel 'the humility of St. Francis was wholly praiseworthy' it is difficult to find the specific content common to both assertions.[28]

On the other hand, it is difficult to believe that a purely attitudinal approach to the generic nature of moral judgments is likely to meet with more success. The history of ethical theory is replete with attempts of this type; yet on every occasion that a specific type of attitude has been used as the unique identifying generic property of moral judgments, criticism has shown that the identification was either arbitrary or unconvincing. Without entering into these controveries it is of course impossible to demonstrate that the attempt to find a specific attitude which can serve as the identifying mark of all moral judgments is likely to fail. Similarly, it is impossible to show, without a long and careful investigation, that there is in fact no common content in all moral judgments. However, the teetering equipoise of the arguments which one finds in both past and contemporary inquiry should certainly suggest that the common property of all moral judgments lies neither exclusively in what is asserted, nor in the attitude which is present when a moral assertion is made. An alternative to either approach is to be found in the method here to be followed, which, for want of a better name, I shall designate as the "structural" approach to the problem of the generic nature of moral judgments.[29]

What characterizes this approach is the fact that it treats moral experience as a complete judgmental act. Not only are the attitudes which are present and the content which is affirmed to be considered, but it is crucial for such an approach to examine each of these in relation to the situation in which the judgment is made. Therefore, instead of abstracting either content or attitude from the total situation, we shall first inquire into the manner in which a situation appears to one who makes a moral judgment; we shall then attempt to interpret the other two elements in terms of their relationship to this situation. What (if any) generic characteristics of moral judgments may be revealed through such an analysis is, of course, an open question. At the outset one can only claim for this approach the advantage of starting from those experiences in which men make moral judgments, rather than confining attention to any one element which such experiences may contain.

It is of course clear that in attempting to discover a common, characteristic relationship between those situations in which moral judgments are made and the attitudes and the content which are involved in these judgments, a structural approach will necessarily involve one form of abstraction. As I have already indicated, we shall not be concerned with the specific content of any particular moral judgments except in so far as this content is directly related to the specific situation in which the judgment is made. However, such abstraction, made in the interest of finding the generic properties of moral judgments, need sacrifice nothing of the concreteness of moral experience. What it does lead one to neglect is the question of which, if any, of the specific moral assertions which men have made are to be considered true.

It may be thought that in neglecting this problem the proposed approach to the nature of moral experience loses all title to be considered as an instance of ethical inquiry. However, to *define* ethics as that discipline which discovers what constitutes the universally valid standard for conduct is not only to exclude from the discipline all of those studies which have attempted to demonstrate that there is no such standard, but it would also leave open the possibility (if these thinkers are right) that ethics has no proper function at all. In place of such a prescriptive definition of its task, one may say that ethics is the attempt to gain a systematic and complete understanding of moral experience. Such a definition of ethics by no means precludes us from saying that in one important sense ethics always has been, and always will remain, a normative discipline: the facts with which ethics deals are (to put it paradoxically) normative facts. Moral experience and the judgments which express that experience contain an inexpungeable reference to norms of better and worse, right and wrong. In short, the essential difference between a normative and a non-normative study may be said to lie in the fact that the primary data of normative studies are normative data, while those of non-normative studies are not.[30] What constitutes a normative datum is simply the fact that it contains as part of its inherent nature some reference to an "ought" or a "norm." Since I believe that all such data are to be found within the realm of human judgments, I shall assume that the primary data of ethics are to be found among the normative judgments which men make.[31]

But here we must guard against error. A mere cataloguing of past normative judgments would not be a normative discipline, nor would, say, a classification of personality-types in terms of their normative reactions. Many such investigations might add indirectly to our understanding of those normative facts which we call moral judgments, and thus be "secondary" data for ethics, but they would not, for this reason, themselves be systematic studies of the judgments themselves. In order to be thus classifiable they must treat of moral judgments in a manner designed to render comprehensible all of their facets, and in particular their normative character. If this be attempted, the study is, I conceive, really an instance of ethical inquiry.

To be sure, having defined ethics in this manner we can no longer, in another sense, ascribe a normative character to it. We cannot claim that ethical inquiry will be able to furnish man with any norms which are not already implicit in his moral judgments. But this, I take it, has rarely been openly avowed to be the aim of ethics.[32] And, for my part, I can only consider it fortunate that the presence of moral norms in human experience has not depended upon the progress which ethical inquiry has made.

The central fact for all ethical study is, then, that men do make moral judgments. These judgments claim, by their nature, to be true, but one quickly discovers that there apparently exist contradictions among them. Thus the search for a valid standard is engendered among moralists. However, the method of attaining and validating such a standard cannot be the method of a simple iteration of our own moral experience if it is to be a standard acceptable to others or, in the end, ideally acceptable to ourselves. Therefore it is essential that we either plunge deeper into the specific content of all moral judgments to find a common underlying standard in them, or we must turn our attention away from their particular content and seek an understanding of their generic traits. I hope to show that out of the latter approach there may arise not only a richer comprehension of their nature, but the possibility of saying—and not only of saying—that one can discriminate between those moral judgments which are valid and those which are not.[33]

CHAPTER

2

DIRECT MORAL JUDGMENTS

If the primary data for ethical inquiry are to be found in men's moral judgments it is imperative that a careful and comprehensive survey of all types of such judgments should be made. It appears to me that there are three basic types which one can profitably distinguish; each has its own nature and raises its own problems, though each is also related to the others in being a case in which something is held to be morally good.

The first of these types I shall term Direct Judgments of Moral Rightness and Wrongness; the second, Removed Judgments of Moral Rightness and Wrongness; the third, Judgments of Moral Worth. By the first I denote those judgments made by an agent who is directly confronted by a situation which he believes involves a moral choice on his part. By the second I denote those judgments made by an observer on the conduct of another person (or by an agent on his own past conduct). By the third I denote judgments of praise or blame which are directed toward specific traits of character, or which concern the total character of a person considered as a moral being.

In all three types of judgment the concept of moral goodness is essential: that act which we as agents feel to be the act which it is right to perform appears to us to be a morally good act; that act which we feel another should do (or which we feel that we ought to have done) is also deemed morally good; those traits of character which we praise, and those persons whose moral character we praise, we regard as being morally good. It is, then, the concept of moral goodness which may be identified as the common characteristic of all moral judgments. However, this concept cannot be analyzed in isolation; it is best approached through an examination of each of the three general types of instance in which it is to be found. The present chapter will be solely concerned with a discussion of Direct Judgments of Moral Rightness and Wrongness, that is with the characteristics of those moral judgments in which an agent feels that he is confronted by a siutation in which he himself must make a moral choice.

i.

IT IS A STRIKING FACT that ethical inquiry has of late paid little attention to the facts concerning direct moral judgments.[1] Under the influence of the teleological tradition which, as we shall see, is primarily based upon an investigation of removed moral judgments, the problems inherent in the structure of direct moral judgments have often been grossly oversimplified.[2]

It will, I believe, be generally granted that direct moral judgments concern the rightness or wrongness of a specific action. The term "rightness" is here taken in a broad sense, including whatever is one's duty, or what one ought to do.[3] Its antonym, "wrongness," is used in a corresponding sense. The term "judgment" as here used must be construed in a loose manner, for in speaking of a direct moral judgment I do not mean to imply that inference is involved. In direct moral judgments one does not look for some characteristic mark on the basis of which rightness or wrongness may be inferred. (As to "implicit inference," it appears to me that such a concept is misleading and had best be abandoned.) One immediately "sees"—or so one believes—the rightness or wrongness of that which is contemplated. It might therefore seem preferable to speak of a "direct moral *awareness*" or a "direct moral *insight*." However, "awareness" and "insight" tend to shift attention from the act of the agent to the specific content of his moral conviction, and both suggest that this content must necessarily be valid. In default of a better term I therefore prefer to use the word "judgment" in an admittedly loose sense.

Having to this extent guarded against misinterpretations of the manner in which the terms "rightness," "wrongness," and "judgments" are to be used, it is necessary to specify what is meant when it is said that direct moral judgments are concerned with the rightness or wrongness of particular *actions*. It is at this point that we reach an analytical problem which is of importance for what follows.

Not everything which in common parlance is denominated as an action can be the object of a direct moral judgment. In contradistinction to removed moral judgments, every direct judgment of rightness or wrongness has as its object what I shall term a "willed" action. It will therefore be necessary to distinguish willed actions and those actions which may be termed "spontaneous."

It is characteristic of willed actions that the agent, even while performing them, feels responsible for them. They are *his* actions in quite another sense than are, say, reflex or habitual actions. When I receive a shock from an electrical appliance and jerk my hand away, I am not aware that it was "I" who acted: the event appears as one that happened to me. I may draw the lesson from the experience that I must be more cautious as to how I handle such appliances, but in the experience itself it was not "I" who withdrew my hand. In the same manner, my eyes may blink at a loud noise in spite of the fact that I am doing everything in my power to keep them from blinking. This feeling of helplessness when we try to control reflex action is simply the extreme case which attests to the fact that reflex action seems not to originate from the self, but has its source elsewhere.

The same is true of habitual action, although in such cases something nearer the phenomenal self seems to be involved. When, upon arising, I follow a particular sequence in dressing, let us say I put on my left shoe before my right, I am not conscious of the specific pattern of the action which I follow; I have no awareness of governing each step in my activity. Thus it is that when attention is called to them, I may be genuinely amazed at the nature of my own characteristic habits, and may fail to believe that I do habitually act in this way. And even when I am aware that I have a particular habit, that pattern of activity does not seem to spring from the self: I am apt to feel and to say that it is due to "something in me." And this remains true even though I may recognize when, how, and for what purpose I came to develop the habit; for, when "the force of habit" exerts itself, the source of the habit is not experienced as lying in the past: my habit has control over me here and now, and is sharply differentiated from the "I" over which it exercises control.

In other cases of spontaneous action, where neither reflex nor habit provides the sole basis for action, the feeling of responsibility is also missing at the time at which the action is performed. I sense the embarrassment of a person, and turn the conversation aside; I see a child in danger and catch hold of its hand; I hear a crash and become alert to help. Actions such as these (of which our daily lives are in no small measure composed) do not, at the time, seem to spring from the self: in such cases I am reacting directly and spontaneously to what confronts me. This is not to say that in looking back upon the action I fail to find that it was directed toward an end: clearly, the action was teleological. But the end which was served was not consciously espoused. In such cases it is appropriate to speak of "reactions" and "responses," for in them no sense of initiative or feeling of responsibility is present.[4]

In "willed" action, on the other hand, the source of action is the self. I act in a specific manner because I wish, or will, to do so. The "I" has a central place in the action; the action is felt as "mine," and is not simply attributed to me. It is in this that the touchstone of willed action is to be found: the "I" is experienced as being responsible for willed action.

To give a phenomenological account of this sense of responsibility is not difficult. It is grounded in the fact that every willed action aims at and espouses an envisioned goal. When we envision a goal which transcends what is immediately given, and when we set ourselves to realizing that goal, we feel the action to be *ours*. Thus, for example, the habitual action of brushing one's teeth may upon occasion give place to willed action, as when, before a visit to the dentist, one realizes that one's teeth demand more care. One does not then merely set about brushing his teeth in the accustomed perfunctory manner: there is a new directedness in the activity, a goal is set, and the individual is aware of the relation between his activity and that goal. It is here that the feeling of responsibility emerges. It is *my* action which I am performing, for the action is explicitly aimed at a goal which I have espoused.

The explicit espousal of a goal, which is characteristic of willed actions, and which accounts for the fact that we feel the action to be "ours," also accounts for another characteristic which can serve to distinguish willed action from all types of spontaneous action: we can give *reasons* for willed actions in a sense in which we cannot give a reason for, say, performing a habitual act. In the case of habit we may explain why we performed this action through pointing to the fact that such acts are habitual to us. This particular pattern of activity may then be explained either genetically or teleologically, or both;[5] but our reason for having performed this specific act is given in terms of a class of similar acts which it is our habit to perform. In the case of other spontaneous reactions which are neither examples of reflex nor habit, our reason does not extend beyond the action itself: if we keep to the point of view which we had when the action was performed, we can only say that we acted as we did because the situation extorted that action from us. In willed actions, however, we can give *a reason*: we acted as we did because we aimed to achieve a particular goal. In giving such a reason we are not appealing to other instances, nor to genetic explanations, but are giving a reason in terms of a purpose which was part of the experience itself. Such a reason, I submit, consists in the fact that the envisioned goal appeared as being valuable: when asked to explain our action, we feel no hesitation in attributing it to the value of the goal which we aimed to achieve.[6]

Perhaps enough has now been said to fix the meaning of what has been termed "willed action." It is obvious, of course, that the preceding remarks have been phenomenological in character, and have not aimed at a psychological explanation of the bases of such actions. The problem of "the will" is therefore left wholly unprejudiced by what has been said. My purpose has been confined to discriminating between willed and spontaneous action, a problem forced upon us by the fact that no person may be said to be aware of the moral nature of his action unless that action is one which he "chooses" to perform.[7]

Now, in every willed action the agent is in effect confronted by at least two alternatives of whose presence he may be said to be aware: at the very least he has the possibility of abstaining from that act which is aimed at the goal which he contemplates. However, a moral judgment is not evoked by all of those situations in which action is willed: many such actions appear to us to be morally indifferent in the sense that they raise no moral problems at all.[8] For example, if I decide to have my hair cut today, or to go to the movies tomorrow, or to reread a particular novel, I will not, under most circumstances, hold that a moral decision is involved. And this is true in spite of the fact that I should not hesitate to say of any of these actions that it was espoused because its end appeared to be in some degree valuable. It is not, then, the mere presence of a contemplated goal, nor the recognition that there is at least one alternative to acting for that goal, which evokes direct moral judgments. Nor is it a matter of the importance which we attach to such goals: the most trivial ends may, under some circumstances, appear as moral ends, while decisions which we know will affect the whole of our lives may be carefully weighed without feeling that we are morally obligated to act for one alternative rather than the other.[9]

What is it, then, which leads us to discriminate between those choices among alternatives which we see as moral choices, and those which we do not? It is, I submit, the fact that in some choices we feel that one of the alternatives places a *demand* upon us, that we are obliged, or bound, to act for it. This feeling of obligation appears as being independent of preference, as many of the alternatives within our experience do not. Where neither alternative has this character, where our choices are wholly matters of preference or desire, the choice which we face does not appear as a moral choice. However, let either alternative appear not as a preference but as an "objective" demand, and I feel myself to be confronted by a moral issue, by a categorical imperative, by an injunctive force which issues from one of the alternatives itself. It is to a fuller characterization of experienced demands that we must now turn.

ii.

WE HAVE COME to the basic element in all direct moral judgments: the phenomenon of a "reflexive demand," that is, of an "objective" demand which is experienced as being directly levelled against the person apprehending it. As most deontological theories have recognized, this is not only an inexpungeable element in our immediate experience, but it is the foundation upon which any adequate theory of the consciousness of our own obligations must rest. However, there are several points at which the following remarks will diverge from traditional deontological interpretations of this element in our moral experience, and it will be well to forewarn the reader of them.

In the first place, it is to be noted that we are here only dealing with direct moral judgments, and it is not to be assumed that the element of a reflexive demand will be found in other moral judgments, nor should it be assumed that it constitutes the most "basic" or "essential" phenomenon with which an ethical theory must deal. If I am not mistaken, many deontological theories have been more impressed by the element of reflexive demand in our consciousness of our own obligations than by any other phenomenon in moral experience. As a consequence, they can sometimes rightfully be charged with having failed to devote adequate attention to our judgments of the conduct of others and to our judgments of the moral worth of specific traits of character. I therefore wish it to be remembered that in placing the emphasis which I do upon the element of reflexive demands in direct moral judgments, I am not necessarily holding that the same element will be found in moral judgments of other types, and I would certainly not contend that such other judgments are in any sense less "basic" or "essential" moral phenomena.

In the second place, it may be said that most deontological theories have taken the element of a direct moral demand as being a phenomenon which is not capable of further analysis. Such will not be my view. In the present and succeeding sections I will in fact attempt to give a phenomenological analysis of this element in our moral experience, and will thereby later be in a position to show how direct moral judgments are related to the other moral judgments which we make.

In the third place, it must be noted that while the feeling of a demand upon the self to act in a certain way is often connected with the acceptance of a general rule, or maxim, of conduct, it is not invariably true that this is the case. Many deontological theories, dominated by the attempt to establish a universally valid standard for conduct, have laid what I should consider undue stress upon these rules. While rules such as "stealing is wrong," or commands such as "Thou shalt not steal," frequently enter into the agent's view of the alternatives, the moral demand which he then experiences as attaching to a specific action is not (in my opinion) different from that which he feels when no rule is present to his consciousness. The reasons which he may give to justify his moral decision when it is challenged may be different in the one case from what they are in the other, but the feeling of obligation to perform or to abstain from performing the action is the same. We shall later have occasion to say more concerning the phenomenology of some cases in which rules play a part in our direct moral judgments;[10] here it is only to be noted that even in such cases the phenomenon of obligation is not merely a matter of action-according-to-rule.

Finally, it is to be noted that deontological theories have almost without exception assumed that the type of experience which gives rise to direct moral judgments is confined to those cases in which serious moral decisions are involved. Because of their concern with the traditional normative problems of ethics, they have not sought to connect our sense of moral obligation with other aspects of our experience, and have treated it as a unique type of fact.[11] For my own part I believe that the phenomenon of a reflexive demand, which is the most essential aspect of our direct moral judgments, is to be found in a great variety of experiences. Many of these experiences are of little or no interest to a theory which defines its task as that of determining a universally valid standard for conduct. However, I do not believe that they can be excluded from a phenomenological inquiry concerning the nature of direct moral judgments if such an inquiry is to yield an understanding of how moral phenomena are related to other aspects of our experience. Therefore, in discussing the element of a reflexive demand upon us to perform a specific action, I shall not hesitate to use trivial and commonplace examples, as well as examples chosen from among those types of case with which moralists have traditionally been concerned.

All four of these points may be summarized in the following way. The reader has been forewarned that in this discussion I shall be concerned with the phenomenology of direct moral judgments, and only later shall I attempt to relate them to the other moral judgments which we make. From the point of view of phenomenology, I find no fundamental difference between the element of demand which is present when I feel that I must weed my garden or tidy my desk, and the element of demand which is present when I feel that I must keep my pledged word. What characterizes each case is a reflexive demand, a demand upon me as agent. And in each case my consciousness of obligation, of what I am bound to (or "must") do, is not a bald recognition of a type of action which any one, under the circumstances, ought to perform; it is what *I*, confronted by this situation with these alternatives, feel called upon to do. In whatever way either general maxims or envisioned consequences may influence my judgment, that judgment contains as its essential element the feeling that *this* rather than *that* is demanded of me.

Because the element of demand, the feeling of being called upon to do this or to refrain from doing that, is common to so much of our experience, arising under so many differing conditions, one is apt to overlook its presence, to take it for granted, and to focus attention upon the specific and varying conditions under which it is manifested. That a feeling of demand may arise in quite different types of situation is clear. I may feel a demand upon me to perform or to abstain from performing a specific action when another person either expressly or by implication demands it of me. Furthermore, it is generally admitted that even when no verbal demand is made or implied, the situations in which other persons find themselves may place demands upon any one who witnesses their plight. It is sometimes held that this is due to the fact that we interpret their unexpressed wishes as being demands on their part; but such is not always the case. When, for example, we watch a person attempting to solve a puzzle or a problem to which we know the answer, we may feel a demand to solve it for him, even though we know that he does not wish us to do so. In such cases the demand issues not from him but from the total situation of which he is but a part. And, in fact, there also are cases in which it is meaningful to speak of demands as issuing from apprehended entities which are not human agents. For example, we may speak of a given state of a scientific problem as demanding a specific experiment, or a given situation in a chess match as demanding a certain move on the part of one of the opponents. Now, it is to be noted that in the latter cases we experience a demand which is not a demand upon us: if we were placed within the situation we would (we assume) feel the demand to perform the experiment or to make the required move; yet we feel the presence of the demand no less when we are not actually placed within that situation. Why this should be the case is a psychological problem, and it is not our present purpose to investigate it. However, it is my contention that no matter how these various experiences of demand originate, or how they are to be causally explained, the use of the term "demand" covers a wide variety of experiences, and it cannot be said to be meaningless, or "merely metaphorical," if it singles out for attention a genuine component in experience. Such I take the phenomenon of demand to be.

Now, a demand is experienced as a force. Like other forces it can only be characterized through including within its description a reference to its point of origin and to its direction. It is my contention that the demands which we experience when we make a direct moral judgment are always experienced as emanating from "outside" us, and as being directed against us. They are demands which seem to be independent of us and to which we feel that we ought to respond.

Not all demands are, of course, of this kind. We often feel called upon to act in one way rather than another because of what we experience "within" us; such are the demands which we feel when we are hungry, or when we desire attention, or when sexual desire has been aroused. In these cases, too, there is a felt demand to act in one way rather than another, but the source of the demand is experienced as lying within us: it is our desire which impels us, and which we feel as the urge-to-act. Such experienced demands we may characterize as "subjective," in contrast to those demands which we experience as having their sources "outside" us and which appear to us as "objective." Of course, in both types of case the experiencing of the demand is *our* experience, and is felt to be our experience, but it is impossible adequately to describe this feeling without taking into account what appears to us to be its source.

But it is insufficient merely to specify the experienced point of origin of a demand; as we have already noted, its direction must also be specified. To specify the direction of such an experienced force it is necessary but not sufficient to characterize it as emanating from within us or from outside us; if it emanates from outside us it might be directed against us, or it might not be so directed. We do, I submit, often have the experience that something is being demanded of another person. In such cases we feel a demand, but that demand is not levelled against us: our tension (which may be extreme) is that *he* should act. And, as we have noted, there also are cases in which we see demands as obtaining within a situation, and not being levelled against any specific human being; and there also may be demands (such as the case of a curve demanding a certain completion) in which an aesthetic or quasi-aesthetic object is seen as demanding something of its parts. However, it is not such demands which are involved in our direct moral judgments. When we make a direct moral judgment, the demands which we feel are objective demands that *we* should act, and demands of this type I am characterizing as being "reflexive."

I see a person unable to start his car, a delivery-boy apparently looking for an address, a child who has lost something, a woman loaded down with parcels and trying to open a door. In such cases I often feel a "pressure" upon me. Such pressures are no less "real" in our experience than are the pressures which we feel when we are hungry or when in anger we wish to destroy that which antagonizes us. Yet, as we have noted, their experienced sources are different, and this difference I have attempted to express by saying that the former types of case involve demands which are apprehended as "objective," while the latter constitute "subjective" demands. It is my contention that we never feel moral obligation unless we feel such objective demands.

However, the awareness of an objective demand is not in itself sufficient to evoke a direct moral judgment. As we have already seen, the sense of being morally obliged to act toward an end only arises when we are aware of alternative possibilities for action and we are forced to espouse one rather than another of these possibilities. When I spontaneously stretch out my hand to help a person in trouble, I may be said to be answering to an objective demand, but I am not aware of an obligation so to act. The sense of obligation only arises when I do not react spontaneously, but am cognizant of an alternative, and must espouse or reject that which I see as objectively demanded.

Now, it is frequently the case that there are barriers to responding to the objective demands which we apprehend. In some cases these barriers are physical impossibilities: we cannot do what we see to be demanded of us. In such cases, I submit, we do feel a sense of obligation, even though we may not at the time—and almost certainly we will not later—blame ourselves for having failed to do what we saw to be demanded. In other cases, we find ourselves caught between two sets of objective demands and cannot respond to both; and in these cases we are clearly involved in making a moral judgment as to what we really ought to do. But perhaps the most frequent type of case is that in which we find that of the alternative courses of action which are open to us, one will satisfy demands which appear as objective, while the other will satisfy some demand which arises from within us. It is in this frequent type of case that we speak of a conflict between duty and interest.

So far as direct moral judgments are concerned, the contrast between duty and interest rests solely upon the phenomenological difference between objective and subjective demands. When both types of demand are experienced, and stand opposed to each other, we find that we face a decision between duty and interest. For this reason it has been held (and not only by Kant) that duty always involves acting contrary to interest.[12] And there are indeed many cases in which we feel this to be true. For example, suppose that I have promised to take my children to the next circus which comes to town, and if when it arrives there is nothing that I myself so much wish to do, will I be inclined to regard going to the circus as an instance of doing my duty? Is it not, after all, what I want to do? Similarly, suppose that I praise a man who has spent the whole of a Sunday with an ill friend, and I say that he has assuredly done his duty; might he not object, saying that I had misunderstood, if he had done it solely because he enjoyed his friend's company? Thus, what we do out of inclination does not appear as our duty, that is, as being morally demanded of us.

My contention is that the demands which appear to an agent to be "moral demands" are seen by him to be objective and independent of his desires. This contention can be further supported by the frequently cited fact that while we find that we feel obligations to promote the pleasures of others, we feel no such obligation toward ourselves. Nor do we feel any obligation to fulfill a desire which we experience as being "subjective" in character, that is, as being something which we want merely because we want it. In order to feel an obligation to satisfy one's desire, the fulfillment of that desire must be seen as a means to some further end which itself appears as "objectively good," that is, as good independently of one's preference for it. It is not what I prefer, what I wish, or what I want, which appears as my duty; duty appears as objective, as independent of preference, inclination, or desire. It is this fact which, without doubt, has led many moralists to offer a rigorous dichotomy of duty and desire, and which also explains the emphasis on the "objectivity" of duty in the whole of the deontological tradition.

However, it is necessary to point out that a recognition of the "objectivity" of moral demands need not lead us into what I, at least, take to be the errors which have beset many deontological theories. The first of these errors consists in the normative conclusions which are sometimes drawn from the fact that the demands of duty so frequently conflict with the demands of interest. The unfortunate rigorism of a few deontological theories arises from the fact that when, in a particular situation, *both* duty and interest are experienced, they do stand opposed. But from this fact it does not follow that wherever duty is experienced, interest must stand opposed to it; nor does it follow that wherever interest is found, duty is also present and must lie in whatever goes against the satisfaction of that interest. When the contrast between duty and interest is seen to be a matter of the "vector" present in the demands which we feel, the necessity for making them antagonistic principles in man disappears, and with it disappears the necessity for the rigorism of these deontological theories.

A second point at which I feel that most deontological theories have erroneously interpreted the conflict between duty and interest lies in the epistemological inferences which they have drawn from the "subjectivity" of interest and the "objectivity" of duty. The fact that the demands of duty are experienced as issuing from outside us does not, of itself, permit one to draw any conclusion regarding the existence of an absolute standard of duty. Nor does it even permit one to infer that what we experience as our duty has any ontological status independently of our experience of it. To acknowledge that such inferences *may be* false, one need merely recall that some philosophers have claimed (without being open to the charge of self-contradiction) that the color red is apprehended as being "objective," but that a color-blind person does not experience red, and that red has no ontological status—does not exist—outside of the realm of the experience of certain groups of percipients.

The third error against which we must guard is the assumption that duty and inclination are ultimately discontinuous by nature, resting on different faculties, rather than being differing modes in which a common substrate of motivational forces manifests itself. It is not my purpose to argue which is the correct view; I merely wish to point out that there is no necessary reason to assume that the objectivity of moral demands and the subjectivity of other demands indicates that there is a separate moral faculty in man: we cannot assume that when we seek causal, psychological explanations of two distinct phenomena, the explanations which can be given of them must be in terms of different faculties or attributes of man. In fact, there seems to be some evidence in psychology that demands *upon* the self are very likely explicable in terms of the same principles as are demands issuing *from* the self.[13] If this be true, we need not appeal to separate principles to explain the vectorial differences any more than we appeal to separate principles in explaining the differences between the rise of a column of mercury in a barometer and the fall of a stone released from a height. While our present task is not one of constructing a psychological theory, it is important to bear this possibility in mind, lest we be tempted to follow the examples of Butler and Kant who, impressed by the concrete difference between desires and the sense of duty, assumed that they were discrete principles in man, and not merely contrary tendencies toward action.

iii.

THE FOREGOING ANALYSIS of our experience of obligation must now be supplemented by an attempt to discover the basis of those demands which we have found to be essential to it. They appeared, it will be recalled, as "objective," issuing from one of the alternatives with which the agent found himself confronted. Our present question (which is still a phenomenological question) is therefore this: Is there any characteristic of a prospective alternative which may be held to provide the basis for the demand which an agent feels?

Two possibilities immediately suggest themselves. The first is that the alternative from which the demand issues has received its injunctive character from a special relationship between it and the past experience of the agent. Such a view would, for example, be upheld by those who explain moral phenomena by the effect of past punishments or childhood fixations. That past experience plays a role in determining what it is that appears as demanding, no one I suppose would deny. However, it is doubtful whether one should pass directly from noting the phenomenon of demand to an attempt to explain its presence in genetic terms. In whatever ways we may reach the point of finding a demanding-character in a specific proposed course of action, it appears to place a demand upon us because of *its* nature, not because of ours. How it acquired this nature for us, is a question on which genetic inquiries may often throw considerable light. But only a phenomenological inquiry into its present mode of appearance can answer the question of whether any characteristic within it serves as the basis for the fact that its demand seems to be "objective," that is independent of us.[14]

Holding fast to the "objectivity" of the demands which we feel, a second alternative is to contend that certain objects, envisioned actions, or states of affairs, possess in and of themselves the property of "demandingness." Such would necessarily be our position were we to follow the guidance of most contemporary ethical theories. Ideal Utilitarianism, the Oxford "Neo-Intuitionists," and writers such as Scheler and Hartmann, all stress the view that the morally relevant aspects of an entity are intrinsic properties of it. And so indeed it initially appears. However, when we recall that many items in our experience (for example the perceived speed of a moving object) are relationally determined even though they initially appear to be inherent properties of specific entities, the assumption that "demandingness" is not relationally analyzable may lose some of its plausibility.[15] And, as we shall later see, there are also theoretical reasons of a properly ethical sort which should lead one to challenge the view that the character of being "morally demanded" is an inherent property of certain entities rather than being analyzable in terms of the "*natural*" relations which they bear to the contexts in which they appear.[16]

Rejecting these two alternatives, we shall now look for the basis of a demand in some relational characteristic which is phenomenally objective. Such a characteristic is, I believe, to be found in the relationship of being "fitting" or "unfitting." The importance of this concept for an analysis of moral phenomena has long been recognized by ethical theories, but the effects of Bentham's attack upon it have only recently begun to wear off. It is now incumbent upon us to examine its meaning. (In doing so we shall also use "suitable-unsuitable," "appropriate-inappropriate," "congruent-incongruent" to denote the relational characteristic here in question.)

When we predicate fittingness of an action we are referring to a phenomenally objective relational characteristic. Like Broad, Ross, and Ewing, I should hold that the relation of "being fitting" is, strictly speaking, indefinable:[17] one can only clarify its meaning through "ostensive definition." But in attempting to make clear its meaning one has advantages which do not always obtain in the case of other indefinables such as "color": one can indicate classes of fittingness (for example, "completion") in which the essential nature of the relation is apparent, and one need not thus be confined to single instances, or types of instance (e.g. "this red," "this blue"; or "redness," "blueness"); and, further, one can utilize correlated phenomena, such as particular experiences of "satisfaction," in calling attention to the indefinable which one wishes to discuss. Thus, the indefinability of the relation of "being fitting" will not force us merely to list examples of the relation in our discussion of it; and I shall assume that each reader will recognize the meaning of the term as he reads it. The problem most apt to evoke difficulties (it seems to me) lies not in identifying the relation of "being fitting," but in specifying from case to case the elements between which this relation obtains.

So far as our present problem is concerned, we predicate fittingness or unfittingness of a particular envisioned action; we do so on the ground that we feel it to be fitting or unfitting in the situation which confronts us. As Ewing says, the relation of being fitting obtains between an action and its environment,[18] and I shall here use the term "environment" to refer to the initial conditions which call forth our action.[19] Among such conditions are to be included not merely the present conditions which we find ourselves confronting, but those past and future events which we recognize as being relevant to the choice which we are to make. Thus, the fact that I am aware of having made a promise or accepted a favor, as well as the fact that I have certain ambitions for the future, are part of the present situation which I face. And potentialities and dispositions of my own, such as the fact that I recognize that I am not well or that I feel animus toward another, are as much a part of my present situation as the fact that a person has just asked me to do something for him. It is not stretching the meaning of "the situation which confronts us" to include within it such elements of past and future, and such states of the self, so long as the agent is aware of them and feels them to be relevant to the choice which he finds himself called upon to make. And if this be doubted, let the reader attempt to specify the situation in which he now finds *himself*, and see whether it can be meaningfully and adequately described without reference either to apprehended relations to past and future or to statements which refer to himself as well as to the page which is before him.

The other pole of the relation of "being fitting" is the envisioned action. As we have already had occasion to note, such an action is not identifiable with mere overt behavior: it includes the awareness and espousal of a terminal state of affairs which is taken as being capable of realization.[20] In acting toward a relatively remote goal the specific form of behavior which is here and now to be followed is seen as connected with the terminal state as means-to-end; in such cases the action includes the end as well as the immediate form of behavior which is related to it as a means. In other cases, where the espoused terminal state of affairs is not remote, and a single step in one's behavior will (presumably) lead to its attainment, we tend to identify the action with mere overt behavior, but in such cases too the being directed toward and espousing a terminal state of affairs is an inexpungeable aspect of willed action.

Now, it may be contended that no state of affairs is in fact "terminal," for any state will be followed by some other, to which, presumably, it is causally related. But though in thought we acknowledge this to be true, in action we do not (and cannot) behave on the basis of it. When we act it is always toward some state of affairs which is envisioned as the goal of our action. Whether or not it be close at hand, it is for us provisionally terminal. When I plan to spend an evening at the movie, or budget next year's income, or act toward a goal twenty years distant, or when a national conservation plan for the next hundred years is charted, there is always in mind some state of affairs which is taken as terminal for that action. Of course, knowledge and prudence dictate that I shall not envision the future in too simple terms, concentrating attention only on the terminal state of affairs which I wish to achieve: contingent possibilities must be taken into account and immediate, inescapable consequences noted. But willed action is not directed toward an indefinitely long future which includes all that will ever happen because the action is taken. Nor, on the other hand, is it merely to be conceived in terms of the momentary conditions which in fact exist when it is initially undertaken: it stretches from the present into the future. Thus, as seen at its inception, it is a continuum of limited temporal scope, reaching from the present to the terminal state of affairs at which it is aimed.[21] And one must further note that within this time-span the action constitutes (as does its "environment") a segregated whole: it is envisioned as a single continuing strand, however multiform may be its relationships to other contemporary occurrents.[22] It is such a single strand, leading from the present to an envisioned terminal state of affairs, and neither some isolated fragment of overt behavior nor an indefinitely long causal chain, which the agent sees as being fittingly or unfittingly related to the situation with which he is confronted.

Having now specified what (for an agent) constitutes an action and its "environment," it will be well to characterize briefly the relation of fittingness which may hold between these terms. This may be done through examples, and, as I have noted, a few should suffice. However, it will be convenient to consider for a moment what holds of aesthetic and quasi-aesthetic[23] perceptual experiences, for these will serve as a useful paradigm in our characterization of the fittingness of actions.

In aesthetic and quasi-aesthetic experience it is extremely difficult to specify why a particular perceived entity appears as having its parts fittingly related to one another; it is far easier to specify in what respect the parts of an entity are *un*fittingly related to one another. In the positive case one can, in the end, only appeal to the particular satisfaction which one feels in contemplating the object. In the negative case one can indicate "gaps," "wrong completions," lack of "relatedness" between elements, and the like. Such designations in the negative cases, as well as the particular satisfaction which one receives from the positive cases, suggest that the relation of being fitting consists in an apprehended internality of relationship among the parts. That this is the ground of aesthetic satisfactoriness, and the nature of aesthetic fittingness, is one of the most persistently recognized facts of aesthetic experience. That it may also be meaningfully applied to the relation between actions and their environments can be shown through a few illustrations.

First, let the situation which I confront be one in which I have a particular desire but can see no means through which I can satisfy it. In such a case I apprehend an unfittingness which I may ascribe either to the initial existing conditions or to my goal. If I discover some mode of acting through which I may presumably reach that goal, the doing of that act will appear as being fitting, or suited, to my end. Or if, in the face of the obdurate initial conditions, I change my goal, my new goal will appear as being fitting, or suited, to the conditions which exist. In either case, the relation of being fitting is ascribable to a "harmony" between some feasible mode of behavior and the end which I seek to attain. This harmony consists in the one case of "leading to," in the other of "being consonant with." In both cases there is the apprehension of an inner and essential relationship between two terms: between the feasible mode of behavior and the goal, or between the obdurate initial conditions and the newly espoused goal.

Second, let the situation in which I stand be one in which I have made a promise, and the occasion for the fulfilment of the promise is at hand. To act in such a way as to fulfil my promise is then fittingly related to the situation which confronts me. That situation, it will be recalled, contains as one of its essential elements the fact that in the past I made a promise to behave in a specific way on this occasion, and to behave in this way is seen as a "completion," or "fulfilment," of what I had promised. Here again, the action and situation are apprehended as internally related: the action would not (in some cases) be meaningful, or would not (in any case) have the same meaning, if I were not cognizant of having made the promise.

Third, let the situation in which I find myself contain as its dominant element the fact that I experience a particular need: I am thirsty or hungry. Further, let there be no drink or food immediately accessible to me, and let no other desires or cognized obligations be present to my mind. In such cases (and they are of course relatively rare), the only "sensible," or fitting, thing for me to do is to attempt to satisfy my need: the action is seen as "answering to my need," and is fittingly related to its "environment."

Such are three types of case in which an action may be said to be fittingly related to the situation which the agent confronts: they should suffice to suggest that when an envisioned action is seen by an agent as being "fitting" it is seen as essentially and internally related to his situation. Terms such as "being in harmony with," "being consonant with," "leading to," "completing," "fulfilling," and "answering to," are indicative of such a relationship. But these terms, as well as the illustrations in which they were used, raise the question as to how, precisely, the element of demand is connected with the relation of being fitting. To answer this question it will be useful to return to our paradigm of aesthetic and quasi-aesthetic experience.

If one examines such quasi-aesthetic experiences as that in which a simple non-representational figure is seen as "incomplete," for example as containing "a gap," one finds that he attributes a demand to the figure: the figure "demands" a certain completion. Similarly, when one finds it perceptually "bad" that a picture is hanging crookedly, or is placed just off-center on a narrow wall, one finds that there is present in his experience an element of demand: the picture ought to hang straight, or ought to be farther to the left or to the right.[24] In both cases what is perceptually given is apprehended as being "wrongly structured": in the first case because something is "missing" in the object, and in the second because the object does not "go with" or "fit with" its surroundings. In other words, the feeling of demand depends in both cases upon the fact that all of the apprehended elements in what is perceptually given are not adequately related to one another, that is they lack fittingness. But it must be noted that if there were not within the object some apprehended internality of relations we should not feel such a demand: we do not experience a demand for completion in all figures, nor feel that all objects must be symmetrically disposed in space. In the cases before us it is only because the object (or the object in relation to its perceptual context) sets up demands that are left unfulfilled that we become aware of these demands. Therefore, so far as these cases are concerned, we may say that the presence of demands presupposes a partial but inadequate fittingness within the object.[25]

In the case of aesthetic experiences proper the same contention may be made. An inadequate or positively ugly aesthetic object seems to demand correction because the elements within it bear a partial but inadequate relation of being fitting to one another. In a *successful* aesthetic object the elements are seen as bearing a positive relation of being fitting to one another. They are not apprehended merely as not-unfitting, but are so selected or disposed as to create demands upon one another; demands of which we are aware, and to which we yet find the answers within the object itself.[26] Of course, these demands within the aesthetically good object only exist for those whose native or acquired perceptual endowments make them responsive to the elements contained in the object. But the necessary cooperation of a percipient does not alter the fact that the demands subsist between the elements as apprehended, and do not issue from the percipient himself. And when we come to characterize what it is within the perceived elements that gives rise to the demands of one upon another, we must, I believe, appeal to concepts of "leading to," "contrasting with," and other terms which equally suggest that we are dealing with an apprehended internality of relationship.

Taking our cue from this paradigm, we may say that in some cases at least the presence of apprehended demands presupposes an apprehended relation of fittingness among given elements: what gives rise to the presence of an aesthetic or quasi-aesthetic demand is an intimate but partially unresolved relationship among perceived entities. (In a positively satisfying aesthetic object this relationship is of course resolved through the effects of further elements.) However, not all motivational examples which involve demands would seem to be capable of being construed in the same manner. When, as in our third example, an urge for food or drink is present, the demand which I feel appears as basic and primitive: it would explain why certain objects are fitting, but cannot (apparently) itself be explained by the concept of fittingness.

I shall not deal with this apparent exception, since an answer to it involves considerations which transcend the sphere of a phenomenological investigation. At this point our paradigm remains useful since, as I shall now show, all cases in which an agent experiences a *moral* demand presuppose an apprehended relation of fittingness.[27] This, if true, is of theoretical importance, since it is not unusual to find theories which reverse this order and seek to account for an apprehended fittingness in moral action through recourse to some demand or need in the agent.

The moral demand which an agent experiences we have already identified as a reflexive demand: it appears as an "objective" demand to act (or to abstain from acting) in a particular manner.[28] Therefore, in the three examples cited, a cautious reader who maintained the point of view of the agent must have been struck by the fact that only the second (that in which I felt obliged to keep my promise) was an adequate illustration of what constitutes a moral situation. And in this case our paradigm proves to be adequate.

When I experience a demand to keep a promise this demand does not issue from me, but is levelled against me: it is not that I want to give X five dollars which motivates me, but the fact that I feel obliged to keep my promise. The promise itself appears as an objective fact which places a demand upon me whether I want to keep it or not. However, "the promise" is not a *simple* fact, and the demand which issues from it is relationally determined. To become cognizant of this we need merely ask under what conditions the fact that I have in the past made a promise fails to give rise to a demand to fulfil it. The cases are of two types. First, there are those cases in which the *present* situation in which I stand seems to bear no relation to the promise which I made. For example, when no precise time for the fulfilment of the promise has been specified I do not constantly feel a demand to fulfil it: I am likely only to feel this demand when I find myself in a situation in which I recognize that the fulfilment of the promise is now possible, or when it appears that the fulfilment of the promise will perhaps always remain impossible, or when other circumstances in my situation remind me of the promise I have made. For example, if I have incurred a debt and have promised to repay it within a certain time limit, and I suddenly find myself in possession of the means to repay it long before the time limit has expired, I may well feel a demand to repay it at that time; or if I have incurred other financial obligations and see no way of ever repaying it, this debt may haunt me with its demand whenever I think of my financial condition. But under many other circumstances I do not feel the demand of the promise: the situation in which I find myself must be seen as being relevant to the promise which I have made. Second, there are cases in which I have made a promise but the conditions which were anticipated by both parties when the promise was made are discovered not to exist when the time for the fulfilment of the promise is at hand. In such cases I feel no demand to fulfil the explicit promise which I have made.[29] In this type of case, as well as the first, it becomes clear that the element of moral demand presupposes an apprehended fittingness: the envisioned action places a demand upon us only because it is seen as connected with and fittingly related to the situation which we find ourselves confronting. Thus, the paradigm of aesthetic and quasi-aesthetic experience in which apprehended demands presupposed fittingness (rather than the reverse) is meaningful when applied to moral demands.

The same point may be made with respect to the first and third examples which were used to illustrate the relevance of the concept of fittingness to motivational situations. These examples, as stated, did not contain the element of moral demand. The demands which were present were in the first case associated with a preexisting desire of mine; in the third case they were contained within that desire. But it is possible to transform either example into one which contains an element of *moral* demand (that is an objective, reflexive demand) by a simple alteration of the initial conditions. For example, in the third case, if I see reasons why I should not satisfy my urge to eat—I am working, or I am short of money—I can attempt to convince myself that the consequences of not now satisfying my urge will be detrimental to my work or my health, and I will then feel (or claim to feel) that it is morally fitting, or "right," to eat.[30] But in such cases the demand issues from the consequences which I envision, not from the urge which I feel.

The demand which is felt when the initial conditions are thus transformed rests upon an apprehended relation of fittingness. This can be seen from the fact that a reflexive demand will not issue from any arbitrarily chosen set of envisioned consequences, no matter how important they may be; they must, on the contrary, be apprehended as being directly and appropriately linked to the situation in which I stand. For example, it is only when I am already working that I can utilize the argument that not to satisfy my present craving will interfere with my work, and can have this argument give rise to a reflexive demand: in other cases the satisfaction of my craving, even though it be related to the supposed success of my afternoon's work, will be seen as "desirable," but not as an obligation. Similarly, we can only attempt to utilize the excuse of health as a means of justifying the satisfaction of a present craving if we can view our health as bound up with our work or with someone else's welfare: otherwise this specious argument leads only to a claim that it would be desirable to eat, not that it is incumbent upon us to do so.

It is then my contention that the basis of the reflexive demand which an agent feels when he is confronted by what appears to him to be a moral situation is his apprehension of a fittingness between a specific envisioned action and the situation in which he finds himself. The relation of being fitting or unfitting is, as I have said, indefinable, but I have attempted to indicate its meaning ostensively and to characterize more precisely than is sometimes done what is meant by "the situation" and by "the action" which are the terms of such a relation. Further, I have attempted to illustrate through the paradigm of certain perceptual experiences that the presence of experienced demands *in some cases* rests upon the apprehension of fittingness among given elements, and I have shown that such a paradigm may be applied to those cases in which the reflexive demand which characterizes direct moral judgments is present. Before going on to more complex examples of such judgments, and the theoretical issues which they involve, let me here draw three important conclusions from what has preceded.

First, as I have already noted, certain theories seek the basis of moral obligation in preexisting demands within the agent, and seek to explain such demands in genetic terms. What I have argued seems to me to throw considerable doubt on these theories, although it does not definitely disprove them. If a theorist is willing to hold that, regardless of appearances, moral obligation *must* be explained in terms of preexisting demands within the agent, no phenomenological evidence could convince him that this was not so. But one could then wonder as to what more substantial evidence he could offer to support his own view. If, however, one is willing to follow the lead of phenomenological evidence in constructing psychological theories, then the foregoing account obviously suggests an alternative psychology of moral judgments. The evidence suggests that the experienced demand in a moral situation arises from the agent's apprehension of that situation and the relation which his envisioned action bears to it. It would still be possible for one to hold that genetic explanations may throw light on the question of why he apprehends his situation or envisions his action as he does, and may therefore throw light on why he sees this specific action as fitting or unfitting, but these explanations would not directly serve to explain the phenomenon of demand itself.

Second, the distinction which has sometimes been drawn (notably by Broad)[31] between the rightness of an act as dependent upon its fittingness and its rightness as dependent upon its utility, can now be seen—so far as direct moral judgments are concerned—to be unfounded. When an agent envisions "an action" he envisions it as leading to a certain terminal state of affairs, and when he regards "his situation" he sees it as including references to the past and the future; therefore, the relation of fittingness which he finds between these terms includes all of the elements of "utility" (that is, good consequences) which are apprehended by him as relevant to the morality of his action. The relation of fittingness may therefore be said to be the sole source of the moral demands which an agent feels.[32]

Third, it is to be noted that while our phenomenological analysis has led us to distinguish between specifically moral demands and other demands, no such distinction has been drawn between "moral fittingness" and other cases of fittingness. And no such distinction was intended. The contention of Broad and of Ross that there is a unique type of specifically moral fittingness seems to me to be without foundation.[33] We were forced to distinguish between moral demands and other demands because both may be present in the same experience while differing from each other. However, the apprehended relation of fittingness which we have found to be basic to the presence of moral demands seems to be identical with apprehended fittingness in other cases, as is testified by the fact that of our three original examples of the fittingness of an action to a situation only one could be said to give rise to a moral demand. That "moral fittingness" should simply be an apprehended fittingness between a situation and an envisioned action, and not a unique type of fittingness at all, is a point of major theoretical importance. For if that which is the basis of a moral demand is not a uniquely moral fact, but an instance of a commonly experienced characteristic, then it may be said that our theory is "naturalistic."

iv.

IN THE PRECEDING phenomenological analysis of the nature and basis of that which appears to an agent as his duty, we have been concerned with only relatively simple cases. It is now necessary to analyze other situations which better represent some of the antinomies of moral experience. In so doing we shall simultaneously be testing the validity of our analysis of the less complex cases and be able to resolve (so far as direct moral judgments are concerned) the conflict between utilitarianism and deontology.

That there is such a conflict among contemporary ethical theories is a fact too well recognized to need documentation. The recent attempts which have been made to resolve it from the side of the utilitarian tradition have, in the main, taken the form of including within the calculation of the total value of an act elements which earlier teleological theories did not include. These additional elements of value have sometimes been the motive from which the act was done (e.g. in Rashdall); sometimes they have taken the form of holding that an act may, because of its nature, possess a "direct" intrinsic value apart from the value of its consequences.[34] And there are indeed a variety of ways in which recent Ideal Utilitarians have modified the traditional teleological position. On the side of deontological theories the attempt has been made to include the promotion of good consequences among the "*prima facie* obligations,"[35] and thus to grant that one's final obligation is not a matter which is independent of the value of the consequences to be achieved by one's action. While each of these types of attempt must be recognized to have been in part motivated by a praiseworthy concern to construct a theory which shall be in accord with our actual moral judgments, each is, in my opinion, open to criticism.

The difficulties with the various teleological attempts seem to me to hinge upon the fact that while they are initially plausible when we examine removed moral judgments, they find no confirmation in our direct moral judgments. For example, it is simply not true that in calculating the value of an action which we contemplate, we do in fact take into account the value of the motive from which we would be acting–nor, if we did, would others think it proper that we should do so. Similarly, I very much doubt that in direct moral judgments our recognition that one course of conduct is obligatory rests upon a summation of (a) all the elements of intrinsic value and disvalue within the act, and (b) the value which will accrue because of the further consequences which that act will have. Such a view may seem plausible when one is examining those judgments in which we attempt to "stand apart from ourselves," attempting to judge as another would judge of our action; but they can scarcely be said to provide a description of what usually occurs when we feel morally obliged not to lie, not to accept a bribe, or obliged to make a personal sacrifice for an ideal. However, since I suppose that those who would give us such analyses are not attempting to remain consistently close to the phenomenological facts of our direct moral judgments, but are attempting to establish how it is that their theories would decide what "really" is right, I shall not press this point.[36]

The deontological attempt to take cognizance of the value of consequences in the estimate of the rightness of an act is of more interest to our present discussion, and I shall consider it at some length. What I find unsatisfactory in it will help to show what I take to be the nature of our more complex direct moral judgments.

As we have already noted,[37] even the strictest of deontologists need not exclude all of the consequences of an action from the nature of that action, and need not therefore hold that all of its consequences are irrelevant to its moral rightness or wrongness. However, in Ross' recent version of the deontological theory something more than this has been claimed. It is Ross' view that among *prima facie* obligations there is the specific obligation to promote good consequences, and this obligation must be weighed against others in attempting to ascertain where our real duty lies. His view may be criticized on two scores.

First, if the promotion of good consequences really constitutes a *prima facie* obligation, it should (according to Ross' theory) always enter into our consideration of what really constitutes the act which we ought to perform. This follows from the following facts: (1) any *prima facie* obligation always has a tendency to be binding, and therefore whenever it is relevant to the situation in which we are placed it ought to be considered in judging what constitutes our real duty; (2) any action which we undertake will, in point of fact, have some causal consequences, and therefore the *prima facie* obligation to promote good rather than bad consequences will be relevant to *every* moral choice which we make. Now, I submit that in our direct moral judgments the value of the causal consequences to be attained by acting in one way rather than another does not *always* enter into our assessment of what is our real duty, and that Ross himself does not argue that it always should. I would therefore hold that however a deontological theory may take the consequences of an action into account in seeking to state what constitutes the moral rightness of an action, it should not do so by holding that we have (in Ross' sense) a *prima facie* obligation to promote good consequences.[38]

My second objection to Ross' modification of the traditional deontological position cuts even deeper. I shall now attempt to show that his employment of the concept of "*prima facie* obligations" is wholly unnecessary, and serves in fact to confuse rather than clarify the nature of our direct moral judgments. It will be my contention that the concept of fittingness, when applied to the relationship between a contemplated action and the specific situation in which we are placed, provides a sufficient basis for the analysis of what constitutes our obligation, and that the notion of *prima facie* obligations need not be introduced even to account for those cases in which we ordinarily speak of "a conflict of duties" or of a conflict between obligations and values.

In the simpler cases of direct moral judgments it was pointed out that what an agent sees as his duty is the performance of, or abstention from, a specific envisioned action. Such an envisioned action is the source of a demand upon the agent, and this demand we found to be based upon an apprehended relation of being fitting (or unfitting) to the situation which the agent regarded himself as confronting. Nothing was said which would characterize this felt demand as merely a "*prima facie*" obligation, and not the agent's "real" obligation. So far as the agent himself is concerned, to feel this reflexive demand is to feel one's obligation.

But it may be objected that in more complex cases of direct moral judgments the agent *does* distinguish between his *prima facie* obligation and his real obligation. These more complex cases would presumably be of two types: those in which a so-called *prima facie* duty conflicts with another *prima facie* duty, and those in which it conflicts with the promotion of desirable consequences (that is, with values).[39] I shall first deal with the former type.

What Ross means by "a *prima facie* obligation" is the tendency of a given act to be obligatory because of the type of act which it is. Thus, to keep a promise or to make restitution for an injury which one has done are *prima facie* obligations. Each *prima facie* obligation has a *tendency* to be binding, but when they conflict one's *real* obligation lies with whichever of these claims is the more "stringent." As Ross points out, which of the claims is the more stringent must be settled from case to case, and no rule of thumb can be given. Nor, according to Ross, are we justified in asserting that our judgments are certain when we find the claims of one *prima facie* obligation to be more stringent than the claims of another. All that we recognize is the tendency of each to be binding, and the fact that to us (and perhaps to others) one *seems* to be more binding than the other.[40]

Taken as a phenomenological analysis of direct moral judgments this position seems to me to be untenable. It is of course true that we may experience two incompatible demands levelled against us. When this occurs each of these demands issues from a different aspect of the situation in which we find ourselves. Thus far Ross' analysis is sound. However, neither of these demands is experienced as having a "tendency" to be binding: each is initially experienced *as* binding.[41] Faced by such a conflict of duties we ask ourselves (as Ross has us ask) which is the more binding, or stringent, of these obligations. To this question we cannot find an answer merely by considering the types of act which are concerned: as critics of the deontological tradition have shown, we do not consistently hold that one type of act, such as promise-keeping, is always more obligatory than an act of another type, such as making restitution for an injury. An answer to the question must, as Ross sees, lie in a comparison of the specific envisioned actions themselves. But on what basis do we find the claims of one of these actions to be more "stringent" than the claims of the other?

In some cases this question is easily solved. When faced by conflicting claims we are led to a reexamination of each in so far as it is affected by the presence of the other. For example, as Ross points out,[42] a prior promise appears as more binding than a later promise which is incompatible with it. Or, again, our promise may lose its claim if we believe (or bring ourselves to believe) that he to whom we made it would wish us to break it under these circumstances. But in many cases we cannot resolve the dilemma which we face by merely reexamining each of the claims, and when we cannot do so we must decide which of the two persistent claims is the more "stringent."

Now, Ross' use of the term "stringent" might lead one to expect that there was in each so-called *prima facie* obligation, or claim, an assessable quantum of force by means of which it was possible to calculate which line of action constituted one's duty. And this in fact sometimes appears to be his position.[43] However, at other times his discussion suggests that our calculations are somewhat more complex: we calculate the respects in which each of the conflicting lines of obligation are *prima facie* right and *prima facie* wrong, and our real obligation then becomes that of setting ourselves to perform that action in which the elements of *prima facie* rightness most outweigh its elements of *prima facie* wrongness.[44] On either interpretation, Ross' analysis of what we do (or ought to do) in reaching a moral decision is not what one would be led to expect him to hold when one notes that he believes that "*prima facie* obligation depends upon some one aspect of the act; obligation or disobligation attaches to it in virtue of the totality of its aspects."[45] The most natural interpretation of the fact that rightness is a toti-resultant property would be that it cannot be calculated by summing the specific rightnesses and wrongnesses of its separable elements. Such, I believe to be the case.[46] I should therefore like to propose, in conformity with my previous analysis, that the ground of the stringency of a claim is the fittingness of answering to that claim, rather than to any opposed claim, in the situation which the agent confronts. Let me illustrate this point through an example.

A certain person, X, did me a great favor: my position was in jeopardy, and he intervened on my behalf. He did so at considerable risk to his own advancement, for we were both under the administration of a person who was determined to have me replaced, and who was vindictive when crossed. Thanks to *X*'s forceful intervention I was retained. Some years later *X* and I are both in other positions. A question arises as to whether he should be retained in his new position. He does not seem qualified to the administrator in charge of his section; and, on the basis of the evidence at hand, I am convinced that he is not so qualified. Should I, when asked my opinion, use my influence to have him retained because of the service which he had courageously done me?

Here there is a clear conflict between two so-called *prima facie* obligations: each taken independently of the other exerts a claim over me. But it is characteristic of such a situation that I must answer to one rather than to the other, and it is in this light that I see my dilemma. I may seek to undermine the apparent claim of gratitude by attempting to hold that when *X* had previously acted in my behalf he had done so not out of an interest in my welfare but out of resentment against our superior, or that if he loses his position he will readily find a more suitable one; or I may seek to undermine the claim of expressing my true conviction by attempting to hold that *X* is not doing any harm in his position and will in all likelihood be replaced by someone no better suited for the work. But if I find myself unable to undermine either claim by such arguments, my dilemma remains unresolved. I may then attempt to escape from it by seeking some means of satisfying each claim successively. For example, I may seek to reassure myself that if *X* loses his position I shall be able to help find him a more suitable one. But this enticing means of escape is not always open to us: we may recognize that the claims cannot in fact be successively met. When this situation obtains we can and do ask ourselves which is the right course to follow, which claim ought to be sacrified to the other, and we find, I submit, an answer to this question in seeing one of the two alternatives before us as being more fittingly related to the situation in which we stand: whichever it is, its claims are the more "stringent."

In the case before us (as I personally envision it) I should decide that it is more fitting to give an honest answer than to act for the benefit of *X*. I should not feel this because honesty is in general a more "stringent" obligation than expressing one's gratitude, nor because in this case there is something more "stringent" in the act of telling the truth, but because telling the truth rather than repaying a debt of obligation is less unfitting in this situation than the act of sacrificing the truth to the past obligation. For the situation in which I stand is one in which I have been asked a legitimate question; he who has asked my opinion either does not know the special past personal tie which binds me to *X*, or is counting on me not to be influenced by it. This is the essential aspect of the situation which I now face. To be sure, the past tie which binds me to *X*, and which is the source of a special concern for his welfare, is also cognized as a factor in my situation; but it is an accidental, not an essential, factor. If I disliked a person concerning whom my opinion was asked, or if that person had done me an injury, I would be expected to discount my bias against him; what I am called upon to do is give a carefully considered and truthful answer. To let a concern for *X*'s welfare lead me to give an untruthful answer is unfitting in such a situation, however fittingly a concern for his welfare may be related to other situations. Therefore, to sacrifice an honest answer to the claims of gratitude would (for me) be morally wrong in this case, not because the claim of veracity is, as such, stronger or more binding, but because it is more fittingly related to the essential nature of the specific situation which confronts me.

But here a possible objection must be anticipated. It may be objected that the views which I have expressed regarding this case must necessarily commit me to holding that to speak the truth when one is expected to do so must always take precedence over any other claim, since the situation which one confronts when asked for the truth is always fittingly related to telling the truth, and unfittingly related to telling a falsehood. Such an interpretation is unwarranted: we often find it fitting to say what we know to be false, even when a true answer is expected of us. Lying is (in a moral sense) easy. But to find it easy we must be able to challenge the right of the inquirer to having the truth at his disposal. When I see the purpose of an inquirer as illegitimate, the unfittingness of his end makes a truthful answer on my part itself unfitting, since it will be used as a means to that end. No matter how insistent on obtaining the truth he may be, I find it easy to deny the knowledge which I possess, for I am not then giving an answer which runs counter to my conviction. But in the case before us I have assumed that my inquirer has a right to the knowledge which he requests, and it is not easy (in a moral sense) to affirm what runs counter to conviction. Thus, the fittingness of a truthful answer presupposes the fittingness of the question asked, and not every demand for a truthful answer leads us to see it as fitting that we should give such an answer.

If this analysis of my own direct moral judgments should be considered too lax, I ask the reader to examine what he would wish himself able to do if he were ever interrogated by a tyrannical secret police; or what he in fact often does (or wishes he had done) when asked a question concerning another person if that question is motivated solely by malice; or whether he does not feel wholly justified in giving evasive or untrue answers to gossipy questions. However, if Ross' analysis of *prima facie* obligations were correct, our view would in fact be too lax. For it is held by Ross that each *prima facie* obligation has a "tendency" to be binding, and is binding if not overridden by another, more stringent claim. According to Ross, even when it is thus overridden it maintains its *tendency* to be binding, and its lack of fulfilment ought therefore to occasion some measure of moral regret.[47] In the cases just cited I fail to find that this holds. In the case of sacrificing a chance to discharge my debt of gratitude to X for the sake of giving a truthful opinion of his capacities, I find no element of moral regret. What I do regret is having been placed in this situation in which I had to choose between a concern for his welfare and telling the truth; I regret the effect which the loss of his position will have on his welfare; I regret that I was in part the instrument of this loss; I regret what he may think of me, possibly viewing me as ungrateful; and I regret that a huge opportunity to show him my gratitude has slipped by. But none of these regrets constitutes the peculiar moral regret which is usually termed remorse. For remorse is that regret which we feel when we contemplate an act which we have done, and each of *these* regrets refers to some specific aspect or consequence of the action, not to the fact that the action was done. In other words, regret is distinguishable from remorse in having as its object a contemplated disvalue, not a contemplated wrongness. If Ross' analysis were correct, and each so-called *prima facie* obligation maintained its tendency to be morally obligatory, we should feel a partial remorse, and not merely regret, when one claim is overridden by another.

It is doubtless Ross' interest in a valid, or "objective" normative system which led him to the analysis of *prima facie* obligations which he gave. It has been my purpose to show that the distinction which he is thereby led to draw between *prima facie* and real obligation is not adequate if considered as a phenomenological analysis of what is involved in direct moral judgments. I have argued that the concept of "stringency" which he employs need not be left unanalyzed, nor analyzed as Ross analyzes it; but that it may be treated in the same way as the original claims (the so-called *prima facie* obligations) which we feel. In my opinion, a strictly phenomenological description reveals that what we take to be the more stringent of two irreconcilable moral demands is that demand which we still feel to be levelled against us after our initial, segmented view of our situation has been replaced by a new view of what constitutes its essential nature. Thus, what we judge to be really obligatory is not the "stronger" of two demands, but that action which is a fitting response to what we take to be the dominant element in the total situation which we face. And I have supported this argument by adducing the distinction which we feel between regret and remorse, for if Ross' analysis were correct we should (I believe) feel some remorse, and not merely regret, when one so-called *prima facie* obligation is overridden by another.[48]

It may however still be objected by those who are primarily concerned to establish a valid normative ethics that the view which I have offered is unsound. For what, they might ask, would happen if some other agent, placed in a similar situation, were to find that "the essential nature" of his situation demanded that he should render a false opinion out of gratitude toward his friend? That this might happen is surely possible, for there are many persons who attach less value to honesty in the field of official relationships. What would then happen?—What would happen is what does happen: confronted by similar situations men reach differing moral conclusions, and each may feel an obligation no less keen than that felt by the other. It is not our present problem to attempt to decide between them. From our present point of view all that is of concern is an analysis of the basis of the obligation which an agent feels, whatever may be the content of that obligation. And if another agent should differ from me, and feel it morally incumbent upon him to protect his friend, an analysis of his judgment would, I submit, reveal that this obligation rests for him on the fact that he apprehends such an action to be fittingly related to what he conceives to be the situation in which he stands.

Thus far in our analysis of the more complex moral situations we have been concerned with conflicts between two so-called duties of special obligation. We must now consider those cases in which one such obligation or claim stands opposed to the promotion of "good consequences." Here again we shall attempt to establish that an adequate analysis of a felt obligation presupposes the phenomenon of fittingness.

That the promotion of good consequences may itself be felt as an obligation is a fact so widely recognized that it is often left undiscussed. Were it not for this fact teleological theories of ethics would, of course, never have arisen. On the other hand, I believe that it is possible to show that there are felt obligations other than the obligation to promote good consequences.[49] If, then, we are to avoid merely listing a number of discrete types of "*prima facie* obligation," among which the promotion of good consequences is one, we must examine the connection between the apprehension of certain consequences as good and the feeling of obligation. In approaching this problem it will be well to consider on what occasions an agent feels an obligation to promote good consequences and on what occasions he does not.

We have already noted certain occasions where the presence of something apprehended as valuable does *not* give rise to the reflexive demand of obligation: these are to be found wherever the value rests upon the existence of a demand which emanates from within the agent himself.[50] Thus, a desire for food, a desire for fame, or the anticipation of some pleasurable experience, do not take on the character of being morally obligatory, for the demands which we in such cases experience are apprehended as "subjective" rather than "objective." On the other hand, certain entities appear to be valuable independently of our own inclinations or desires. Thus a courageous act does not appear valuable because I admire it, but I feel that my admiration is based on the valuable quality of the act. And I do not feel that the relief of another's pain, or the fulfilment of my friend's ambition, are states of affairs which are valuable because I desire them; on the contrary, I believe that I desire them because of the value which they contain. It is only in this type of case, where the value of an entity is apprehended as being independent of us, that we feel an obligation to promote this value.

However, not every case in which we apprehend an entity as being valuable independently of us is a case in which we feel that a demand for action is placed upon us. The recognition of the value of a painting or of a courageous action may seem to us to demand admiration, but we should hardly hold these to be cases of a felt moral obligation. What is missing in them is the fact that they do not concern the espousal of an envisioned goal: they are not what we have called willed actions. But when I see that I can relieve the pain of another or aid a friend in attaining his ambition, I am contemplating a future state of affairs which I recognize as valuable, and which I believe some effort on my part can help to actualize. It is only then that I feel obligated to act for that end.

Yet not even all cases of this type are cases in which an agent feels obligated to promote good consequences. We may recognize a certain future state of affairs as valuable, and we may believe that through some action we could help to actualize that state of affairs, but we may still not feel obliged to do so because we find it be "none of our business": the state of affairs which might be achieved bears no relation to the situation in which we stand. For example, a parent's awareness of the dependence of his child upon him makes the incidental pleasures of his child a source of concern to him, while the incidental pleasures of a stranger, an acquaintance, or a neighbor are not.[51] Similarly, one's vocation, be it teacher, lawyer, doctor, policeman, clerk, makes certain states of affairs relevant to our situation, whereas others, no matter how good, seem not to be within the province of our action: it is only the former which give rise to a sense of obligation in us.

In summary we may say that the apprehended goodness of certain consequences only gives rise to a feeling of obligation to promote them when the following three conditions are fulfilled: first, the goodness must appear as independent of our own inclinations or desires; second, this goodness must attach to some envisioned future state of affairs which we feel we can help to actualize through action; third, this state of affairs must be seen as relevant to our situation. When these conditions are fulfilled we feel a demand which emanates from the apprehended value of the envisioned state of affairs and places an obligation upon us to act for that state of affairs. This experience, I submit, is qualitatively similar to the feeling which we have when we see that we ought to tell the truth or that we ought to keep a promise which we have made.

It is not my present purpose to seek to explain why there should be this similarity between the felt obligation to promote good consequences and such other obligations as keeping a promise.[52] I have merely contended that in those cases where an agent does in fact feel an obligation to promote good consequences, he would not be inclined to view this obligation as different in force or in status from other obligations. It is now necessary to show that this obligation rests upon the apprehension of the fittingness of the action to the situation which the agent sees as confronting him.

Suppose that I promise a friend that I will attend to his affairs while he is away, and I realize when I make this promise that its faithful execution will involve my staying at home all summer. If, after he has left, I am invited to the shore, I will not feel it right to go, even for a brief stay, if his affairs need my constant supervision. I may become chagrined that I made the promise, and irked at him because he allowed me to do so, but the obligation to remain continues to have all of its binding force. (And if I do accept the invitation, taking the risk that nothing of decisive importance will arise during my absence, I do so knowing full well that what I am doing is not what I ought to do.) However, suppose that during my friend's absence a political or academic investigation is being conducted, and I believe that such testimony as I might volunteer would be of crucial importance in establishing the competence or loyalty of one of the individuals concerned. Under these circumstances I would feel it to be proper to relinquish the affairs of my friend to the care of another—whether or not I was wholly convinced that they would be properly attended to—and act for what seemed to be the more important objective, establishing the competence or loyalty of a person who has been unjustly accused.

If in such a case I were asked to state on what grounds I reached my decision as to the rightness of abandoning the promise which I had made, I might answer that it was more important to defend the innocent than to protect my friend against such inconvenience and loss as my absence might occasion him. This, it would appear, is a frank and explicit appeal to the relative value of the two sets of consequences to be achieved. Yet, what occurs in such a case is not precisely what most teleologists would have us believe.[53] We do not alternately weigh the values attaching to each set of consequences and reach a decision on the basis of which will promote more value than the other. For example, in reaching my decision I need not assume that I know that the unhappiness of the innocent man will exceed the unhappiness occasioned to my friend. What we do in fact mean by appealing to the relative "importance" of the two sets of alternatives is that the situation in which this man will lose his position and reputation on the basis of false charges is a worse situation than the one in which my friend will suffer inconvenience and loss. What makes the one situation "worse" than the other is the greater "wrongness" or unfittingness which I find to be present in it.[54]

If these phenomenological remarks are correct, it will be seen that, so far as this case is concerned, the way in which we apprehend an obligation to promote what are usually termed good consequences is identical with the way in which we apprehend an obligation to keep a promise or to speak the truth. To apprehend such an obligation we must be cognizant of something being wrong in the initial situation which we confront, and we must recognize that some action of ours can serve to correct this wrongness. The action which we envision as a corrective then seems to place a demand upon us, for it serves as a fitting answer to the demands which we see within the situation itself. And when, as in this case, we are faced by a complex situation containing two incompatible sets of objective demands, our decision as to which is the morally obligatory course of action rests upon our apprehension of the degree of unfittingness which will characterize the resulting situation if we sacrifice the first claim to the second, or the second to the first.

That this analysis as yet provides no clue to a distinction between "valid" and "invalid" moral judgments is a fact which has already been recognized. Our present problem is not to establish what constitutes a correct or an incorrect apprehension of obligation, but to show the conditions under which a sense of obligation is felt. For this purpose our preceding example seems to me to be a significant and fair test. However, there may be those who would take exception to it, since it treated the defense of an innocent man as an example of the promotion of good consequences, and it might be objected that his innocence introduced some special obligation other than the promotion of good consequences into the case. To such an objection the following reply can be made.

We have already noted that not every case in which an entity appears to us to be valuable gives rise to a feeling of obligation. In order that this feeling should arise three conditions must be present: first, the value must appear as independent of our inclinations or desires; second, the entity to which it attaches must be some future state of affairs which can be the goal of a willed action; third, this state of affairs must be seen as relevant to our situation. Now, whenever these conditions are fulfilled we in fact find that we can equally well refer to the valuable state of affairs which we feel obliged to promote in terms of its value, or in terms of some so-called special obligation. For example, when I feel obligated to help a stranger who is in difficulty or who is suffering, I would surely be said to be feeling an obligation toward his welfare, but I could equally well be said to be feeling the obligation to help another. Or when I feel obligated to act for the benefit of the community in which I live, I can equally well be said to be moved by the value of that which I seek to promote or by an obligation to my community.[55] It is only in those cases in which the presence of value does not in fact give rise to a feeling of obligation that we can find a "pure" case of action in accordance with value—that is, a case which cannot also be described in the more deontological language of everyday moral experience.

The truth of this contention can be seen in the following way. Suppose that I am faced by a situation in which I am aware of the possibility of acting for either of two incompatible ends, both of which appear as good to me. Suppose also that these ends are in no way connected with one another save for the fact that they cannot both be attained—that is, the circumstances which I face make it impossible to realize both. An example of this type would be the fact that I can choose between buying a new car or taking a vacation: I should like both and can have either. In such a case I merely decide on the basis of "preference," and no feeling of obligation will arise. But now suppose that my choice lies between taking a vacation and spending the summer at some remunerative work. In this case the two alternatives may be seen as having an inner connection with each other, and not merely as being related through the fact that they are incompatible: the one appears as pleasant but costly, the other as unpleasant but financially rewarding.[56] As soon as they are thus brought into a single context I am aware of the possibility of an obligation: I ask myself what I "ought" to do, not merely "what do I want to do." Now, if my financial situation were such as to cause me no concern whatsoever, I should feel no obligation to act in one way rather than the other: what I ought to do would depend upon what I would like. Thus, I would again decide on the basis of preference. But it is to be noted that even though under these circumstances I should feel free to consult my preference, the mere fact that the two alternatives were seen as inherently connected within a single context gave rise to the idea of an "ought." Now suppose that I am in fact concerned about my finances; in this case I should immediately feel an obligation to forego my vacation in favor of the remunerative work. This obligation would be felt to rest upon the relation of fittingness: considering my finances it is fitting that I should earn rather than spend money. When I see the alternatives in this light the demand which I experience issues from the envisioned action of earning the money, and can equally well be described in terms of an obligation to better my financial condition or in terms of an obligation to act for what I apprehend to be valuable: having the additional money at my disposal.

Now I may of course decide that what I really ought to do is take the vacation, and not work. But if this is my decision it will be because I see the vacation as being more fittingly related to the situation which I confront. For example, I may hold that though I need the money I also need a vacation for reasons of health; or I may hold that I should go on the vacation in order to refresh myself for my other duties, or because my family will profit more by the vacation than by the improvement of my financial condition. In other words, the situation in which I stand may be seen to contain other demands which would cause taking the vacation to appear as more fitting than obtaining an additional income. But in that case, too, I can equally well describe the grounds of my obligation in terms of a duty or in terms of the value of the state of affairs to be achieved. So long as we are cautious enough to distinguish between those cases in which we act for an apprehended value without feeling an obligation to do so, and those cases in which the pursuit of a valuable end does appear as obligatory, there is no difference between finding the ground of obligation in the value of the envisioned goal of an action and finding the ground of obligation in the fittingness of this action to the situation in which the agent stands.

We shall later find other examples in which there is this equivalence between an obligation to promote valuable consequences and an obligation which is describable in deontological terms.[57] Here it has only been of importance to note that in both cases the ground of obligation is the same. And now, as a final test of the adequacy of the concept of fittingness when used to describe the ground of an apprehended moral obligation, we may adduce the explanations which it affords of the following apparently puzzling facts.

The first of these facts is that we often feel an obligation to act for the pleasure of others, but no obligation to act for our own pleasure. We feel such an obligation, I submit, when we are cognizant of another as being "unhappy," or when we feel that he will be made unhappy by our failure to act on his behalf, or when through personal ties with a person we become sensitized to each of the desires which he experiences. In each of these types of case our feeling of obligation to act for his pleasure rests upon the fact that we see something "amiss" in his situation. For example, we are moved to act for the pleasures of others in such situations as those in which we see a person suffering, or think of him lying ill abed; we feel an obligation to confer a pleasure upon some one when we realize how easily we might do so, and envision him as being rendered less happy by our failure to do so (a feeling which may persist even when we recognize that he may not be cognizant of what we might do for him); and we find it our duty to promote pleasure when through love or constant association we feel each successive beat of another's desire and wish to save him the frustration of unfulfilled desires (in our solicitude often feeling desires which the other does not feel, and might even reject). In all such cases the common factor is not merely the possibility of pleasurable experience, but the awareness on the part of the agent of something which appears to him amiss, of some demand on the part of another which he himself can fulfil.

But when we are cognizant of some way in which we can bring pleasure to ourselves, we feel no such obligation. We do not see the situation which we confront as containing something amiss, but only as not conforming to subjectively experienced demands. The "subjective" origin of these demands makes the object which could satisfy them appear as fitting (that is, as good),[58] and the pleasure which might be derived from their satisfaction will appear as morally innocent if its attainment does not conflict with any demands which appear as "objective." However, when we think of our own future pleasure we find that its attractiveness rests upon our inclination toward it, and this fact differentiates it from our experience when we feel moved to act for the pleasure of others: the reflexive element of demand is absent. Thus, though our own pleasures are no less instances of value than are the pleasures of others (each being apprehended as "fitting"), we do not feel an obligation to promote them.

The second apparently puzzling phenomenon which is explained by the analysis I have given is why, although we feel no obligation to promote our own pleasure, we do in fact feel certain other obligations to ourselves. To explain this fact we need not follow the theory of Butler and Broad that our selfish propensity to promote our own pleasure is so strong that it needs no reinforcement from the sense of obligation, while our concern for others (and presumably also for our own nonhedonic values) must be supported by a further prop. Such a theory would not only introduce metaphysical assumptions concerning extra-natural or evolutionary causality into our discussions of the moral consciousness, but would substitute genetic speculations for an analysis of present facts. The answer to the question is to be found elsewhere.

So far as our present discussion is concerned, where we are dealing only with direct judgments of moral rightness and wrongness,[59] it may be said that whenever we feel an obligation to ourselves we are viewing some particular action as obligatory because of its relation to an ideal which we espouse. When I feel it obligatory to work rather than to go to the movies or play bridge, when I feel it obligatory to spend a sociable evening rather than be seclusive, or to have a solitary evening rather than be sociable, I feel I owe such actions to myself; but I feel this because I see the action in relation to an ideal with which the alternative action is not consonant, and which the action felt to be obligatory will serve to uphold. If I merely wish to work, or to be sociable, or to be alone, I do not feel it to be a duty to do so; the fact of obligation emerges when some ideal stands threatened, and it is the ideal, not my present interest, which places the demand upon me. Therefore, to speak of such cases as instances of obligations to one's self is apt to be a misleading characterization of them. They are, of course, distinct from our obligations to others, but they are not felt as obligations to guard and promote our own welfare, but as obligations to act in accordance with our espoused ideals.

That this contention is phenomenologically correct can be seen from the fact that not every instance of such an obligation can be understood in terms of the future consequences which will be fostered by it. For example, to attempt to work rather than go to the movies is not necessarily seen as important with respect to that to which it will lead: I may feel the obligation very strongly though I do not anticipate achieving any important results through my work. On such occasions the obligatoriness of the action is felt to be connected with a larger issue than the results to which my evening's work can be expected to lead: I feel that my life has somehow taken a wrong turning, that I have become lazy and shirked work, and my present choice then appears as a crisis, as a test of an ideal—no matter how trivial the occasion appears to an outsider to be. And if this is true of the felt obligation to work rather than to seek entertainment, it is even more obviously true of those cases in which I feel it incumbent upon me to become more sociable, or to explore some field of knowledge with which I am unacquainted. It is not the ultimate good consequences of so doing which is the source of my feeling of obligation (in fact, if challenged, I would be unable in many cases to point to a single ulterior good consequence which my action would promote); the source of the obligation is in the feeling of incompleteness which a recognition of my lack of sociability, or of this knowledge, imposes upon me. Thus, when we say that we owe it to ourselves to pursue some course of action, it is not because we have a direct desire to do so, but because this course of action seems prescribed by an ideal which we accept.

Once it is recognized that our so-called duties to ourselves are to be understood, not in terms of the particular good consequences which they promote, but in terms of their relation to an ideal, any supposed difference between them and other obligations disappears. For an ideal does not operate upon us in the form of a subjective wish: it appears as "inherently" good, and as the source of demands upon us.

Having thus explained the commonly accepted facts that we feel an obligation to promote the pleasures of others, but not our own pleasures, and that we nonetheless do feel other obligations to ourselves, it will be well to draw together what has been said in the present section.

It will be remembered that we have been concerned to show that the concept of fittingness is of use in understanding those more complex moral situations in which one felt obligation comes into conflict with another. Dissatisfied with Ross' theory of *prima facie* obligations, I have suggested that when an agent feels that two parts of the situation in which he is placed level incompatible demands against him, the reason why he finds one of these demands to be morally obligatory, and the other not, is that he finds that to answer to *this* demand is more fittingly related to the total situation in which he is placed. In the case of a conflict between two "duties of special obligation," such as is involved in a conflict between the claims of veracity and gratitude, his feeling of obligation will follow what he takes to be the *essential* nature of the specific present situation. In the case of a conflict between a "duty of special obligation" and the promotion of what he takes to be good consequences (and the apprehension of certain consequences as good does not always, it will be remembered, give rise to a feeling of obligation), he will find his duty in whichever course of conduct is seen as leading to a less unfitting result. Thus the two supposedly different types of case (the one most frequently cited by deontologists, the other by teleologists) turn out in the end to be susceptible of a common analysis. What might be called the "structure" of the situation will differ in the two types of case—in the one the agent's attention is primarily focussed upon the initial conditions which he faces, in the other upon the terminal states of affairs to which each alternative will lead; but regardless of this difference in structure, a common factor lies at the root of the feeling of obligation; this factor is the apprehended fittingness of one rather than the other of the envisioned actions when each is viewed in the light of the situation which the agent finds that he faces.

That it in fact makes no difference whether we speak in terms of specific obligations or in terms of the goodness of consequences, *so long as we hold fast to the data provided by our direct moral judgments,*[60] can be made clear by the following considerations.

First, what appears to the agent as an obligatory act also appears to him to be valuable. When I feel obliged to speak the truth no matter how disastrous the consequences of speaking the truth may be, I attach value to that act and find it to be a *better* act than its alternative would be. (There is, so far as I can see, no case in which an agent would say that an act was morally obligatory but was really a bad act: so long as we are speaking of an agent's own apprehension of duty and value, a good act and a right one, a bad act and a wrong one, are identical terms.)

Second, when an agent feels it to be his duty to speak the truth, "veracity as such" will appear to him as a worthy ideal. (To feel this he need not hold that regardless of circumstances one should always speak the truth; but the example before him may seem to him to exemplify a principle the force of which he on that occasion feels—just as he may attribute the goodness of a particular painting to some principle of pictorial composition without holding that the same principle must be exemplified in all paintings.)[61] If in such a case he were to be asked "What is the good of speaking the truth?" he would doubtless characterize "veracity" as being inherently good. However, there is no essential difference between characterizing veracity as inherently good and saying that "veracity as such tends to be obligatory"; nor is there any difference between holding either of these and holding that veracity is a worthy ideal. The language of inherent moral values, of general principles of obligation, and of moral ideals, may be used interchangeably, for an accepted principle of obligation is an ideal, and an ideal cannot be characterized without saying that it appears as inherently valuable to him for whom it is an ideal. Thus, in so far as an agent may attribute the obligatoriness of a given action to some general principle of obligation which he finds exemplified in the choice before him, it is immaterial whether this principle be characterized as a peculiar "*prima facie* obligation," as an "intrinsic moral value," or as a moral ideal.

Third, in those cases in which an agent may feel it to be obligatory to act for some value which is not usually classified as being a specifically "moral" value, the source of his obligation does not lie in his preference, but in an apprehension of the relation of the action which will achieve this value to the situation in which he stands. Whether he describes his obligation in terms of the fittingness of his envisioned action to the situation in which he is placed, or whether he describes it in terms of the values which he hopes to achieve through his action, is again immaterial. Every willed action, as we have seen,[62] involves the envisionment and espousal of a particular terminal state of affairs, and the apprehension of an obligation to promote certain values rests, as we have also seen,[63] on the fact that these values are viewed in relation to the situation in which the agent stands. So long as we consider only direct moral judgments and are careful to exclude cases in which the apprehension of value does not in fact give rise to a feeling of moral obligation, we may say that there is no difference between apprehending a particular course of conduct as morally binding and apprehending it to be obligatory for us to attempt to achieve certain values by acting in a specified way.

In the language of the traditional schools of ethical theorizing we may therefore say that while the theory of moral obligation here propounded is a variety of perceptual "intuitionism,"[64] it is compatible with every fact that a teleological theory of obligation can cite.

C H A P T E R

3

REMOVED MORAL JUDGMENTS

Removed judgments of moral rightness and wrongness are closely related to the direct judgments which we have previously considered. The concepts which we have already employed will also be applicable to them. On the other hand, we shall find certain differences between those judgments which are made by an agent who feels himself to be confronted by a moral decision, and the judgments with which we are now concerned.

Removed judgments of moral rightness or wrongness are the moral judgments of an observer, not of the agent himself. (As we shall later see, the judgments which we make concerning the rightness or wrongness of our own *past* actions are identical in principle with them.) However, not all of the moral judgments of an observer belong to this class: an observer may also make judgments of *moral worth*. A judgment of moral rightness or wrongness concerns the application of moral criteria to a specific action; a judgment of moral worth predicates a particular type of value (moral value) of a person, or of a trait of character exhibited by him. While both types of judgment are "removed," that is, neither is made by the agent in the situation, there are differences between them. They may, in fact, seem at times to conflict. Thus, we can praise the courage of a man, or his forebearance, and yet not believe that he acted in the right manner. We may also consider him to be a morally good man, and yet not approve of some acts for which he was responsible. Our present concern, then, is not with the whole range of moral judgments on the actions of others, but solely with those removed judgments which concern the moral rightness or wrongness of specific acts.

i.

IT IS A BASIC FACT of perceptual experience that some things belong or fit together, and that others do not. A curve may demand a certain completion and seem to reject all others; this completion appears as appropriate to the nature of the curve. Whatever may be our explanatory hypotheses, the facts are incontrovertible. In perceptual experience we find things belonging together, demanding and rejecting certain completions, appropriately and inappropriately organized. We have already seen that these concepts possess meaning when applied to direct moral judgments; in fact, when applied to possible actions they serve as the ground for such judgments. If this is not already clear, I am at a loss to know how to proceed. Perhaps I can simply point to the long tradition which claims to find fittingness and suitability to be the basis of moral obligations: no such tradition should be casually dismissed.

On the other hand, there is also a strong teleological tradition in ethical theory. This tradition would not have survived were it not true that we frequently base judgments of moral rightness and wrongness upon an assessment of the comparative value of two alternative courses of action. In our present analysis of the nature of removed moral judgments we shall have an opportunity to examine this principle of judgment in detail.[1]

All judgments of moral rightness or wrongness have a categorical character. This is as true of removed moral judgments as it is of those judgments which are passed by the agent himself. When I say that it is right that someone should do this, or refrain from doing that, I mean that he ought to do it, or that he ought to refrain from doing it. I feel that he is absolutely obligated to do so, if he is to do what is right.

When I judge in this manner I always have before me a situation in which an agent is seen as confronted by alternatives for action. I am aware of this agent as being part of that situation. I am also aware of the state of affairs to which I believe each alternative will lead. When I say that it is right for the agent to act in one manner, and wrong for him to act in another, I am judging that it is right that he should bring about, or attempt to bring about, one state of affairs rather than another.

This may appear to be obvious, but it in fact calls for several comments, each of which will later be considered in further detail.

First: When I see a person confronted by a situation in which there are alternatives for action, I may make a moral judgment on his action even if the agent is not cognizant of these alternatives. For example, I may judge that it was right that he should have acted as he did even though he acted spontaneously, for example through habit. The fact that the agent was not aware of alternatives at the time of his action is not decisive; all that I must suppose is that an alternative was in fact there.[2] Thus I may make a removed moral judgment when no obligation was felt by the agent, that is, when no direct moral judgment was involved.[3]

Second: It is not sufficient that an act should merely contribute to a good or bad result in order to be termed right or wrong. If by happenstance an act were to produce a most fortunate state of affairs, we should not therefore call it a right act. In order to be the object of a removed moral judgment an act must be seen by us to be related, because of its own nature as a goal-directed action, to a good or a bad state of affairs. It is only in the light of the state of affairs which it of itself tends to produce, that an act of another is judged to be morally right or wrong.[4]

Third: In order to be judged right or wrong, it is not necessary for an action to bring into existence the state of affairs at which it aims. I may hold an act to have been a right act because I see that an agent attempted to bring about certain consequences through it, though in fact he was unsuccessful in doing so. As has frequently been pointed out,[5] obligation concerns not the actual achievement of an end, but the attempt to achieve it—the setting or exerting of oneself to achieve it. In some instances it may be that a person is deemed culpable for setting himself an end which, in the nature of the case, cannot be achieved, but this does not alter the fact that an act, in order to be right or wrong, need not always be successful in bringing into existence the state of affairs at which it aims.

Fourth: In making a judgment of the rightness or wrongness of the action of another person, I view him as a "part" of the situation. I do not simply judge that a certain action should have been undertaken in order to bring about a particular state of affairs, but that *he* ought to have taken such action. In some cases this is a matter scarcely worth noting, since in certain situations we feel it to be right for *anyone* to act in a particular manner, and wrong for anyone who is cognizant of that situation not to do so. In other cases, however, notably where there exist ties of "special obligation" (for example, in family relationships), our judgment of the rightness or wrongness of a specific action takes into account the relation of the agent to the situation of which he is a part. It has been one of the regrettable mistakes of teleological theories to have singled out for attention the goodness or badness of the consequences of action and to have neglected the fact that when we judge of another's action we view his action in terms of what we take to be his relationship to the situation in which he appears to stand.[6]

Fifth: In making a removed moral judgment I am always cognizant of the state of affairs to which I believe each of the alternatives will lead. Now, I cannot possibly expect to know the ultimate future causal consequences of any action, and it is not in fact on the basis of these that I judge the rightness or wrongness of that action. In making such a judgment I only take into account those consequences which, in the light of its nature and my knowledge, I believe that such an action may be expected to bring about. From the point of view of moral judgments, such states of affairs may be characterized as *terminal.* Of course, they will themselves bring about further consequences. However, it is not with these that the person who makes a moral judgment is concerned.[7]

These five observations should aid in interpreting what was meant when it was held that in removed judgments I always have before me a situation in which an agent is confronted by alternatives for action; that this agent is viewed by me as a part of the situation; that I am aware of the state of affairs to which I believe each of the alternatives will lead; and that I judge it to be right that he should bring about, or attempt to bring about, one state of affairs rather than another. It is now necessary to analyze the relation which the phenomenon of value bears to this apprehended obligation.

It is an indisputable fact that in our judgments of the conduct of others we take into account the comparative value of the alternatives which we find to be open to the agent. In this the teleological tradition is correct. However, it is necessary to proceed with care if we are to determine the locus of the morally relevant value. Among the older teleological theories some identified this locus with the *intended* consequences of the action. Others identified it with the value of the consequences to which the action in fact led. More recent forms of the teleological principle hold that certain actions, taken in themselves, possess intrinsic value or disvalue, and that this value must be added to the value of the actual or intended consequences when judging which of two alternative courses of action was (or would have been) the morally right one for the agent to perform. As we have seen, the locus of this further value is sometimes held to lie in the motive which the act evinces, sometimes it is held that the act as a whole, because of its intrinsic nature, possesses "direct" value.[8] In my opinion none of these variant forms of the teleological theory is adequate. I shall attempt to show that the morally relevant value of an action does not depend upon the value which either the actual or intended consequences of the action would have, if these consequences were to be considered by themselves—that is, as mere existent states of affairs. And I shall then attempt to show that it is also not the case that the morally relevant value of an action is the sum of the value of these consequences together with the value of the motive, or of the "direct" intrinsic value of the action itself. It will, on the contrary, be my contention that removed moral judgments are based upon the value which an observer finds in the fact that an agent, in a particular situation, sets himself to achieve a given state of affairs. However, as we shall in the end see, to say that one action is, in this sense, "better" than another is not to have given a ground for its rightness: its rightness and this value are one and the same. This opinion I shall now begin to defend.

Let us suppose that one man has an opportunity to serve another, and does so. If no further stipulations are added, one would doubtless say that he had acted rightly. At the same time, one would doubtless be willing to say that it is better that he should have acted in this way than that he should not have done so. In fact, in ordinary parlance these statements appear to be equivalent. But upon what grounds do we say that it is better that he should have done so: where does the value lie?

That the value of the act does not rest upon the value of the benefit conferred can be seen from several considerations. First, our praise of the act does not depend upon the fact that the benefits which were aimed at were actually conferred. If by chance the benefits intended did not materialize, we would not change our estimate of the value of the act in any sense which is relevant to its moral rightness. We should of course say that it would have been better had the intended benefits materialized, but so long as the agent was in no way responsible for this failure, so long as he showed neither lack of foresight nor effort, we do not deny that his act was right. This fact of our moral judgments shows that the morally relevant value of an action is not to be found in the state of affairs to which it actually leads.

What is true in such a case is even more obviously true if one considers not merely the immediate state of affairs which an action in fact produces, but the long run effects to which it may contribute. In making a moral judgment these remote and intricate causal consequences are not seen as part of the action and are not relevant to the judgments which we make regarding the fact that a given person performed it. For those who do not immediately find this to be true of their own removed moral judgments, I should like to point out two facts. First, if the ultimate causal consequences of an action were relevant to its moral value we should always have to say that an action is *probably* right or *probably* wrong: the evidence of its rightness or wrongness would not all be in. This would be true not only of present actions, but also of actions which have already been done, since we are never in a position to trace *all* of the causal consequences (nor even all of those consequences which have already transpired) of a given action. Yet we do not believe that our moral judgments are merely probable in this sense. We may hold that they are merely probable because we may have misunderstood the nature of the action, but we do not believe that the future may transform what was wrong for a person to do into something which was right. (If one were to judge on the basis of ultimate causal consequences, one might even plausibly contend that Judas' betrayal of Jesus was a right act.) Second, if we, as observers, are shown that our view of the terminal state of affairs at which an action was aimed is mistaken, we will be forced to reexamine our judgment; if, on the other hand, we are told that our view of that state of affairs was correct, but that new circumstances have unforeseeably arisen, rendering the effects of the agent's action nugatory (while he might have acted otherwise and have achieved his ends), we would not for that reason hold that he had acted as he should not have done.—These two considerations should be sufficient to show that the locus of the morally relevant value of an action does not lie in the ultimate causal consequences to which it leads.

Nor is it possible to hold that the value of an action is to be estimated in terms of the value of the state of affairs to which it was *intended* to lead. The value which we see in one person's trying to help another, lies in the attempt to confer a benefit, not in the benefit itself. Other things being equal,[9] we do not say that the greater the benefit which an agent attempted to confer, the better is the act: when only a small service is called for, the rendering of that service is as good from the point of view of our removed moral judgments as, under other circumstances, is the rendering of a far greater one.

To these points it may be answered that a kindly act does possess a certain value because of its intrinsic nature, but that its total value is enhanced when it is successful, and when the immediate or the ultimate state of affairs to which it leads are of greater, rather than lesser, value. To this I believe the answer is clear. There is no reason to assume that the value which would be ascribed to a state of affairs were it considered by itself is part of the total value of an action directed toward realizing that state of affairs. In this matter we must follow the guidance of our actual judgments. And since we are here solely concerned with problems of moral rightness and wrongness, the judgments on which we must rely are moral judgments. One must therefore ask whether in our moral judgments concerning the actions of others we do or do not ascribe greater value to an act because of the independent value of its actual or intended consequences. The answer to this question is negative. If it were not negative we could not explain the value which we attach to small acts of kindliness, to the sensitive attention of a mother to the needs of her child, or to noble but recognizably futile acts of protest against an injustice.[10] In our actual moral judgments we do not judge a small benefaction to be less good than a large,[11] nor a mother's attention to the needs of her child to be proportionate in value to the importance of these needs, nor self-sacrifice in the cause of justice less good when it is doomed to fail rather than succeed. Our view of the value of an act varies with the circumstances under which that act was done, but it does not vary with the value which its consequences would have were they considered by themselves.

What may seem to be the paradoxical character of this contention will disappear if one bears clearly in mind what constitutes the nature of an action. In speaking of an action I am not referring to the mere fact that overt behavior of such and such a nature has taken place; I refer, rather, to instances of what are seen as being goal-directed behavior. In an action an agent is placed in a situation to which he reacts; his mode of reaction is aimed at a target, this target being what we have called the terminal state of affairs. So far as removed moral judgments are concerned, such actions need not be willed, that is, the terminal state of affairs need not be consciously espoused.[12] But any behavior which is not seen to have this "intentional" or goal-directed character is not the object of a removed moral judgment.[13] Now, the value of an action (when taken in this sense) is impossible to assess without taking cognizance of its goal, for without this goal it would simply not be the action which it is. Thus it should be clear that I am not contending that the nature, and therefore the value, of the state of affairs toward which an action is seen to be aimed is *irrelevant* to the value of that action. It would be nonsense to say that we value "an action" regardless of what may be its end. I have simply contended that the value which an action is seen to possess does not depend upon the value which this end would possess if it were considered by itself or as the terminus of another action.

Before attempting to elucidate the significance of this contention through recourse to examples, it will be advantageous to press home our criticism of the teleological view. Having urged that the value of an act is not a function of the value of either its actual or its intended consequences I shall now briefly consider the attempt on the part of recent theories to include the intrinsic value of the act itself among the "consequences" which must be considered in assessing the total value of that act.

Ideal Utilitarianism has recognized that it is impossible to interpret our judgments of rightness or wrongness exclusively in terms of either an action's intended or its actual effects. To the value of its actual effects the Ideal Utilitarian has therefore added the value which resides in some aspect of the act itself. For Rashdall this aspect was (primarily) the fact that an act was done from a certain motive; for Moore the doctrine of organic wholes opened the possibility that the relations between different aspects of an act could themselves be considered as value-components in the act as a whole.[14] What is characteristic of such views is the fact that they assess the total value of an act by means of summing its own "direct" value and the value of the causal consequences to which it leads.

In summing these two components the Ideal Utilitarian is forced to treat the motive from which the act was done, or any other element of value inherent in it, as being an *effect* of the act. Were it not so treated, it would not conform to the general Utilitarian view that rightness depends upon the value of the total consequences of an action. Thus, Ideal Utilitarians are inclined to speak as if in their calculus of value they were able to assume the perspective of the seraphim and cherubim, calculating whether the world as a whole is better or worse for containing an act of this sort. Whether such a manner of speaking can be squared with the nature of our moral judgments seems to me to be open to grave doubt. But here it will suffice to show that, when we make a removed moral judgment, the value which we attach to an act is not the sum of isolable elements.[15]

In order to say whether an act is good or bad we need not tot up the values of its various individual causal consequences and add this sum to a sum obtained by assessing the values of its various inherent properties. For example, if I judge that it is bad that a bully torments a child, the badness inherent in such an action is not based on the net balance of disvalue among its various components. I do not weigh the pleasure of the bully against the displeasure of the child and then add to my reckoning the factor of cruelty—that is, the pleasure taken in the misery of another. The badness of such an action is wholly located within the relation between the bully's enjoyment and the child's angry misery. If the bully were to derive ten times the pleasure from his action, the state of affairs would not be one whit better, for the cruelty would remain. And if we were to say that under these circumstances the evil remained constant because the cruelty grew as the bully's pleasure increased, we should merely be calling attention to the fact that our moral appraisal is based on the cruelty evinced, and on nothing else. This can also be seen in what happens to our appraisal if the child's misery increases. It is not the misery as such which we have in view, but the cruelty of inflicting this heightened misery. And if we upbraid the bully for not only having tormented the child but for having *hurt* him, our sense of the evil involved is guided not by our appraisal of the hurt itself, but by the lengths to which the bully's cruelty took him.

Even more importantly, however, an examination of such cases easily demonstrates that our appraisal of a state of affairs does not rest upon affixing a name to a type of act and assigning to it a specific degree of value. Our appraisal of the evil depends upon the particular nature of the cruelty evidenced, and this is a function of the situation in which it is displayed. There are innumerable forms of cruelty: the bully's enjoyment, the savage joy of inflicting pain in physical combat, the calculated infliction of an indignity, the violent satisfaction of a long enduring hatred. Our judgment of the degree of evil in the state of affairs at which any such instances of cruelty aim will vary from case to case, depending upon the relation of that cruelty to the rest of the situation. (I for one do not feel that the murder of Mussolini, and the indignities to which his corpse was submitted, constituted a wrong act, whatever might be my judgments concerning the character of the agents involved.) Thus, while cruelty is indeed a discriminable component in an action, its disvalue is not a fixed quantity. We cannot therefore reckon the total value of an action merely by adding the disvalue of "cruelty" to the action's effects.

Other examples will illustrate the same point. Whatever may be our judgments of the moral worth of agents who act in a courageous, or generous, or self-effacing manner, the value which we assign to any one of these components will vary from instance to instance. He who exemplifies courage in fighting for a lost cause, or he who is always generous, or always self-effacing, may seem to us to merit praise. Yet we may feel it to be wrong of him to sacrifice life for a particular lost cause, or to be generous to those who will misuse what is bestowed upon them, or to be self-effacing when others will be able to interpret this as weakness and make capital of it in achieving unscrupulous ends. In such cases the wrongness does not arise merely because, for example, the loss of life is a disvalue outweighing the value of courage (we do not always hold that it is); rather, we feel the courage to be *misplaced*.[16]

It has been my aim in these illustrations to suggest that the value of an action is not to be reckoned in the fashion claimed by those Ideal Utilitarians who seek to take into their accounts the "direct" intrinsic value of actions. It is to their credit that they have recognized the inadequacy of calculating an action's value solely in terms of either its actual or intended causal consequences. However, they have in my opinion mistakenly conceived of the "additional" element of intrinsic value or disvalue as merely another component to be added in the calculus of effects. It appears to me that the truth in the teleological interpretation of our removed moral judgments can only be saved if we abandon the assumption that the value of an action is analyzable into the value of its discriminable components. I shall soon attempt to show that if we assume the morally relevant value of an action to lie in the fact of its performance, we can indeed interpret removed moral judgments in terms which are consonant with all of the facts concerning our moral judgments to which the teleological principle appeals.

However, before proceeding to justify this view of the relation between the value of an act and its moral rightness, it will be necessary to raise the question of whether removed moral judgments may not best be interpreted in terms of the value which an observer finds in the motive of the agent. Upon such a view the judgment that an act was either right or wrong would depend upon the judgment that the motive from which it sprung was a better motive than that from which any alternative to that action would have sprung. Such a theory might assume a variety of forms. As we have noted, in Rashdall's form of the Ideal Utilitarian theory, the value of a motive is to be included along with the value of the causal consequences in calculating the total value of the act. With such a position I have, in effect, just dealt. However, it is now necessary to deal with the more general view (of which there are many variants) that removed moral judgments of rightness or wrongness are based not upon consequences, but upon the value which we assign to the motive from which the action was done.

This view certainly has great plausibility. When we say of an action that it was a morally right action for *X* to have done, we must know (or think that we know) what *X*'s motives were in performing that action: neither a knowledge of the actual results, nor a knowledge of the intended results, is the sole basis upon which we make our judgments of rightness and wrongness. As we have seen in cases such as acts of kindliness, acts of protest against injustice, and acts of cruelty, the rightness or wrongness which we predicate of these actions is not independent of our judgment of the motivation evinced in these actions. Therefore it might appear as if our removed moral judgments were based upon the moral value of the traits of character evinced in the action.[17] However, there is an alternative explanation of these facts.

It must again be recalled that, in making a removed moral judgment, what we are judging is not mere overt behavior, but is what we regard as the goal-directed act of a human agent whom we see placed in a situation which contains alternative possibilities for action. Our judgment of his action does indeed involve us in a consideration of his motive, but what constitutes his motive is not definable without reference to the end which he sets himself to achieve. (If this be doubted, let the reader attempt to characterize a concrete motive exemplified in a specific situation, or a dispositional trait such as "cruelty" or "generosity," in wholly "subjective" terms, i.e., without reference to that toward which it is aimed!) Therefore, to the extent that our removed moral judgments involve us in a consideration of the motives of the agent they also involve us in a consideration of the state of affairs at which the action was aimed. What we are doing, then, is making a judgment about whether it is better or worse that the agent, placed in this specific situation, with these alternatives for action presumably open before him, should have acted for one state of affairs rather than the other. And it then seems to me immaterial whether we say that one action would have been "better" than another or whether we say that one action was "right" and the other "wrong."

Thus, when we examine our removed moral judgments with a view to determining whether they are grounded upon the value of the motives evinced in the action, we reach the same conclusion as when we attempt to determine whether they are grounded upon the actual or the intended consequences of the action. What we find in each case is that the value which we attribute to the action does not reside in any one of its aspects, but in the fact that this agent, under these circumstances, sets himself to perform this action. This value, I take it, is what has been called the "direct" value of an act.

Now, the "direct" value of an act does apparently provide us with the ground of the rightness of an action: when we say of the action of another that it was right for him to have performed this action, or that he ought not to have performed it, we do attempt to justify our statement by an appeal to the fact that it was better to have done this, or that it would have been better had he not done this. And, in the first instance, we may even be considering the actual consequences of his action. However, if this judgment is challenged on the basis of what constituted the agent's intention or his motive (and such challenges frequently arise), we cannot continue to confine our attention to the value of the actual or even the intended consequences. What we do, I submit, is attempt to justify our judgment of the action's rightness or wrongness by an appeal to the "direct" value of one of these actions as compared to the "direct" value of the other. We attempt to get our opponent to agree that, considering the nature and knowledge of the agent and the nature of the situation which he confronted, it was morally better for him to have set himself to achieve one goal rather than another. But this, of course, is merely to say over again that this action was right and the other was wrong.

In summary, then, it may be said that in our removed moral judgments we do not (upon reflection) seek to ground our judgment of the moral rightness of an action in a consideration of the value of its *actual* consequences, but that we often do seek to ground our judgment of its rightness in either the value of its *intended* consequences or in the value of its *motive*. However, such attempts are not, in one sense, successful: we are not in all cases willing to judge that an action is right or wrong on either of these grounds. It is only when one or another of these factors is the particular aspect of the alternative actions in which they are strikingly dissimilar (and therefore stand in contrast to one another) that we use its value as a means of justifying our judgments. But if we are to have a means of justifying our judgments that will be acceptable in all cases, we must appeal to the "direct" value of one action as compared with another. However, when we do this we are not, I submit, providing a ground for the rightness of the action, but merely saying in other words that the action *is* right.

Now, if this is the case, one may wonder why the teleological tradition has seemed so plausible when applied to our removed moral judgments. The first reason is obvious: there are in fact many cases in which two alternative actions differ significantly from one another solely with respect to the value of their consequences, and in such cases we make judgments on the conduct of others in terms of the value of the consequences which they did or did not set themselves to bring about. The second reason why the teleological interpretation of our moral judgments is plausible is that in our removed moral judgments we look at the alternative actions as if they had been completed,[18] and ask ourselves whether it would not have been "better" if the agent had done *this* rather than *that*. (Even when the action has not yet been undertaken, our removed moral judgments involve imagining the two alternative states of affairs which we think will result if one or another course of conduct is espoused by the agent.) Therefore we are apt to speak as if there were some further ground of rightness to be found not in one of these actions or the other, but in some contrast between the end results of each. Thus we are apt to speak of the rightness of one action as being based upon its being "better" than the other. However, as we have seen, this being "better" means that it has a greater "direct" moral value, and this value, I have argued, is merely its rightness stated in other terms.[19]

ii.

HAVING ATTEMPTED to state in general terms where, so far as our removed moral judgments are concerned, the morally relevant value of an action resides, it is now necessary to supplement my argument by concrete phenomenological analyses. It will be my purpose to show that not only have the foregoing generalizations been correct, but that the concept of fittingness is the basis upon which we judge the morally relevant value of an action. That action which we see as being fittingly related to the situation in which we apprehend the agent to have been placed we regard as the right action for him to perform, and his performance of this action, contrasted to his performance of any other action, appears to us to be good. Thus, what has already been shown regarding direct moral judgments will also be seen to apply to removed moral judgments.

Suppose that you witness a man sitting quietly on a park bench. Is what he is doing good or bad; is it morally right or is it wrong? In order to answer you must know something of the situation in which he is placed: is he waiting to keep an engagement, is he avoiding an obligation, is he simply there to take the sun? The moment you have an answer to such questions, you feel something about the value of what he is doing. And if you assume answers to other questions concerning his situation, you feel in a position to say whether what he is doing is right or wrong. This case merely points to the fact that it is not overt behavior, it is action—interpreted action—which is valuable or disvaluable from a moral point of view.[20] And that which is necessary for our interpretation is to see the relation between the initial situation and the goal at which action is aimed.

The truth of this may further be tested by reverting to the case in which we are simply told that one person has conferred a benefit upon another. If no further stipulations are added, and we assume none, we find it good that such an act should have been done. The value which we attach to the act does not, I have claimed, rest upon the value of the benefit conferred, nor on the remote causal consequences of having conferred the benefit.[21] To be sure, with so little information at our disposal, it would not be unnatural to hold that its value rested upon the specific intrinsic value of, say, "benevolence." However, in terms of our hypothesis it is possible to push analysis beyond this point. I should claim that in such a case we are assuming the existence of an initial situation in which the agent might either have conferred the benefit or have abstained from doing so. But this is not enough. If we think of the agent abstaining from conferring the benefit when he has no justification for doing so, there is aroused in us a feeling of a situation which has been left incomplete.[22] It will seem as if the agent had overlooked something, that he had merely passed by without having *seen*. Thus the value of the act depends upon a contrast-effect: we should not consider it good were we not aware that its alternative was in some measure bad.

This provides an interesting parallel to the demands which are present in those quasi-aesthetic perceptual experiences with which we are already familiar. In them we are not aware of demands unless a non-completion or wrong-completion is given. In apprehending a circle the presence of demands is not experienced; but when the norm of circularity is violated by an irregularity or a small gap, their presence becomes clear.[23] Similarly, that element of value which is relevant to the rightness of the act which we are considering, depends for its apprehension on the disvalue of abstaining from it.

In a case such as this, phrased as it is without recourse to any stipulations regarding attendant circumstances, it is likely that we will be more inclined to think in terms of the character of the agent than in terms of the rightness of the act. Nevertheless, in the absence of further information the act appears to be right. Its rightness, I claim, is correctly explained when we say that it was *better* that the agent should have acted thus than that he should have acted otherwise. And the reason it appears to us better is, I believe, because the terminal situation toward which that action was directed, the conferring of the benefit, appears as a natural fulfilment of the initial situation. We see it in this light because the failure to confer the benefit would have left the initial situation as it was: something might have been done and was not.[24]

If this analysis seems arbitrary and unenlightening, one need merely think of what we would feel if we saw an agent confronted by a situation in which he might confer a benefit on another and we found that he quickly busied himself in doing something else. That which he did as an alternative to conferring the benefit may have been trivial or genuinely important, it may have been in his own interest or in the interest of a third person, but when we witness him doing it we do not find that whatever value it has (considered in isolation) makes it the right act. On the contrary, we feel that it could have waited, that it was merely an escape. This is because it was not related (except as escape) to the initial situation confronting the agent: seen in the light of this situation we do not consider it a valuable act. Perhaps better than anything else, such a case suggests the strong part which is played by our apprehension of the initial situation when we judge the morally relevant value of an act.

In order to substantiate our thesis it will be well to consider further cases.

Let us now suppose that I witness one man helping another, and judge that it is good that he should be doing so. But then let someone point out to me that he who is helped will thereby more easily carry out a wrong act which he intends, and that the agent knows this to be the case.[25] What then happens is that I change my original judgment. This obvious fact is important, for it shows the changes brought about in our removed moral judgments when the horizon of the situation is altered. It is impossible to understand the character of such shifts in our judgments if the nature of the situation which confronts an agent is left out of account. It would, of course, still be possible to hold that the agent's action was "wrong" because in helping the malefactor he actualized less value than if he had not; however, as we have seen, we do not in all other instances deem such actions to be wrong in any morally significant sense of that term. Nor do we always deem them to be bad with respect to that type of value which is of moral concern to us; yet in this case we would in fact look upon this agent's action as being both wrong and bad. And we view it not merely as bad "on the whole." What would under other circumstances have positive value, the act of helping another, now becomes the very locus of its badness. Thus, the character of the initial situation by which an agent is faced is determinative not only of whether the action is right or wrong (as traditional teleological theory would hold), but whether it is good or bad. This fact, once admitted, can only be interpreted by assuming that the situation places demands on the agent to which his action must answer if it is to possess value as a whole. If there are other interpretations which do justice to this fact, I am at a loss to know what they are.

In terms of our thesis the shift in judgment in this case can readily be explained. What was seen as fitting in one situation, the conferring of a benefit, became unfitting, and therefore bad, when seen as part of another situation. The fact that our judgment should change in this way need occasion no surprise. Unless one were to interpret an action merely in terms of the overt bodily behavior involved, one must immediately recognize that the action judged was a different action in the second case than it was in the first. And while it would seem to us unfitting not to help another (when no further stipulations are added) it may also seem unfitting to help this person when what he is attempting to do is to perform what is itself seen as a wrong act.

But now let us alter the case. Suppose that an agent is called upon to help another person accomplish something which is not judged to be a wrong act, and suppose that the agent himself is faced by a quite unrelated but incompatible task. Such cases are by no means rare: a person is often called upon for aid when he is otherwise occupied. On what basis does an observer judge which of the alternatives the agent ought to follow? The answer seems to me to involve a judgment of comparative value, and to this extent the general thesis of teleological ethics is correct. However, we must specify further where the morally relevant value resides.

According to the older interpretation of the teleological principle we should, in such a case, carefully consider the value to be achieved by following each one of the two alternatives, and our judgment of rightness would fall on whichever side had the greater positive value. While judgments based upon such a calculation would often coincide with our actual judgments, the latter are not arrived at in this fashion.

For example, a person may have planned a trip which he knew would be pleasant, would refresh him, and would be of some help to him in his professional career. However, he receives a telegram from his parents asking him to do something which would make such a trip impossible. Let us suppose that he complies. Now, in such a case we do not determine whether he ought or ought not to have complied merely by estimating the value which each of the two alternatives would have were it independently considered. We do not weigh the value which the trip has for him against the value which complying with the request would have for his parents. Nor do we reach our final judgment by adding into the reckoning a specific value-component derived from the special ties of obligation involved in the parent-child relationship (as the Ideal Utilitarian would hold), for such a component does not possess a fixed degree of intrinsic value.[26] What we ask ourselves is this: given these alternatives, which is a better state of affairs, that the trip should be taken and the request not granted, or that the request be complied with at the expense of the trip? This means, of course, that we are comparing the value of acting for each of the two alternative terminal states of affairs. However, in doing so we view each of these states of affairs as a whole, in which what is gained is gained at the expense of the rejected alternative. Our judgment is based not on a weighing of the value of one alternative and then a weighing of the value of the other, but on an apprehension of the value or disvalue of acting for one alternative at the expense of the other. When we do this we are in fact asking whether it is fitting for an agent who is placed in this situation to further his own good at the expense of not granting the request; and our answer will depend upon the particular character of the demands which we see in the situation which confronts him.

We are not here concerned to indicate the concrete nature of the specific demands which may confront an agent, nor to attempt any classification of them. But it is obvious that in the case before us, the demands which we see will vary with the importance which the trip may have for the agent and with both the nature of the request and the past relations of his parents to him. We should in some cases consider it right, in other cases wrong, for the agent to comply with the request. But our judgment of rightness or wrongness, I have argued, rests upon what we see to be the value of each of the acts, and not upon a separate weighing of each component in the alternative terminal states of affairs.

The importance of this distinction, and, to my mind, one of the strongest arguments in favor of the analysis proposed, lies in the fact that the fundamental teleological principle no longer need be considered to exclude a recognition of the role played by "special obligations" in our removed moral judgments. For when the rightness of an act is appraised in terms of the value of that act, and not in terms of its "results," a bond of special obligation is as relevant to the nature and value of that act as is the goodness or badness of any other characteristic of it.

Finally we may note one further argument in favor of the analysis here proposed. If it were true that we estimated the rightness or wrongness of an action in terms of a calculus of its actual effects, *every* overt act would be either right or wrong.[27] (The chances that either of two alternative acts will, in the long run, have causal consequences of identical value is very slight indeed.) However we do not in fact find that we make moral judgments concerning all actions. For example, no question of moral rightness or wrongness arises from the fact that a man frequently spends an evening with friends rather than staying at home reading for entertainment; nor would we find it wrong for him to read rather than visit friends. The actual consequences (and doubtless their value) would probably be different in each of these cases, but so long as we introduce no special element of fittingness or unfittingness into the situation each action, as an action, appears to be equally right.[28] It is only when we see an agent performing or refraining from performing certain actions that a moral judgment is evoked; what it is which constitutes these actions is, I have argued, the fact that the terminal state of affairs at which we see his action as aimed is either fittingly or unfittingly related to what we apprehended his situation to be.

iii.

UP TO THIS POINT our consideration of removed moral judgments has been confined to an analysis of that toward which such judgments are directed. However, a phenomenological analysis must also seek to ascertain what, if any, unique characteristics are present in the act of making these judgments. In considering removed moral judgments this problem is important, for one whole type of ethical theory, the "emotionalist" theory, has its primary source in an hypothesis concerning these acts.

Now, in *direct* moral judgments it is not difficult to analyze the fundamental characteristic of the act of judging: this we have found to lie in the element of reflexive demand. This characteristic, it appears to me, obtrudes itself as soon as one centers his attention on these judgments: it is a phenomenon which no one is likely to overlook. With respect to *removed* moral judgments we are less fortunate. A judgment concerning the moral rightness or wrongness of another person's conduct possesses no attributes which immediately strike one as being uniquely characteristic of this particular type of judgmental act. Like other judgments, for example in the mathematical realm, our own removed moral judgments not only seem to us to be formed by, and to follow from, objectively given characteristics in the conduct with which we are concerned, but they also seem to be free of any reference to ourselves. And it certainly does not appear to us as if the moral predicates which we use in describing that conduct are in any sense dependent upon our own judgmental act. Yet as soon as we inspect the removed moral judgments of those who disagree with us, we incline to give up the belief that the act of judgment is always irrelevant to the character of what is judged. Candor then demands that we investigate whether we too may not be deceived in thinking that our own judgmental acts are a pellucid medium through which the moral aspects of conduct are directly and unmistakably discerned. This, I take it, is a chief reason why "emotionalist" theories, among others, feel it to be essential to investigate the nature of acts of moral judgment. And there is much to be said in favor of the hypothesis that affective elements play a significant part in moral judgments. Direct evidence seems to be afforded by the fact that we speak of approving and disapproving of moral actions, of admiring them, of finding them despicable or loathsome, and the like. On the basis of such descriptions of our judgmental attitudes, it is not implausible to think that moral judgments are by nature "emotional" reactions or that they are based upon such reactions; and indirect evidence has also often been cited for such a view.[29] What we shall in this section attempt to do is assess the role of affective elements in removed moral judgments.

The theoretical issue which gives weight to this problem is clear. In judging of the conduct of another we find ourselves approving or disapproving, admiring or despising; we also speak of the actions themselves as being worthy of approval, or admirable, or contemptible, and the like. In what way are such characterizations of actions related to our attitudes toward them? Shall we say that our attitudes are determinative of whether the action is admirable, or should we view our admiration as a response to the admirable quality which we find in the action? This, as is well known, has often been thought to be the fundamental problem of moral and axiological theory. And to this problem there has also become attached the conviction (shared by all recent writers until the time of Scheler) that if we find that our moral judgments depend upon feeling, "relativism" inevitably results.[30] The problem of how such attitudes as admiration are related to the objects toward which they are directed, has therefore become not only a matter of interpreting the epistemological status of value-qualities, but has assumed the proportions of a controversy over whether there can or cannot be valid ethical standards.

In dealing with the problem of the role of affective elements in removed moral judgments we are as seriously handicapped by a lack of an adequate phenomenological classification of affective experiences as we are by the absence of adequate psychological theories in this field. The term "affective," as contrasted with conative and cognitive, is commonly used to embrace hedonic tone, moods, and emotions; it is also often used to include those aspects of conative and cognitive experiences which are termed "attitudes." For our present purposes some of these phenomena may be disregarded, since we are only concerned with those states which are directly and invariably connected with judgments of the rightness or wrongness of the conduct of other persons. Such states are primarily to be found among those which are designated as "attitudes," and it is these that we shall consider here.[31]

The concept of an attitude has been employed in many senses by social psychologists and by those who are concerned with the problems of personality. We shall here depart from what has almost come to be the prevailing usage, in which "attitudes" are treated as entities which inhere in persons as parts of their personality. We shall on the contrary use the term to designate whatever, at a given time, may be the "set" of a person toward the objects of his experience. Thus, in our usage, we would not speak of "radicalism" or "conservatism" as attitudes, but we would speak of attitudes of anticipation, boredom, disgust, hatred, anxiety, admiration, disapproval, and the like.

In this usage the term attitude embraces a wide range of phenomena, even including the emotions. However, not all attitudes are relevant to our problem. For example, attitudes such as anticipation or boredom or anxiety do not possess any intrinsic connection with our judgments of moral rightness or wrongness: they are never experienced as parts of these judgments, nor are they ever claimed to furnish the grounds for them. If they in any way actually influence our moral judgments it is in an indirect, covert manner, as when, perhaps, anxiety leads us to place hidden constructions on actions which would otherwise appear innocent. Similarly, emotions such as fear may exert an indirect, covert influence, but do not form part of our moral judgments nor provide them with explicit grounds. On the other hand, there are certain attitudes such as admiration, contempt, and disgust, which may plausibly be held to be linked to our moral judgments. For when we characterize actions as admirable, contemptible, or disgusting we are often saying something about the moral rightness or wrongness which they appear to us to possess.

In order to understand these morally important attitudes it will be necessary to proceed by pointing out what all attitudes have in common. I have spoken of an attitude as being the "set" of a person toward the objects of his experience. This demands elucidation. Attitudes, in our usage, are simply modes of experiencing. As such, they belong to the experiencing subject. However, they are not to be conceived of as merely "subjective" states, for they contain a relational element. To speak of an attitude is to say something about the relation in which a person stands to an object which he experiences. Thus, the concept of an attitude involves a polar reference, that is a reference to both the experiencing subject and to objects as experienced by him. The particular relationship which is involved in any attitude always issues from the person and is directed "outward" toward experienced objects. It is for this reason that attitudes have been characterized as "centrifugal," and have been spoken of as "flowing" from the person toward objects, or as being "aimed" at objects.[32] In conformity with non-psychological usages of the same term, we may say that when one defines any type of attitude he is defining a type of *stance* which persons assume toward objects of their experience.

It is a generic characteristic of attitudes that we are able to describe them as being of positive or negative "valence": some attitudes contain the element of being "for" the objects which we experience, others are "against" them.[33] This highly suggestive fact is universally recognized. It is evident in the emotions, as all classical theories of the passions attest; it is present in the twin concepts of desire and aversion, and it is to be found in such other attitudinal states as boredom and interest, admiration and contempt, in hope, anxiety, disgust, despair. As has often been noted, this polarity of being "for" or "against" is intimately connected with all value-experience,[34] but at this point we need merely note it as a generic characteristic of attitudes.

In order to distinguish between other attitudes and those with which we are here concerned, we must note that some attitudes are directed toward specific objects, while others are "objectless."[35] To say that an attitude is "objectless" does not signify that it is not directed toward the objects which a person experiences, but merely that it is not tied to a specific object. Thus, in euphoric joy our attitude is an attitude toward objects, but it is not directed at any specific object; it covers whatever objects we are experiencing. On the other hand in the most usual instances of fear or of anger, our attitude is tied to definite objects: it is an attitude toward them in particular. Thus, we might speak of "tied" attitudes, in contrast with those which are usually referred to as "objectless."

Objectless attitudes are by no means rare: one need merely think of *ennui*, resignation, anxiety, a sense of expectancy, and the like, to find examples of them. Further, in so far as "moods" are attitudes, they too belong to this class. However, it is obvious that such "objectless" attitudes do not constitute the affective element in removed moral judgments, for these judgments are directed toward individual specific actions. We need not therefore concern ourselves with them here.

It is also the case that not every "tied" attitude is relevant to removed moral judgments. For example, the terror which an action may inspire in us does not constitute an essential part of a moral judgment; neither does the envy which we may feel when we witness the bestowal of a favor constitute a moral condemnation of that act. Some distinction must therefore be drawn between those tied attitudes which are morally relevant and those which are not. This distinction exists in the fact that "moral" attitudes are, in a sense, "selfless." To be sure, every attitude belongs to a person: when I admire something, the admiration is mine no less than is the fear which I experience when I am afraid. Yet the attitude of admiration, though it be mine, is not experienced as a *state* of the self, it is only a relational stance. This may be noted when we consider the fact that in speaking of fear, or anger, or boredom, we not only have in mind a relation between the set of a person and an object which he finds frightening or hateful or boring, but we think of him as *being* afraid, or angry, or bored. On the other hand, in speaking of admiration (so far as it is involved in removed moral judgments) we are only concerned with the relation between the person and the object which he finds admirable: his admiration consists in this relation and we do not think of him as *being* in a state of admiration comparable to anger or fear. Similarly, when we approve or disapprove of an action, our approval or disapproval only characterizes a relation in which we stand to that action; no one would be likely to speak of us as being in a state of approval, nor use any other locution which would refer to something transpiring within ourselves.

Now it must not be assumed that attitudes of admiration and approval and disapproval are always "selfless" in this sense. One need merely think of how we speak of someone as being "lost in admiration," or of what it means to say that someone "cast an admiring glance" at a person, to see that admiration may also, sometimes, refer to a state of the self. And when we say that a person (for example a guest at a party) was very "approving" or "disapproving" we are referring to a state of the self. The point which I am making is merely that these states *may be* selfless, detached, contemplative; fear, anger, and boredom never are.[36]

With respect to other attitudes which make their appearance in removed moral judgments, the same point may be made. Disgust or contempt, for example, may upon occasion be "selfless." When I find a fawning, hypocritical act "disgusting" my attitude is one of disgust; but I would not characterize myself as *being* disgusted in the same sense as that in which I am when I see a disgusting sight or am "fed up" with my failure to achieve some end which I had set for myself. Again, when I find a cheap trick "contemptible," I feel a contempt for the action; but I am not contemptuous in the same manner as when I feel myself superior to someone on whom I look down. In moral judgments concerning the rightness or wrongness of the actions of others, we possess attitudes which, whatever they may be on other occasions, are selfless, contemplative, detached.

It is important to note this fact, for moral judgments are not, in the usual sense, "emotional experiences." As Hume pointed out,[37] a moral feeling "is commonly so soft and gentle that we are apt to confound it with an idea": in short, it does not seem to be an *emotion* at all. Unlike emotion proper it is "detached"; the self does not stand in the center of it. It is for this reason that even those who base their ethical theories on affective attitudes can resort to an appeal to "the impartial spectator," that is to the judgments of a person who stands detached from the situation and yet shares the attitude appropriate to the act.[38]

In spite of this detached aspect, our moral attitudes are continuous with other affective states. If they were not, it would be difficult to understand why the same terms are consistently used to designate both. Therefore while it is misleading to speak of *emotions* as being present in removed moral judgments, the problem of the relation between these judgments and affective attitudes still remains.

This problem, as I have already suggested, is usually formulated by asking what relation exists between the fact that I find an action admirable or contemptible, or the like, and the fact that I feel admiration or contempt for it. On the one hand, this relation has been conceived in terms of my attitude of admiration as being a response to the admirableness of the action; on the other hand, it has been argued that my act of admiration is the generative source of the admirableness which seems to reside in the action.

In attempting to deal with this question two facts must be held firmly in mind. First, when I say an object is admirable or contemptible I do not merely mean to say that I do in fact admire it; my meaning is that the object is a fitting object of admiration.[39] My meaning thus involves the expectation that others too will admire it, and that, if they do not do so in fact, they should. In moral discourse, therefore, to denominate an action as "admirable" means not that it is admired by me (or by others), nor that it is merely capable of being admired, but that it is worthy of admiration, that is, that admiration is a fitting attitude to take toward it. Second, it must be recalled that in speaking of any attitude bipolar reference is involved: we refer to the stance of the person toward the objects which he experiences. In "tied" attitudes we refer both to the stance of the person and to the object toward which he has this stance. Thus, in the case of admiration, the quality of being admirable and the act of admiring are correlatives: in any "original" judgment[40] it is always the case that when we call an action admirable we do in fact have the attitude of admiration toward it, and that when we do in fact admire an object we find it (in that respect) admirable. Bearing these two facts in mind, I should say that the question of whether the admirableness of the object serves as the ground for our attitude of admiration, or whether our admiration is the ground for our calling the object admirable is misconceived.

To demonstrate this thesis let me first deal with the analogous case of a boring lecture.[41] When I go to a lecture which I find boring I am of course bored. But if someone were to ask me *why* it was boring, I should not answer "because I was bored." The reason why a lecture is found to be boring is because it has certain other qualities: it is, for example, felt to be trite, or repetitious, or poorly delivered, or abstruse. It is in such qualities that we find the ground of both the boringness of the lecture and the boredom we experience. Thus, although boringness and boredom are correlative terms, the predication of boringness depends upon the lecture's appearing to possess some further quality which (phenomenologically speaking) we find to be the causal ground of our boredom.[42] The same thing may be said of fear. An object which we fear possesses a frightening quality. To ask whether we fear it because it looks frightening, or whether it looks frightening because we fear it, is to pose a false genetic question. The frightening quality of the object is always referred by us to some harm which it threatens, or to some physiognomic quality which it possesses; and either of these may be taken by us to be the causal ground of our fear.[43] Therefore the correct genetic question to ask would be why the frightened person sees the object as threatening harm, or why the specific physiognomic quality which he feels to be an adequate ground for fear is connected with a fear-reaction.

When we now consider states such as admiration and contempt we will no longer be inclined to ask whether our admiration leads us to call an action admirable, or whether we discern that it is admirable and therefore admire it. In an original judgment, as we have seen, admiration and admirableness imply one another. However, we find an action admirable because it is loyal or generous or courageous, and we believe that we admire it for the same reason. If ethical theory is therefore to pose the problem of why certain actions are admirable, it will have to investigate the reason why qualities such as generosity, loyalty, courage, and the like, evoke our admiration. Such an investigation does not appear to me to be unfeasible, but it would carry us far beyond what is required in the present context. All that I here wish to establish is the fact that any explanation of why an action is admirable (that is, is a fitting object of admiration) must take into account the specific quality because of which we find it admirable, and toward which our admiration is directed: one cannot give an adequate account merely in terms of the attitude of admiration itself.

This conclusion becomes of importance to an evaluation of "emotionalist" theories as soon as we confine our attention to the area of removed moral judgments. Our previous illustrations —the boringness of a lecture, the fear of an object, the admiration of a courageous or loyal action—did not fall within the scope of these judgments: they either contained no moral judgment or they were concerned with judgments of moral worth. But in our judgments of the rightness or wrongness of an action, what quality or qualities of that action provide the grounds of our admiring it and calling it admirable, feeling contempt for it and calling it contemptible, and the like? The answer is, I believe, the apprehended rightness or wrongness of the action. When, in a removed moral judgment, we find ourselves holding that an action is admirable we also hold it to be morally right, and if anyone were to ask us why it was admirable, we would answer because it was right. Thus, if we look for the ground of our admiration of what we see as a morally right action we find this ground precisely in the fact of its rightness.

Now, this point may be made clearer (and its significance as an argument against the phenomenological adequacy of an approbationist form of ethical theory will be strengthened) if we examine those attitudes which are denominated as "approval" and "disapproval."

The terms "approval" and "disapproval" are, of course, sometimes used to designate a specific type of attitude which differs either in kind or in degree from attitudes such as moral admiration or moral indignation: for example, we may correct someone who in commenting upon one of our judgments remarks that he was pleased that we had approved of the action, and we may say that we did not merely approve of it, but that it evoked our admiration. On the other hand, the terms "approval" and "disapproval" may be used in a wider or generic sense, in which moral admiration or moral indignation, as well as mere approval and disapproval (in their narrower sense), are included. However, it does not appear to me that there is any reason to make much of this difference in usage, since when we experience moral admiration (or any of the other "stronger" moral responses) such an attitude *is* our approval, and is felt to be continuous with the "mere" approval which another may feel. While these differences in affective response may, perhaps, lead to some controversies regarding the degree of rightness or wrongness which an action possesses,[44] they are not, I believe, taken by anyone to generate differences in opinion as to whether the action judged is right or is wrong. In fact, it should not occasion surprise that there are such differences in affective attitude either within the same person toward different actions, or between different persons toward the same action: such differences seem to parallel differences in other aspects of our emotional lives. Just as no one would expect the same affective response when a person is the recipient of a small benefit and when he is overwhelmed by a huge stroke of luck, so no one should expect our affective responses to be the same when we witness a heroic action, involving great emotional strain on the agent himself, and when we see a person merely set an unpleasant situation to rights again. Nor need our affective response be the same as either of these when we see a person tactfully confer a gift upon another. We need not hold that the heroic act was a morally better act than conferring the gift in a manner designed not to injure the self-respect of the beneficiary, but we should surely not expect that our own emotional responses to these actions would be the same—nor should we be surprised if the emotional responses of others were in some ways different from our own. The diversity in affective attitudes would only pose a serious problem for an ethical theory if it were not the case that all of these attitudes formed a single genus. Yet I believe it is clear that they do. As I have already indicated, it is not only the case that we use the terms "moral approval" and "moral disapproval" in their wider, generic sense to cover the "stronger" moral emotions as well, but it is also the case that when we feel moral admiration or moral disgust or moral indignation, we do not *also* have an attitude of approval or disapproval: these attitudes themselves are our approval or disapproval. Like "mere" approval and disapproval, these "stronger" moral attitudes (in so far as they are denominated as "moral") are attitudes which are not merely "for" or "against" a particular action or state of affairs: they are "detached" and "selfless" in precisely the same sense as are approval and disapproval. Thus I should say that there are common general properties in the attitudes which are involved when we make moral judgments concerning the actions of others; and while there is a difference between merely approving of an action and admiring it, or merely disapproving of it and finding it despicable, or between attitudes such as moral indignation and moral contempt, these attitudes may be said to belong to the same genus: the genus of what have been called "the moral emotions."

All such attitudes, I have claimed, share the characteristic of being experienced as having their causal ground in what is seen as the rightness or the wrongness of the action judged. What we take to be (and, phenomenologically speaking, what *is*) the cause of our admiration is the fact that the action is admirable because it is a right act; what we take to be (and what, in the same sense, *is*) the cause of our contempt or indignation is the wrongness of the action. Thus, those who would speak as if it were our approval or our admiration or our contempt which made actions right or admirable or contemptible are not holding fast to the experienced characteristics of our moral judgments. And if they wish to construct a psychological theory to explain our moral judgments in terms of "emotions" or approbative "attitudes," these emotions or attitudes must, I believe, be construed as being very different from the emotions or attitudes which we actually experience when we make moral judgments.

iv.

UP TO THIS POINT we have failed to consider one species of removed moral judgment which might be held to furnish evidence against a perceptual intuitionism. Such judgments are those which an agent makes regarding his own past actions, finding them to have been right or wrong. Why judgments of this type are to be classified among removed rather than direct moral judgments must now be made clear; we shall then be in a position to deal with the substantive issue of whether in fact they serve to support the teleological principle.

Direct and removed moral judgments may be said to differ in at least two respects. First, although the object of both is the moral rightness or wrongness of a specific action, a direct moral judgment only arises in the case of willed actions while a removed moral judgment is often made when an agent acted spontaneously and was therefore himself not aware of an alternative.[45] Because of this fact the range of removed moral judgments is wider than that of direct moral judgments. This difference in range, and the disparity in judgment which it entails, should have been sufficient to have made ethical inquiry more sensitive to a second difference between the two types of judgment. This is to be found in the affective element which each contains. Removed moral judgments, as we have seen, involve attitudes which may be denominated as "selfless" or "detached";[46] they are "contemplative" rather than being states of the self. On the other hand, in a direct moral judgment the element of reflexive demand evokes emotion; this emotion, like fear or anger, is experienced as a state of the self and is directly related to action. Thus, the stirredupness and pressures which are present in direct moral judgments have no counterpart in removed moral judgments. In the latter we approve or we disapprove, or we may feel admiration, disgust, contempt, or loathing; but even when these stronger affective states are present they appear as by-products of our acts of moral apprehension, and not as direct manifestations of what are experienced to be motivational forces.

In both of these respects it is clear that when we contemplate our own past actions we are making a judgment similar to those which we make when we view the actions of others. For not only is it the case that we have before our minds a completed action which we can view as having been done by a given agent (who merely happens to have been ourself), but we find ourselves praising or blaming many actions in which we were not originally cognizant that a moral choice was involved. Furthermore, the attitude which we have when we resurvey a past action is usually that of approval or disapproval;[47] it is by no means the same as our original affective response to the choice which we confronted. Aside from remorse (which is obviously not present in direct moral judgments), the only emotions which are inherently connected with judgments of our own past actions are pride and shame,[48] and these emotions are clearly different from the affective side of an agent's experience when he feels a compulsion to perform or to abstain from performing a specific act.

This difference in the type, and often the degree, of the affectivity which is involved in the two forms of judgment is one factor that has probably led most writers to ground their ethical systems in the data of removed moral judgments. When one seeks a norm for conduct and assumes moral phenomena to be cognitive, those attitudes which are detached and selfless will be considered to be more valid than attitudes in which emotion is involved and decisions are called for.[49] Thus, traditional normative systems have tended to gravitate toward the data of our removed judgments.[50] Furthermore, the fact that a removed moral judgment concerning our own conduct comes *after* the direct judgment has been made (and comes at a time when we have seen some of the consequences of our action) leads one to expect that it will be of greater validity. Therefore traditional ethical theory has usually been more concerned with our removed, retrospective judgments on our own conduct than it has been concerned with the direct judgments which we make when confronted by a moral dilemma.[51]

Since our removed moral judgments on our conduct have played so great a role in traditional ethical inquiry, it is necessary to show that they are not inconsistent with that form of perceptual intuitionism which is here being defended. This is the more important because it may be thought that these judgments provide an exceptionally clear demonstration of the truth of the teleological principle.

At first glance it would appear that when we review a past action and find it to have been morally wrong, our change of mind rests upon our present apprehension that the consequences of having acted as we did were less good than they would have been had we acted in a contrary fashion. Similarly, there are times when we feel doubts that an action which we are about to perform is morally justified, and yet when we later appraise this action we believe that it *was* right. In such cases too the ground for the newly found assurance of its rightness seems to rest upon the goodness of the consequences which were promoted by it.

There is no doubt that there are many such cases which apparently support the teleological principle. And since these cases involve what appears to be not only a revision but a *correction* of our direct moral judgments, it would seem that the teleological principle is the ultimate principle to which—when an action has been done and the strain and involvement of a direct moral judgment are over—we make an appeal which is final. However, such a conclusion is unwarranted.

It is unwarranted because a teleological interpretation of these cases rests upon a confusion. When we review a past judgment in the light of the knowledge of those consequences which ensued from our action, we tend to confuse two different and distinct actions, one of which occurred, the other of which we now feign in our imagination. What I as an agent actually did was to behave in a certain way because I saw this behavior as directly linked to certain consequences. If I now see that the envisioned consequences did not ensue, I may ask myself what course of conduct would have been right had I known what I now know. Naturally, my conclusion will in this case be different, for the situation in which I was originally placed was different from the feigned situation concerning which I am now judging. So far as the validity of my original moral judgment is concerned, I cannot say that I have now made a more valid judgment; I can only say that because I now have knowledge which I did not then possess I would now—if called upon to do so—make a different moral judgment. Thus, I have not, in such a case, correctively altered my original moral judgment; what I have done is to substitute another judgment for it. The problem posed by the later, retrospective judgment is whether it would have been right or wrong to have knowingly acted for the consequences which in fact followed from what I did. This question, I submit, is susceptible to precisely the same analysis as has previously been given in the case of other removed moral judgments.

Further evidence against the view that our judgments on our own past conduct support the teleological principle can be seen when we consider those cases in which our past action was spontaneous, and not consciously espoused for the sake of envisioned consequences. Once again it would appear as if we might meaningfully say that the action was either right or wrong because of the consequences to which it in fact led. Yet here we must again guard against the illusions of a feigned past. We only say that such an action was right or was wrong because we now have in mind the fact that it might not have been done. This is evident when one notes that our retrospective judgments are in such cases confined to those spontaneous actions which flow from habit or are direct, unthinking responses evoked by the situation: we do not make similar judgments if what we did was due to an uncontrollable reflex reaction. Viewing the action as one which *did have* an alternative, we look at the situation in which the action took place and ask ourselves whether this action was as fittingly related to that situation as its alternative would have been. In many such cases the alternative which we consider in our retrospective judgment is merely the abstention from the habitual or direct response; in other cases it is some unrelated willed action of which we were not cognizant. In either type of case, however, we are passing judgment as to whether, given a choice between the alternative and the action which we performed, we ought to have acted as we did.

These illustrations should make it clear that removed moral judgments concerning our own past actions do not force a revision of what has been said regarding removed moral judgments in general, and do not lend any special support to the teleological principle. However, our discussion of this point has raised a further problem regarding the relation between direct and removed moral judgments, and it will be convenient to deal briefly with this problem before going on to analyze judgments of moral worth.

The problem is this: when an agent confronted by a situation reacts spontaneously, or acts on the basis of envisioned consequences which he fails to achieve, and when in such cases we as observers (or he at a later time) judge his action to have been wrong, which judgment are we to allow to stand, the direct or the removed judgment of the action's rightness or wrongness?

This problem is among the oldest and has been among the most discussed problems of ethics, but the answers which have been given to it tend to converge whenever the data of our moral judgments, rather than systematic preconceptions, are taken as a basis for its solution. It is widely agreed that we do not hold it proper to blame a man for an unavoidable action nor for an action whose consequences he was not himself in a position to foresee. Yet, such actions may appear as wrong to an observer if he views them as having had an alternative, or if he sees what their morally relevant consequences have been or are likely to be. Since in such cases the action is seen as morally wrong, the agent who performed them will in some sense be "blameworthy." This apparent inconsistency in our judgments disappears when one notes that our blame falls on the man not because he did this particular act, but because of some trait of his character or because of some past choices which he made. For example, if a man who radiates a cheery optimism and tends always to put everything in its most favorable light is asked advice and encourages another to embark on a disastrous venture, we will blame him. Our blame does not attach to this particular act in itself; if it did we should have to revise our censure if it were pointed out to us that the habit of construing everything in its rosiest light had become so ingrained in him that he could not act otherwise in such a situation. However, instead of causing us to drop our blame, such an answer merely focusses it upon what we find blameworthy: a particular trait of character for which we hold him responsible.[52] Similarly, the incidence of our blame of a man who fails properly to assess the consequences of some envisioned action lies not in the action which he has conscientiously done, but in whatever past actions or traits of character led him to be culpably ignorant of what the consequences would be.[53] In short, if an agent finds a particular action not to be wrong, upon reflection we do not blame him for this action but for the trait of character or the past actions from which this wrong action flowed. Thus, our removed judgment of the moral rightness or wrongness of a specific action does not take precedence over the direct judgment which the agent made unless a judgment of moral worth is seen as supporting it.[54]

Even if this contention is granted so far as our removed judgments on the conduct of others is concerned, it might be held that when we look back upon our own past conduct we blame ourselves for having done a particular thing even though, at the time, we thought we were acting rightly or were not aware that any alternative was involved. Thus, once again our removed judgments on our own past actions might seem to serve as an exception to the generalizations here made.

Now it is true that when we look upon certain of our past actions and find them to have been wrong, we experience an emotion which is different in kind from our disapproval of an action done by another. In fact, this emotion seems to be qualitatively the same whether we are blaming ourselves for possessing a particular trait of character, for having given way to a temptation, or for having performed a specific action which appears wrong in retrospect but which, at the time it was performed, either did not seem to involve a moral decision or seemed innocent. Because of this similarity it might be argued that in retrospective moral judgments we do not draw a distinction between those innocent actions which had bad consequences and actions for which another would hold us to be blameworthy. If this is true, the teleologist may say that in this one type of case at least we judge the rightness of an action wholly in terms of the consequences which ensued.

However, there is in fact a recognized difference in our judgments regarding the two types of case; this difference is to be found in the distinction between remorse and regret, or as it sometimes is put between "repentance" and "sorrow."[55] Now, these two states differ even though the particular affective element which they contain may be the same. This affectivity is a state of "sorrow"[56] directed toward an action for which we see ourselves to have been causally responsible: the vision of ourselves performing the action is one which we cannot with equanimity face. In both types of case self-deprecation is present, and within each type of case there can be wide variations of affectivity, ranging from that mild state which we usually think of when we speak of "regret" all the way to violent self-hatred. However, the difference between the two types of case lies in the type of response which is evoked by the act of contemplating what we have done. The vision of ourselves performing the action will in both cases evoke the same typical affective state (and in either case it may lead to a resolve to make amends for what we have done), but only in the case of moral remorse does it lead to a resolution concerning what the patterns of our action *should be*. When the thought of our past action evokes in us the resolve not to act in this habitual manner again, or to review probable consequences more thoroughly, or to set ourselves goals which we had not previously espoused, we are accepting moral blame for what we have done and are not viewing our past action only as a misfortune. Thus, remorse leads to a reappraisal of our selves, while even the most haunting and violent regret remains attached to the specific action which occasioned it.

We may therefore say that in the case of removed moral judgments on our own past actions (no less than in the case of our judgments of others) it is the supervenience of a judgment of moral worth which transforms what is seen as a consequentially "wrong" but morally innocent action, into an action which is blameworthy. With such judgments of moral worth we must now deal.

CHAPTER

4

JUDGMENTS OF MORAL WORTH

The moral judgments with which we have thus far been concerned have predicated moral rightness or wrongness of specific actions; we must now consider those judgments which predicate moral goodness or badness of some attribute of a person's character, or of his character as a whole. Such judgments I am terming judgments of moral worth.

In one respect judgments of moral worth are similar to removed judgments of moral rightness or wrongness: they are always passed upon the character of another, or upon our own character when viewed as another might view it. Among them there are no analogues of direct moral judgments, for it is only by distancing ourselves from our actions, observing them as we would the actions of another, that we can judge what our own moral character may be. However, there is a significant difference between judgments of moral worth and removed judgments of rightness and wrongness. This difference does not lie in the fact that in the one case we use the predicates "rightness" and "wrongness" and in the other the predicates "morally good" or "morally bad"; as has already been noted,[1] when an action appears to be a right action its performance also appears to be morally good. Rather, the difference between judgments of moral worth and all judgments of rightness and wrongness lies in the fact that the former directly refer to the character of a person, or to some attribute of his character, and not to the moral quality of a specific action performed under specific circumstances. To what extent (if at all) there is mutual involvement between these two types of judgment we shall later have occasion to inquire; here they are to be distinguished, since the moral quality is in one case predicated of an action, while in the other it is predicated of the character of a person.

In examining the problems which arise when we speak of the moral worth of a person or of some aspect of his character, I shall follow the method which I have previously prescribed: I shall attempt to uncover the generic, structural properties of the judgments which are involved, rather than dealing directly with the qualities of character to which these judgments purport to refer. Here, if anywhere, this method must seem perversely oblique. The qualities concerning which these judgments are made are either traits of character which persons possess or they are the persons themselves, considered as moral agents. Why, then, should we not simply examine the intrinsic nature of such attributes or over-all personal qualities, educing their common characteristics through a direct inspection and comparison of them? To do so would be to specify what, in itself, constitutes a virtue or a vice and what constitutes a morally good or bad person. This direct approach has usually characterized aretaics, and it would indeed seem to be the most natural way to proceed. However, there are several considerations which favor an oblique or "judgmental" approach.

The first of these considerations, which is by no means decisive, is that any "direct" approach must none the less return in the end to an examination of the judgments which men make concerning moral worth. This follows from the fact that no philosophical ethics can rest content with a mere delineation of specific virtues and vices, nor with a statement of what constitutes a morally good man. It is an essential feature of the philosophical approach that one should investigate whatever serves as the ground for the praiseworthiness of the virtues and the blameworthiness of the vices, and whatever serves as the ground for the moral worth of a person. However, here as elsewhere in ethical theory, there is reason to suspect that the grounds of these moral characteristics are not wholly obvious; and here, as elsewhere, the existence of what appear to be conflicts among men's judgments makes it imperative that we should not assume that our own attributions of moral worth reflect a universally valid standard, while the judgments of others are falsely based. To rule out the judgments of others we must show wherein they are inadequate, totally apart from the fact that they happen not to agree with our own. Here as elsewhere, then, an ethical theory must seek its confirmation in the adequacy with which it can interpret the existence and the nature of the moral judgments which men make and which, upon reflection, they willingly accept. Thus it is that, in the end, any theory faces the problem of analyzing the nature of these judgments in order to offer confirmation of its adequacy: to postpone such an analysis does not obviate the necessity for making it.

Now there is, I believe, reason to suspect that the direct approach to aretaics has tended to make some ethical theorists neglect the need for this sort of confirmatory analysis. For example, when the virtues or the vices have first been sharply distinguished from each other, and when each is directly examined in an attempt to depict its essential nature, the common properties of the virtues and of the vices usually shrink to nothing more than the fact that each virtue appears as intrinsically good and each vice appears as intrinsically bad. But if it is taken for granted that this is all that can be said about the grounds on which traits of character are deemed to be virtues or vices, a confirmatory analysis tells us nothing which we did not already know: that the characteristic in question appeared to the judger to be intrinsically good or intrinsically bad. Whatever other aspects the judgment contains will then seem to be irrelevant, and the analysis of these judgments stops short; in fact it stops before it has begun.

Whether this has not usually been the case in the history of direct approaches to aretaics, I leave to the reader's own judgment.[2] Believing that a theory of moral worth must be confirmed through showing that it accords with all of the facts concerning both our judgments of the virtues and vices and our judgments of the goodness or badness of a person's whole character, I propose to examine these judgments at the outset, and confirm my theory of their nature by asking whether, if it is accepted, it does not provide an adequate interpretation of the existence of these judgments, of the nature of what we denominate as morally good or evil attributes of character, and of the role which such attributes play in our moral life.

The second consideration in favor of approaching the problem of moral worth indirectly rather than directly is, I believe, decisive. That of which we predicate moral worth is either a person or an attribute of a person. These persons differ from others, and these attributes differ from other attributes of the same or other persons, only in the fact that their natures are such that they are deemed to have moral worth. The person whom we consider to have outstanding moral worth, or the person who is judged to be evil, is generically like all other human beings; the attributes which we denominate as virtues and vices are natural psychological attributes of the person's character, and are related to other natural psychological attributes which he possesses. It is not, then, an ontological difference, but a difference in value, which distinguishes between personal characteristics which we find to be virtuous or vicious and those which we do not judge to be so.

Now, if we attempt to treat the virtues and vices "directly," insisting that the proper function of aretaics is confined to inspecting their intrinsic natures, we shall be forced to treat them as a special class of personal attributes: the class of those attributes which are necessarily good or necessarily evil. This, however, involves that we should view the attributes as ideal essences which are embodied in some persons and not others, for it is impossible to view a particular psychological attribute of a specific individual as being under all circumstances necessarily good or necessarily evil. Thus, the direct approach to aretaics has always led to a Platonizing tendency, in which all virtues and vices are considered to be ideal entities rather than natural properties which characterize some, but not other, human beings.[3]

On the other hand, if one seeks to escape this Platonizing tendency and holds fast to the fact that the virtues and vices are natural psychological attributes of a person, one must make clear why they appear to have a specifically moral character while other of the person's attributes do not. Direct inspection of these two types of attributes does not illuminate this difference. When treated as natural properties which some people possess, one cannot find in them any *intrinsic* characteristic which would serve to explain why the virtues appear to be inherently good, the vices inherently bad, and why just these natural attributes, and not others, are to be denominated as virtues and vices. In the absence of any such intrinsic characteristic, those who have sought to escape a Platonizing tendency have generally been forced to assume that the moral worth of the virtues and vices (or of certain over-all attributes of character) must be grounded in certain relations which are *extrinsic* to them: for example, that their moral worth depends upon their relations to the consequences of action or upon the act of judgment which finds worth in them. Thus, a direct approach which is "naturalistic" tends to commit one to a utilitarian or to an approbative theory.

If, however, we approach the problem of what constitutes the nature of a virtue or a vice by examining how they appear to a person who predicates them of another, we remain uncommitted either to a quasi-Platonic or to a utilitarian or approbative theory. We can treat them as being precisely what they appear to be to one who makes a judgment of moral worth: natural elements in a person's character which merit praise or blame. Why these natural elements are seen as meriting praise or blame is then our first question, and this in fact is the question which all theories must in the end answer. The decisive advantage of our judgmental approach is that this question is directly answered, rather than being deduced from prior commitments regarding other problems. It is therefore an apparently oblique approach which actually proceeds most directly toward the ultimate goal of a philosophical aretaics.

A third consideration, which is supplementary to that which has just been advanced, is that a judgmental rather than a direct, or "objective," approach permits us to understand why a particular trait of character should be considered a virtue or a vice under some circumstances and not under others. That some traits are so considered I take to be a fact: what are seen to be virtues and vices in some individuals (for example, in individuals who have a particular vocation) are not held to be either virtues or vices in others. Further, a particular psychological trait which we attribute to a given person may upon some specific occasion appear virtuous or vicious even though it is not so regarded upon other occasions. Finally, it appears to me to be the case that what are considered to be virtues or vices in one cultural community may not be so considered in others, or—at the least—that the usual rank-order of the virtues and vices may be different in different communities; such a fact would demand explanation in any theory of aretaics. In short, if we are to be able to consider non-universal cases, rather than confining attention to those traits which may seem to be virtuous or vicious under all circumstances, it will be useful to inquire into the structure of judgments of moral worth.

For these reasons I shall continue to follow the method which I have proposed, and shall inquire into the generic structural properties of judgments of moral worth. Among these judgments I shall first consider those which attribute specific virtues and vices to specific individuals, delaying until later an inquiry into the judgments which concern the moral goodness or badness of a person's character considered as a whole.[4]

i.

TO SPEAK of virtues and vices is to use language which has gone out of fashion; in contemporary ethical writing the term "moral values" is preferred. However, if one wishes to discover why courage, loyalty, generosity, or the like, should be considered to be both morally relevant and valuable, it is as well not to use the term "moral values." The latter designation immediately suggests that the object of one's attention is the courageous, the loyal, or the generous, as ideal, achetypal forms of behavior; whereas "virtues" and "vices" help to fix attention upon the important fact that one is concerned with certain attributes which some people, and not others, are held to possess.

When we speak of a virtue or a vice it is clear that we are intending to refer to some attribute which we believe that a person possesses, and in the one case we hold this attribute to be morally good and in the other to be morally bad. Among the commonly acknowledged virtues I would cite courage, prudence, temperance, loyalty, generosity, and fellow-feeling. As a few examples of vices I would cite cruelty, self-centeredness, sloth, vindictiveness, and jealousy. Now, such characteristics by no means exhaust the traits which we attribute to people, nor would they do so even were we to expand our list of the commonly acknowledged virtues and vices. It is therefore necessary to distinguish the class of those personal attributes which are generally taken as examples of virtues or vices from other attributes which are not usually held to belong to this class.

When we refer to a virtue or a vice which a person possesses, we are referring to what we take to be an ingrained aspect of that person, a relatively persistent trait. Upon reflection, we are of course willing to acknowledge that these traits are not present at birth in the same forms in which they later appear, that they are probably a product of all the processes which enter into "development." In spite of this malleability we regard them (and have reason to regard them) as persisting rather than transitory.

Further, these are traits of the person's *character*. While in ordinary thought we do not explicitly distinguish between personality and character, it is useful for the sake of analysis to do so. We may use the latter term to refer to the relatively persistent forms which a person's motivation takes, and designate by the former *all* of the persisting attributes which we predicate of him. According to this usage, "personality" would include "character," but would also include such other aspects of a man as his interests, endowments, sentiments, and temperament. Granting this distinction, I believe that it is clear that when we make judgments concerning a person's virtues or vices it is to his character, and not to his personality as a whole, that we directly refer.[5]

If this convenient distinction is acceptable, it may furthermore be said that the attributes of character with which we are here concerned are those which are general rather than specific: they are not exemplified with respect to one object alone. When we predicate courage or generosity or cruelty of a person we assume (though we may be mistaken) that this trait is so ingrained a part of him that he will respond in the same manner whether it is his child, his neighbor, or a stranger, who is involved in the situation which confronts him. It is thus to the general forms of a person's motivation that we look when we speak of those traits which we deem to be virtues or vices.

Finally, in this connection it is to be noted that the traits with which we are here dealing are responses to *types of situation*, that they characterize the person's reaction to certain states of affairs. For example, he who is courageous does not think of himself in times of danger; he who is generous responds to the needs which he apprehends others to have; he who is cruel enjoys the infliction of suffering upon others. Thus, in attributing any such trait to a person we have in mind how he behaves in a particular type of situation. Of course, within what we think of as a type of situation there may be discriminable varieties, and the person who exemplifies the virtue or vice in one sort of situation may not exemplify it in another. For example, a man who appears to us to show "physical courage" may not also show what is termed "moral courage," and a man may appear to be generous in a wide variety of cases and still be acknowledged to display a specialized meanness when dealing with persons whom he regards as unworthy. Similarly, a person may be judged by us to be loyal or considerate when dealing with his family or his friends, and yet be seen to be disloyal to others who trust him, or to be inconsiderate in his associations with other men. Thus, a trait which is consistently displayed in one type of situation, and is attributed to a person on these grounds, may not be displayed when the situation is changed. This does not signify that the trait is limited to a specific situation: it applies to a variety of situations of the same type. What we gradually learn is just how narrow or how wide the type may be.

In dealing with the virtues and vices one is, then, dealing with persisting forms of response which characterize an individual when he is in situations of a given type. Such forms of response we may term "character attributes." Among them it will be useful to distinguish two sub-classes, one of which I shall term "actional traits," the other "dispositions."[6] In order to suggest the difference which distinguishes these two classes, let us first take a clear case and compare the actional trait of courage with the disposition of gratitude.

Courage is to be termed an actional trait since it can only express itself in action. When we attribute courage to a person we are not making any reference to the state of his feelings: he may be terrified or calm, angry or coldly despairing, and yet show courage.[7] Furthermore, when we hold that a man is courageous we do not attribute any particular motive to him: his courage may be due to ambition, to emulation, or even to a fear of certain forms of opprobrium, and yet his action may justly be called courageous.

In speaking of gratitude, on the other hand, we are involved in attributing certain feelings and motives to the agent. Unlike courage, gratitude is an "inward" state whose essence does not lie in action. While it is true that a grateful man will give evidence of his gratitude in his actions (and if he does not we suspect that he is not genuinely grateful); we do not attribute gratitude to a person merely because he acts in a certain way toward someone who has conferred a benefit upon him. In order to say that a person is grateful we must assume that he acts out of a gratitude which he genuinely feels. Thus, in attributing gratitude to a person we attribute to him an attitude toward the fact that another person has bestowed a benefit upon him. Such an attitude, I am terming a disposition.[8]

This distinction between actional traits and dispositions may seem artificial, since we sometimes use the same word to denote both types of instance. Thus, when we speak of "generosity" we may have in mind the actional trait which is also called "liberality," while at other times we use the term to denote an "inward" disposition which expresses itself (so far as it can) in liberal gifts. Similarly, when we speak of "loyalty" we may have in mind either of two persisting characteristics: the actional trait which is also termed "fidelity," and that inward disposition which leads a person to place the interests of people or ideal objects to which he is attached above any interests which come into conflict with them. In this case, as in the case of generosity, the disposition may be the basis of the actional trait, for an inward loyalty may be the source of a person's fidelity; however, the actional trait may exist even in the absence of such a disposition: he who consistently fulfills his trust may be known by us to be motivated by reasons other than an attachment to the persons or institutions which he serves.

Even when ordinary language does not distinguish between actional traits and dispositions, there is a touchstone which serves to discriminate between them, and this is suggested by our discussion of courage and gratitude: if the actual feelings and motives of a person are relevant to our judgment as to whether or not he possesses this attribute, then the attribute is a disposition, and otherwise not. Thus it appears to me that some of the traditionally cited virtues and vices, such as courage, prudence, temperance, or sloth, are unambiguously to be termed actional traits, while others, such as gratitude, humility, forgiveness, self-centeredness and cruelty, are always dispositional traits.

This distinction between actional traits and dispositions may also be indicated and made more plausible through recourse to the concepts of moral training and moral education. If we wish to foster an actional trait in a person, we may attempt to *train* him to act in this fashion.[9] But we cannot develop a new disposition in a person by training: we must make him see new possibilities in his relations to others, to himself, and to the world. This insight can only be indirectly imparted. We can make a man act "humbly" through discipline; that is, we can train him to keep to "his place," but we can only impart to him the attitude of humility through awakening in him a sense of what lies beyond the sphere of any individual's self.

In the cases of generosity and prudence one can examine the relation, and lack of relation, between these two types of character-attributes. A person of generous disposition will perform actions which exhibit this disposition, and generosity as an actional trait will therefore also characterize him. Thus, in this case, the disposition serves as the foundation of the actional trait. However, as we have already noted, this actional trait may also spring from other sources. To bestow gifts upon others, to be generous with money, to seek to do favors, bolsters the self; therefore, a persisting attitude of self-assertion, when coupled with feelings of inadequacy, may lead to the actional trait of generosity. In this case, too, a disposition underlies the actional trait; but it is a disposition which is qualitatively unrelated to the form of behavior which is grounded in it. Similarly, the actional trait of prudence may spring from a disposition of timidity, or from self-centeredness; which, if either, of these sources it may have is not always made clear when we simply state that a man is prudent.

Now, these cases might be taken by the reader to suggest that one or another dispositional attribute always underlies an actional trait. However, even this generalization would not be true. As the case of physical courage shows, a particular actional trait may spring from a temperamental characteristic such as an explosive combativeness, or from a specific desire, if that desire is sufficiently strong and the performance of courageous acts is seen as a means to its satisfaction. Such temperamental characteristics and such desires are not what we have termed "dispositions," although they may be connected with them. Thus, in such cases, dispositions may play a role in determining an actional trait, but they will do so only indirectly, as parts of the character as a whole. This fact, together with the previously noted fact that otherwise similar actional traits may not reflect similar dispositional attributes, makes it necessary for us to avoid assuming any necessary relation between actional traits and dispositions. Even when an actional trait and a disposition bear the same name, this only reflects the fact that the disposition will of itself give rise to the actional trait; it does not signify that the actional trait is always grounded in that disposition.[10]

For these reasons it will be well to examine the two types of virtues and vices separately. We shall first consider those virtues and vices which are actional traits.

ii.

IN DISTINGUISHING between actional traits and dispositions we have seen that the presence of a particular actional trait does not allow us to infer the presence of a particular disposition; on the contrary, different dispositions, or other motivational forces which are not themselves dispositions, may give rise to such traits. It is now necessary to show that the moral worth which is attributed to a particular actional trait does not necessarily vary in accordance with its source.

This fact is already implicit in some of our previous observations. For example, we have noted that the actional trait of "fidelity" may spring from an inward disposition of loyalty, but it may also have arisen from other sources, such as a desire to avoid censure or a desire to retain one's position. When such desires have given rise to the settled trait of fidelity, the fidelity itself is not, I submit, regarded as morally indifferent, but is granted to be a virtue. Similarly, "liberality" as an actional trait may spring from that attitude in which the needs of others are more acutely felt than one's own; yet, whatever its source, when it is considered to be a settled attribute of character, and not a mere unique reaction to a specific situation, it too is considered to be a virtue. And the same point may be seen when we note the approval which is widely given to the attribute of physical courage, regardless of the source from which it springs. This trait may be grounded in such disparate conditions as combativeness, a calculated use of daring to attain certain personal ends, a craving for self-aggrandizement through social approbation, or a readiness to sacrifice one's self to an ideal. Any one of these may lie at the root of the bravery which a man shows in battle or which a child shows when he fights another of whom he is afraid. Yet even if we hold that an action is wrong, and even if we despise the total character of the agent who performed it, we may still see his action as exemplifying courage and regard *this feature* of his action as worthy of admiration. The worth of the courage is therefore not dependent upon its motivational source. While we doubtless prefer to see courage which springs from devotion to an ideal, we do not find that a man is *more courageous* because he acts out of principle. A citizen-soldier who is absolutely steadfast because he believes in the righteousness of his cause, is neither more nor less courageous than an equally steadfast mercenary. To be courageous each must perform in the same manner; even in the face of death each must persevere in fulfilling the responsibilities which he has assumed. To be sure, there *are* degrees of courage. As obstacles and dangers mount, the requisite perseverance mounts as well. But the degree of courage which a man manifests is a function of these obstacles and dangers (and perhaps of the fear which he feels), but not of the motivational source of the perseverance he is called upon to have.

If this be granted, our judgments of the moral worth of character traits cannot all be reduced to judgments of the moral worth of dispositions. We must therefore analyze those judgments which concern actional traits independently of our judgment of the dispositions which may underlie them.

When we turn to examine the actual judgments which men make concerning the actional virtues and vices, we immediately note that that with which the judger is faced is merely the fact that this individual, under these circumstances, has behaved in a specific way. If nothing more than this is given, how can a man judge that another possesses an enduring, morally valuable trait?

It might be thought that the attribution of an actional virtue or vice, such as courage or cowardliness, is merely the result of the fact that one has learned to apply these terms to certain forms of overt behavior. And this, of course, occurs: our stereotypes of the courageous or cowardly act sometimes lead us to say that a particular act exemplified courage or cowardliness merely because, in all external respects, it resembled other acts so denominated. But this form of judgment does not exhaust all relevant instances: if it did, we would never withdraw our attributions of courage or cowardice—as we sometimes do—when we later think that we have better understood the situation with which the person felt himself to have been faced. The fact of the matter would seem to be that our judgment that a person possesses a particular actional virtue or vice rests upon our view of how he responds to a particular type of situation which confronts him, not upon what his overt bodily behavior may be.

Nor must it be thought that we attribute a particular actional virtue or vice to a person only on the basis of having observed, in a variety of instances, how he responds to situations of this type. Though we are making a judgment concerning what we take to be an enduring trait, a single instance is often sufficient to reveal it. For example, it takes no more than Othello's first speech—"put up your bright swords for the dew will rust them" —for us to know that we are confronted by a man of action and courage. Nor do small boys need to experiment repeatedly in order to attribute courage or cowardice to a newcomer among them. What we see in a single instance is the manner in which the variant vectors in the situation are deflected or absorbed when they impinge upon the agent. To be sure, we may in such cases be mistaken, and a repetition of instances is useful both for the sake of forestalling gross misapprehensions and for the sake of making sharper discriminations as to the precise type of situation in which this trait will be evinced. In principle, however, it is to be insisted that one does in fact judge of actional virtues and vices on the basis of single cases, and that, as it turns out, these judgments need not always be revised.

If these two points are granted, we are in a better position to analyze the nature of those judgments which attribute a particular actional virtue or vice to a person. The first point shows that since this attribution is not merely a matter of observing and classifying overt behavior, he who makes the judgment must view the action in relation to what he sees to have been the situation in which the agent found himself placed. The second point shows that when viewing the action in this light the person judging is concerned with the specific nature of this particular action, and not with a class of actions: although he assumes that the agent will behave in a similar way in other situations of the same type, his belief that this action reveals a character-attribute need not wait upon corroborative evidence from a variety of cases. For the purposes of this analysis we may therefore confine our attention to the relation which a person apprehends as existing between a specific action and the situation in which it is seen as having been performed.

However, not all relations between the individual's action and the situation are relevant to the judgments with which we are here concerned. For example, the final rightness or wrongness of having performed this action under these circumstances is not the basis on which actional virtues or vices are ascribed to persons: if it were, we should never have cases in which we admire, say, a man's courage and yet condemn what he did. The crucial relation, it is safe to assume, must on the contrary be one which specifically includes a character-attribute as one of its terms, for it is with such attributes that our judgments of the virtues and vices are concerned. Now, we can easily exclude the possibility that the relevant relation is one which obtains between such an attribute and the action which followed from it. All other reasons apart, this is evident from the fact that we are here investigating the judgments which people make on the virtues and vices of others, and their own knowledge of these attributes in any individual case is given through their observations of the actions themselves. It is therefore to be concluded that the relevant relation must be one which is seen as obtaining between the situation and the actional trait.

A clue to the nature of this relation may perhaps be found in the concepts which were used in analyzing the nature of judgments of moral rightness and wrongness, since our judgments of actional traits also appear to us to be moral judgments. However, it will be necessary to avoid subsuming either class of judgments under the other. When we examine the relations between the two classes of judgment we find that in making a judgment of rightness or wrongness we are not involved in attributing any specific virtue or vice to the agent. Furthermore, as has just been noted, we may find that an action which evinces a specific actional virtue may not be judged to have been a right action. Nor, in the case of actional virtues, are we even able to say (as we can say in the case of dispositional virtues)[11] that if we restrict our view of the situation in which the action was taken to one of its aspects, excluding from consideration any other demands which it may contain, this aspect of the action would have been a right action. We cannot assign such a so-called *prima facie* rightness to an act which manifests an actional virtue because the moral rightness of an act is not independent of its "motive," that is, of what the agent set himself to do. But, as has been pointed out, the nature of an actional virtue *is* independent of the nature of its motive. Thus the fact that an action reveals what we regard as an actional virtue does not involve that we should in any sense consider it to be a morally right act.

However, this sharp separation of the actional virtues from moral rightness is obviously unsatisfactory in two respects. In the first place, when an action which we regard as courageous is also regarded as being a morally right action, its moral rightness and the courage which it displayed are not taken to be two independent factors which lack all connection with each other. In the second place, when an action reveals what we take to be an actional vice, such as cowardice, our removed moral judgment of that action seems always to hold that it was in some degree wrong (i.e., had a *prima facie* wrongness). Therefore, although we may praise a trait of character which to us represents an actional virtue without becoming involved in a judgment that the action which evinced that trait was in any way morally right, there must be some reason why, in other cases, there is an intimate relation between judgments concerning rightness and wrongness and judgments concerning actional traits. This suggests that the same factors which lead us to denominate an action as morally right or morally wrong have *some* applicability in our judgments of moral worth. It will be on the basis of this assumption that I shall now proceed.

We have seen that in removed moral judgments an action is judged to be right if it answers to the objective demands which the situation is felt to contain.[12] Our present question therefore becomes one of specifying how we can apply the concept of providing an answer to objective demands in the case of the materials now before us. The answer, I submit, lies in the fact that certain traits of character seem to provide adequate responses to the objective demands within certain types of situation. Just as it may be said that certain temperamental characteristics or certain aptitudes provide a fitting answer to the demands which a particular vocation places upon a person, so enduring actional traits may provide a fitting answer to recurring types of demand. The traditionally acknowledged virtues are, I submit, precisely those traits of character which provide fitting answers to the ever-recurring demands which all men face; the specialized virtues—the virtues which apply primarily to one vocation or which are only sporadically seen as virtues—are actional traits which provide fitting answers to less universal demands. And those forms of action which do not appear to spring from any enduring trait of character are not denominated as virtues, since they do not represent to the observer any generalized form of response to demands which recur from situation to situation. These are the theses which I shall attempt to render plausible by showing how, on the basis of them, some of the traditionally acknowledged actional virtues and vices are to be interpreted.

A suitable starting point for such an analysis will be provided if we compare a single actional virtue such as courage with its related vices of foolhardiness and cowardice, or prudence with recklessness and timorousness. In this discussion I shall not attempt to give an exhaustive analysis of these actional traits; my sole concern is to show that my hypothesis concerning the generic nature of actional virtues and vices provides a reasonable and plausible interpretation of our judgments concerning these virtues and vices.

It is generally acknowledged that the border between courage and foolhardiness is a sinuous one, and that two acts which outwardly resemble one another may fall on different sides of the line. This fact has led some moralists to differentiate between courage and foolhardiness on the basis of the dispositions which underlie them, or on the basis of the value of the end which the action seeks to obtain. The first of these two alternatives (which are not themselves mutually exclusive) we have already rejected, and the second is no more plausible than it. The mercenary (or the reluctant or cynical citizen-soldier) may be courageous although he does not believe in the cause for which he is fighting; and the man who out of pride accepts a frivolous or contemptible challenge may be courageous even when he does not believe that the end to be gained is of positive value in itself.[13] The mercenary or the egoist may be courageous when he resolutely faces the danger in which he is placed: he need not do so out of a commitment to a higher cause.[14] What characterizes foolhardiness is the defiance of danger when the situation in which one is placed makes no demands upon one to run any risk. Thus, he who seeks out dangers to show that he is not afraid of them is foolhardly: but he who accepts dangers because he faces a situation which demands that he accept them or retreat, is courageous and not foolhardy, regardless of what importance may be attached to that for which he runs this risk. And if it be objected that this depiction is too cavalier, for according to it a man would be courageous if he threw away his life for some trivial promise, I can only answer that however wrong his action may be he *is* courageous if he can prevent himself from stepping aside at the last moment.[15] (If we were to be called foolhardly for taking a serious risk when the end which we might thereby achieve is not equally serious, then many acts which evoke admiration which is indistinguishable from the admiration of great heroic acts would have to be called foolhardy, and foolhardiness itself would be seen as a virtue. Yet we do condemn the foolhardy, but admire and would seek to emulate the man who is ready to run risks which threaten to destroy him when the situation in which he sees himself to be placed demands that he should take such a risk. However wrong we may hold any particular action of this sort to be, we still hold that it exemplifies courage, and we admire it as we do not admire what appears to us a foolhardly action.) Foolhardiness, then, is the wanton assumption of risks; courage is unfaltering perseverance (however wrong it may ultimately be) in facing the risks to which a man's situation commits him.

According to this view foolhardiness is not an excess of courage, but a structurally different phenomenon. Cowardice, however, is a deficiency of courage. The coward fails to meet the challenge which he recognizes as confronting him because he fears the consequences to himself. In cowardice the self stands at the center of decision. The coward attempts to purchase immunity for himself; he will seek to save himself regardless of what his act will cost, either to others or to his future.

The prudent man is not a coward, though he may lack courage. In prudence we may retreat from the challenge of the moment because we envision the future, which also contains demands. The prudent man refuses to be carried away either by the imperative demands of his own desires or by the demands which the needs of others make upon him. He who fails to take cognizance of the actual demands of the future we term reckless; he who neglects its possible demands we term imprudent.

(And in financial matters we speak of the prodigal and the improvident.) But he who constantly overweights the actual or possible demands of the future, and neglects the demands with which the present confronts him, is timorous.[16]

In these few remarks on courage, prudence, and their allied vices, I have attempted to show how a direct approach to the nature of specific virtues would confirm my view that the essence of an actional virtue lies in the fact that such a trait is seen as a means of meeting an objective demand which the situation is held to place upon the agent. Similarly, it is my view that an actional trait is seen as a vice in so far as it appears as the cause of an agent's failure to respond to those demands which, in the view of an observer, confront him. Such an analysis differs markedly from those traditional views which insist that specific virtues and vices are to be understood as embodiments of intrinsic, subsistent "moral values and disvalues." It is the essence of my hypothesis that actional traits which are termed virtues and vices are natural psychological attributes of persons which receive their specifically moral character from the fact that through them a person meets the demands which we see as inhering in certain types of situation which we view him as confronting. According to my hypothesis their value resides in this relationship, and is not to be interpreted in terms of specific moral values which subsist independently of them.

In order to make this hypothesis more plausible it is now necessary to show how it comes about that when we speak of courage or prudence or cowardice we are referring not merely to a specific actional trait of a given person, but to a trait which has a more general moral significance. This is not difficult. Since the situations to which people must respond possess diverse structures, the attributes which will enable them to meet the demands which these situations contain will also be diverse: there will be a pluralism of virtues and vices. But these virtues and vices will not vary endlessly, for frequently the over-all structural aspects of different situations will be identical, and the type of demands which they involve will therefore also be the same. For example, we have seen that courage involves a resoluteness in following out an action despite the impingement of danger, and this type of trait may be evidenced in many different situations and with differing motivations. It is equally applicable to "physical" and "moral" courage, however different are the dangers which impinge. What remains the same, and what we refer to in speaking of both as courage, is the resoluteness of the action, the defiance of the threat to the self. Thus it is that we can use the term "courage" substantively, and not merely as an adjective which is ascribed to one form of a given individual's behavior.

In the light of this hypothesis we can also understand why we attach so great a significance to the judgments which are made concerning those actional traits of a person which are traditionally viewed as virtues and vices. Any judgment of an enduring factor in a person's personality will, of course, be important for us if we seek to understand his past behavior or are concerned to forecast what he may do in the future. However, those specific traits of character[17] which are viewed as possessing intrinsic moral worth seem to have an especially great importance for us, an importance which in most cases transcends that which we assign to the person's other actional traits. This fact, it seems to me, deserves explanation.

The conviction that the traditional virtues and vices are of special significance in understanding a man's behavior and forecasting what, in general, he will be inclined to do, does not spring from any wish on my part to rest the whole of our interpretation of character upon an assessment of moral worth. Such a subordination of all phases of a man's character to an ethical sovereignty seems to me to be false. However, the conviction that the virtues and vices[18] are highly significant character-attributes receives confirmation on every hand. Any letter of recommendation is hollow if it does not contain some estimate of morally relevant actional traits; our gossip is sprinkled with attempts to find the particular moral "go" of a person; in our relations with our children we are full of concern for those actional traits which have moral significance. And it is not difficult to see why this should be so. The crucial actions of men are those in which conflict is present, in which objective demands contradict impulse, or contradict one another; the virtues and vices are actional traits which serve as responses to, or avoidances of, the commonest types of these demands. They are, therefore, the critical actional traits of men. We may know that a man always shows ingenuity when confronted by obstacles, or that he is characteristically reserved or forceful in dealing with others, or that he is gregarious, but these traits, unless they are specifically related to the demands of a particular vocation, tell us little of how he will meet the situations which he will face. The traditional virtues and vices, however, have reference to types of *objective* demand which recur in the experience of all, and thus give broader and more general topographical indications of what lines his action will take.

The fact that the traditional virtues and vices designate the types of response which individuals make to recurrent types of conflict should not lead one to assume that the possessor of a particular virtue always experiences the conflict which leads us to predicate that virtue of him. The judgments which we make concerning the moral worth of actional traits are the judgments of observers: the courageous man himself may not see (much less seriously entertain) any alternative save that of acting as he does. The demands of the situation by which he is faced may seem to him so direct and imperative that considerations concerning his own welfare play no part in his decision. And such a man we may deem even more courageous than others. This is the meaning of the paradox of the virtues: we wish to become so imbued with the virtues as not to be tempted by the vices; we wish to transcend our own freedom to err.[19] This is also true of virtues other than courage: he who appears to us as wholly temperate may not be tempted by the desire for an excess, and he who exemplifies prudence may always be looking only to the future. And in this we see the reason why the person who presents an extreme embodiment of a particular virtue may at the same time be subject to our moral censure, as well as being personally distasteful to us. For the development of such an automatic response to certain demands, to the total exclusion of others, is apt to stultify any flexibility and tact in one's moral life. Nonetheless, in such cases of a hypertrophy of a particular virtue we cannot deny that the virtue in question is present, and is present in a pure though exceptionable form.

However, the agent may himself be aware of the conflict by which he is faced, and may wittingly choose what seems to us to be the courageous, or loyal, or prudent part. In such cases we are likely to find that if we approve his action for the courage or loyalty or prudence which it exemplified, he will reject our praise and say that he has only done what seemed to him to be right. This is as it should be: the objective demands which lie at the basis of our apprehension of his courage or loyalty or prudence, are the same demands which led him to view the action as right. And if he himself, in making his judgment, should have apprehended that his action was the only courageous or loyal or prudent thing for him to do, it would be because he had already cognized these demands. Thus it is that we find fault with moral judgments in which an agent attempts to throw one of the virtues into the scale in order to offset the balance of what he would otherwise judge to be right: when an action appears to be right to the agent, the situation no longer contains for him other equally important objective demands. Even in those cases in which an agent takes thought concerning whether his action embodies a particular virtue or vice, the fact that this virtue or vice might be attributed to his action is not the basis upon which he can validly reach a decision concerning what his duty may be.[20]

In most cases, it seems to me, a person who is said to have exemplified a particular virtue is not himself, at that time, aware of doing so. However, the same is not true with respect to most actional vices. It is true that a man may be judged to be imprudent when he fails to recognize the possible demands of the future, even though he is not aware of these demands. But we do not term a man a coward unless we feel that he is aware of a demand to take a risk. If he feels no such demand, he is simply acting in response to a danger, which is not what we mean by cowardice. Similarly, we do not characterize a man as disloyal or intemperate unless he feels that there is some demand placed upon him to refrain from acting out of self-interest or to curb his desires. Instead of attributing the vices of cowardice, disloyalty or intemperance to the person who is unaware of the demands with which we feel he is faced, we blame him for other vices—and in fact dispositional vices—which make him insensitive to the demands which we see. Thus to the person who is lacking in courage and yet is not a coward, or who lacks loyalty and yet is not wittingly disloyal, we attribute self-centeredness, or the like. In almost all cases the actional vices are vices of which the agent himself is aware, though he may later seek to justify himself by holding that the act itself displayed no persisting actional trait, or by using the artful ruses of self-deception whereby almost any given situation may be transformed into what it was not.

Now it must be noted that our judgments concerning the actional virtues as well as the vices are often subject to dispute. In terms of our analysis of the nature of these virtues this wide variability may readily be understood. A judgment concerning the presence of any actional virtue or vice rests upon our perception of the demands inherent in the situation which confronts the agent. And different observers may apprehend this situation differently, or both may apprehend it differently from the way in which it appeared to the agent. For example, the prudent man, who is keenly aware of the demands of the future, will be called cowardly by those who are inclined to live solely in the present. The man who is judged to act recklessly may be so judged because we are not aware of the demands which the situation, as he experiences it, levels against him. Thus, we must once again say that we cannot tell whether a man is courageous, foolhardly, or cowardly, or whether he possesses any other actional virtue or vice, if we simply observe his overt behavior; we can only make such judgments on the basis of recognizing demands (or their absence) in the situation by which he is faced. Whether we should or should not take into account the nature of the situation as *he* sees it, poses a problem which we shall later discuss.[21] Here it is sufficient to note that it actually seems to be the case that in some of our judgments of moral worth we do judge on the basis of what the situation appears to us to contain (regardless of what the agent believed), while at other times we modify our judgments to take into account what he believed the nature of that situation to be.

iii.

TURNING NOW to those moral judgments which are concerned with dispositions, we find that many of the traditional virtues and vices refer to dispositions rather than to actional traits. Humility, gratitude, generosity, modesty, forebearance, compassion, cruelty, self-centeredness, vindictiveness, are typical examples of these.[22] Our task will be to understand the generic nature of those judgments which attribute moral worth to such character-attributes, or which find them worthy of condemnation.

There are many parallels between actional and dispositional virtues and vices. For example, not all dispositions are usually thought of as being virtues or vices. Shyness, a pervasive cheerful optimism, or stubbornness, are dispositions which, in accordance with the context within which they are placed, may appear as virtues, or vices, or as morally indifferent traits. This we also found to be true of actional traits. Furthermore, as in actional traits, the dispositional virtues and vices are to some extent particularized: for example, a vocation such as that of the trained nurse makes special demands for "buoyancy," which we do not regard as a universal virtue. However, there is one significant difference between our judgments concerning dispositional and actional traits. We have seen that we may praise an actional virtue such as courage, and yet believe that the action to which it gave rise was morally wrong. In such cases we believe without qualification that the person ought not to have performed the act, in spite of the moral worth which we judge his courage to have. In the case of the dispositional virtues no exact parallel of this is to be found. When we praise a man's generosity or gratitude or sincerity we may judge that the action which sprang from this disposition did not adequately meet the demands which he faced, and was thus "objectively" wrong, but we do not without qualification blame him: the action itself does not appear to us to be *wholly* wrong. This difference, with which we shall later deal more extensively,[23] is here worthy of note since it is based upon what we have found to be an important difference between the relations of actional traits and of dispositions to the specific actions which follow from them. The same actional trait, it will be recalled[24] may result from different motives, but a dispositional virtue or vice always is grounded in the particular disposition which bears its name. It is for this reason that an action which is seen to exemplify a particular dispositional virtue is not held to be wholly wrong: even if we believe another possible action would have been more fitting to the situation, the fact that the agent acted from what appears to be a virtuous motive makes his action in some sense right. Conversely, if the action exemplifies a dispositional vice, even the fact that it corresponds to what we believe to be the objective demands of the situation will not make it appear right. However, the same is not true of the actional virtues (although it appears to me to be true of actional vices). The moral worth of courage does not mitigate our judgment of the wrongness of certain actions. Until we know the source of the courage our moral judgment of the action is not affected; we have only made a judgment regarding one of the attributes of the agent himself. Such judgments on character, however important they may be, are different from judgments regarding the moral rightness or wrongness of the specific action. A problem is therefore posed by the fact that judgments concerning the dispositional virtues and vices do affect our judgment of the rightness or wrongness of the actions which exemplify them. In analyzing the generic characteristics of dispositional virtues and vices, we shall discover the ground of this connection.

In order to ascertain what constitutes the generic nature of dispositional virtues, let us first examine the nature of gratitude, and ascertain why we attribute moral worth to it.[25]

Gratitude may be characterized as benevolence (a willing of good, as the etymology suggests) toward another person because of the fact that that person has conferred, or has attempted to confer, some favor upon us. It is natural that when we genuinely will good to another we should try to confer some benefit upon him, but, as has already been pointed out, the essential mark of gratitude is the inward willing, not the outward result. In extreme cases, such as that in which our benefactor is anonymous, we may be grateful though we are in no position to show toward him the gratitude which we feel. And, of course, we may return a benefaction and yet be ungrateful. In the case of dispositional virtues everything depends upon the feeling, not upon the outward act. But what is it about such feelings that one should be called upon to praise them?

The commonly accepted answer to this question is that gratitude and other dispositional virtues are praised because they are the sources of right actions. Though an act which springs from such a virtue may not always be judged to be wholly right, nonetheless (it is argued) such dispositions are, in general, conducive to the performance of right acts and are therefore praised. This theory, which is characteristic of earlier teleological systems (and is to be found in other systems as well) is psychologically implausible.[26] Furthermore, if it were true, the worth which we attached to a disposition would in no case be more important than the worth which we attach to its corresponding actional trait. This, however, is plainly false. For example, the disposition of generosity is more important to us than is the trait of liberality, and the worth of the disposition of loyalty is not exhausted by the fidelity to which it gives rise. If it be thought that this fact is to be explained by holding that the dispositions of generosity and loyalty not only give rise to these actional traits but are also conducive to other right acts, it may be pointed out that at least some worth seems to attach to the disposition itself. If this worth were wholly a function of the consequences to which the disposition tends to give rise, it would be impossible to explain why cruelty is judged to be more evil than callousness to suffering, for, as a matter of empirical fact, it would seem that the latter produces at least as much misery as the former.[27]

Yet it must be admitted that we would never praise a dispositional virtue such as gratitude were it not for the fact that we regard it to be right that a person should make recompense for a favor which has been conferred. If anyone were to deny that the repayment of a non-contractual debt was a morally right act, he would also, I believe, fail to find anything praiseworthy in the feeling of gratitude. The moral rightness of this type of act therefore in some manner serves as the ground for the moral worth of gratitude. But since gratitude has moral worth even when we do not believe the action to which it gives rise is *wholly* right, the relation entailed is not a simple one.

I suggest that the case is as follows. In viewing those situations in which a favor has been conferred on a person, we find that a demand is placed upon him to make some form of suitable return for this favor. This, as has been suggested, is equivalent to holding that the action of making such a return is, *pro tanto*, morally right.[28] Now, being grateful is the having of a specific feeling toward the fact that another person has conferred a favor upon one: it is the attitude of benevolence toward the person who conferred this favor because he did confer it. Thus, the grateful person is he who is sensitive to those demands which are the source of the moral rightness of our attempting to repay non-contractual debts. It is for this reason that one who failed to find any obligation to repay such a debt would also fail to find gratitude to be a virtue. But our conclusion is that the praiseworthiness of the disposition of gratitude rests on the fact that gratitude is simply a form of *moral sensitivity*, an awareness of those demands which make the grateful act a right act. In finding moral worth in gratitude, and therefore in praising a person for having this attitude, we are commending his character because it is permeable to a certain type of demand.[29]

In this there is both similarity and difference between dispositional and actional virtues. The similarity consists in the fact that both types of virtue are character-attributes which are specifically related to the demands which exist in certain types of situation. The difference consists in the fact that an actional virtue is defined in terms of a form of action which meets these demands, while a dispositional virtue is an attitude of sensitivity to the presence of such demands. Thus, both refer to persisting types of response, rooted in the agent's character, but the one refers to actional responses, the other to the feeling which this type of situation evokes.

This hypothesis concerning the nature of dispositional virtues may be tested against other examples. First let us examine humility and generosity, and then turn to a consideration of cruelty as a dispositional vice.

Humility is that attitude in which one feels his own self to be small when compared with other realms of being.[30] When we feel the weight of the totality of nature, or the magnitude of science, or the greatness of God, and when through that feeling we find that our own self is not the focal point of reference for other things, we experience humility. This attitude of the self does not lead to any specific mode of action, though it may be expressed in whatever one does. And since it is not expressed in any specific mode of action it cannot be claimed generally to lead to morally right acts. Why then does one find it to be morally good?

In terms of our hypothesis concerning the moral worth of dispositional attributes, its worth derives from the fact that this attitude involves a sensitivity to the demands in situations which confront one. And this is true of humility. Nothing so obscures objective demands as does the centering of attention on one's own self: so long as one makes oneself the focal point of attention to which all things are referred, the demands which arise in variant situations are taken out of the context in which they are given and distorted to fit the pattern of one's interest. And this is the reason why humility, unlike gratitude or generosity, can shine through any action: it is a condition of openness of the self to whatever demands may arise.

However, though we recognize the importance of this dispositional virtue, the man who possesses only humility, or in whom humility overpowers all else, is not necessarily a man whose conduct always appears as morally right. Nor is humility a virtue the possession of which can compensate for a lack in other dispositional virtues. The man who possesses humility may be lacking in gratitude, or even in modesty, toward his fellowmen; he may also lack many of the actional virtues, such as the perseverance which is courage, or the foresight which is prudence. Thus the man who is characterized by humility is not a man who is thereby possessed of the key to all virtues, but he is freed from the most serious bar to right action—the preoccupation with one's self.

Generosity, as a dispositional virtue, is that attitude in which one is sensitive to the needs or wishes of another, and feels, within oneself, gratification in witnessing their satisfactions. It is thus an affective response to a type of situation; furthermore, it is based on a sensitivity to the demands which a situation possesses. The generous man does not create these demands, but he is alert to their existence: if he were not, he could not feel gratification in being instrumental in satisfying them. Further, we speak of, and recognize, "a generous spirit" in one who takes gratification in witnessing the satisfaction of another's wishes, even when he himself had nothing to do with the fact that they were satisfied. To such a spirit the term "generous" is applicable, since generosity, as a dispositional virtue, is a type of affective response to the satisfaction of the needs of others, and is contrary to the self-seeking attitude in which it must be *I* who am the instrument of another's satisfaction.[31]

Like other dispositions and actional traits, generosity has natural affinities with other virtues, such as compassion: like other virtues it also stands in need of complementary sensitivities. The man who is generous but lacks a particular attitude toward others (an attitude for which we unfortunately have no adequate distinguishing name), will continually embarrass the recipients of his generosity. In this complementary attitude a lively sympathy and restraint are mixed; it is a sensitivity to the feelings of others, "a listening with our capacity for feeling"[32] to the wishes of others, a paying-attention to their self-respect. This sort of sensitivity to human dignity (which, in one sense of the word, might be called "tact"), this modesty on the part of the generous man, makes a person no more generous, but it makes his generosity assume a morally more adequate form. Once again, then, we see that no specific virtue can make a man virtuous in the broader sense: no single actional trait or disposition, however praiseworthy, can satisfy all of the variant types of moral demand. The concrete investigation of these demands and the specific virtues and vices which are correlated with them is not our present problem, however important it may be. Nor can we now examine the affinities among certain virtues, or among the vices, or between virtues and vices, though this too is a problem which deserves careful treatment in any systematic ethical theory. Our present problem has been limited to suggesting a hypothesis concerning the generic characteristics of dispositional virtues and vices. Our hypothesis that these are intelligible in terms of a sensitivity or lack of sensitivity to moral demands will be made more plausible if we now turn to an examination of one characteristic dispositional vice.

Cruelty, or the enjoyment of the suffering of another, is without question a dispositional vice. Like other dispositions, it may find expression in action—in causing suffering for the sake of its enjoyment—but it need not do so. In terms of our hypothesis concerning dispositional virtues and vices, cruelty would be understood as an insensitivity to certain demands, and this is precisely what it is. But we must not interpret the nature of cruelty in too simple a fashion. The vice of callousness, which is sometimes confused with it, is also an insensitivity to moral demands. The physical pain, or anguish, or discomfiture, of a person are sights which, when witnessed, seem to call upon us to offer relief. If we do not feel a demand to give succor, we are in fact callous: we have failed to be sensitive to the demands which we face. But the person who is cruel is not insensitive to the suffering of others: in fact, his enjoyment rests upon his awareness of it. To what demands may we then say that he is insensitive; is cruelty not rather a positive vice?

It is easy to think of cruelty as being an underived vice, intrinsically vicious, not blind but perverse. But the cruel man can reap his positive, malicious enjoyment of suffering only because he lacks sympathy. Constituted as we are, the suffering of another seems to demand a certain feeling response in us; were we otherwise constituted no one could convince us that cruelty was a vice. But the cruel man—for whatever reasons: a total lack of sympathy, or resentment, or sadism—does not respond to the suffering as we feel that the sight of suffering ought to make him respond. Thus, in cruelty the insensitivity is again an affective one: it is an impermeability to demands for a certain type of affective response. The demands which we find to be left unanswered are not in this case demands for a specific action: the failure to relieve distress springs equally from cruelty and from callousness. Rather, they are demands for that sympathy which we believe to be a fitting response to apprehended suffering, the ability and the willingness to be sensitive to another's pain.[33]

The difference between callousness and cruelty is paralleled among other dispositional vices. Among such vices there are many cases in which an insensitivity may take either of two forms: a failure to see certain positive demands in a situation, or a failure to be moved by them when they are seen. Thus, in self-centeredness we fail to see demands because of an inability to be open in our responses to what any situation may in itself contain; while in selfishness we see these demands but are impervious to them. And once again we may note that if we were otherwise constituted, if we could feel no demand to respond to the needs, desires, or wishes, of others, selfishness would not be deemed by us to be a vice.

So far as I can see, the hypothesis that one predicates a dispositional virtue or vice on the basis of viewing the agent as sensitive or insensitive to the existence of specific types of demand is a hypothesis which holds in all cases, and not merely in those which have here been discussed. In these cases, as in our judgments regarding actional virtues and vices, we are aware of demands in the situation which we view the agent as confronting, and we make our judgment of his character on the basis of how he reacts to the presence of these demands. The sole important difference in the two cases is that in judgments regarding an actional virtue or vice we are concerned with actional traits, while in our judgments regarding a dispositional virtue or vice we are concerned with the affective responses—the sensitivity or lack of sensitivity to these demands—which the agent's behavior suggests.

Before leaving the question of the specific virtues and vices and turning to a consideration of judgments concerning a person's character as a whole, it will be well briefly to suggest the advantages which the present hypothesis appears to me to possess when compared with some alternative views.

A) When compared with many contemporary Ideal Utilitarian theories (for example, those held by Rashdall or Scheler or Hartmann) our hypothesis has two distinct advantages. *First*, it offers a theory of why certain actual psychological traits are seen to have moral worth, and does not commit us to saying that these traits are judged to have worth because they represent specific archetypal forms of behavior each of which possesses the indefinable and unanalyzable quality of intrinsic value (or to each of which there is attached an ideal ought-to-be). Upon our hypothesis it is possible to understand each judgment concerning a virtue or vice in terms of what is apprehended as constituting the character of this agent who, in a specific situation, acts in a particular way: for this understanding no intuition of essences in which the actions participate is needed. Further, our theory affords an intelligible explanation of the following facts concerning the virtues and vices: first, that all virtues and vices seem to belong to a single genus, yet that there are differences between two major classes of virtues, those which are actional and those which are dispositions; second, that the specific virtues are not only distinct from one another, but that each virtue may have connections with others, and with certain vices; third, that to each virtue there is allied more than one correlative vice. These facts, I submit, are not concretely explained by the usual forms of Ideal Utilitarian aretaics: in them a generic theory of the virtues and vices can scarcely be said to exist.

Second, upon our hypothesis it becomes intelligible why some attributes of character are regarded as having universal moral worth, while the worth of others is relative to the situation in which the individual is placed. For most contemporary forms of the Ideal Utilitarian theory such facts are unintelligible. Rather than acknowledge that particular virtues are relative to the situation in which the person stands, any judgment concerning a non-universal virtue is explained by the hypothesis that this alleged virtue is merely an embodiment of some ultimate, universally applicable one. For example, the probing curiosity of a scientist or scholar, or the punctilious neatness and attention to detail of a laboratory technician, are not themselves considered as traits which possess moral worth. Rather, for the Ideal Utiliarian theory, their worth (when it is not conceived to be merely a case of "instrumental value") is deduced from a more general virtue, such as fulfilling the duties of one's station. But such a "virtue" is not a virtue. Fidelity or loyalty are virtues, but the traits which are here in question need not be examples of them. Rather, the so-called virtue of "fulfilling the duties of one's station" is a moral generalization—a statement of what a man ought to do. Thus a gap is created between traits of character which are viewed as essentially moral and traits of character which are viewed as merely psychological and which may, but need not, take on moral import. Such a dichotomy not only falsifies our actual judgments of moral worth, but it leaves unexplained why courage, generosity, and humility, which are themselves natural psychological traits, should possess a "non-natural" quality which other traits lack.

B) The more traditional Utilitarian theory, especially in its hedonistic form, does not suffer from having created any such dichotomy. Like approbative theories, it insists that the virtues and vices are natural psychological attributes, and it insists that our judgments concerning their worth are not absolute, but vary as the relation between the agent and the situation which he faces varies. With these points I agree. But when compared with a utilitarian or approbative theory the present hypothesis possesses one distinct advantage: it is not "recessive."[34] Instead of holding that the source of the worth which is predicated of a trait of character lies in either its relation to the consequences which it will presumably (or in general) promote, or in its relation to the affective attitudes of the person making the judgment, our theory, like Ideal Utilitarianism, holds that the worth attaches to this trait because of what we apprehend to be its intrinsic nature. To be sure, I have claimed that the ground of the worth of the virtues is to be found in the fact that they are seen as providing fitting answers to those objective demands which we see in the situation which the agent confronts, but this is part of what we take to be the nature of the trait: as has been noted, not even an actional trait is to be identified with a specific form of overt behavior. Most hedonistic Utiliarians,[35] on the contrary, hold that worth attaches to a trait of character not because of its own nature, but because of the consequences to which it actually or presumably gives rise. Further, the theory here maintained differs from most approbative theories. I have admitted that if an observer did not in fact possess a particular affective nature, or did not see certain demands as characterizing a given type of situation, he would not make the judgments which he does regarding dispositional and actional virtues and vices. However, this fact does not localize the ground of their worth in him: his judgment of the worth of a trait is based upon the moral relations which it appears to him to have. Now, these implications of our theory square with the mode of appearance of the virtues and vices when we actually make judgments concerning the worth of some aspect of the agent's character: the virtues appear to be intrinsically good and the vices appear to be intrinsically evil. If this were not their mode of appearance, the traditional Utiliarian theory would not have had to rely upon the hypothesis that the continuing praise of a useful trait will of itself lead men to believe that the trait is intrinsically good, nor would approbative theories find difficulty in separating the "real" meaning of a judgment of worth from its ostensible meaning. It is, I submit, no small virtue in what can be taken to be a naturalistic hypothesis concerning moral judgments for that hypothesis to remain faithful to the facts of what we directly experience when we make such judgments. This I believe our hypothesis does.

iv.

IT IS NOW TIME to turn to the second major class of judgments of moral worth. These judgments concern the moral character of a person as a whole. When we speak of a man as good or as virtuous, or when we speak of him as bad or vicious, or when we say that his character is noble or corrupt, we are making such a judgment.

There are, it seems to me, three inadequate types of theory regarding that aspect of a man's total character which we call virtue: each is based upon an attempt to derive our judgments of either virtue or vice from one of the other types of moral judgment.

The first of these inadequate theories would hold that a man is virtuous only if he habitually acts in accordance with what he conceives to be his duty. This theory, held in its most extreme, or Kantian, form, would insist that the sole motive of the virtuous man, *qua* virtuous, would be a sense of duty. In a modified form the theory would hold that the paramount motive of the virtuous man, although not his sole motive, would be to act in accordance with what he sees to be his duty.

In either form this theory has much to recommend it. The virtuous man does seem to be motivated by a sense of duty which the vicious man either lacks or disregards. Although the Kantian form of the theory has made it difficult to interpret a sense of duty as a psychologically satisfactory motive for action (and the modified theory has done little to further our interpretation on *this* point), it is true that men often do appear to act out of a sense of duty. It is also true that this motive may so regularly be present in the actions of a man that a sensitivity to it is one of the most significant of his character-attributes. This attribute we may term "conscientiousness." It has two aspects: a readiness to experience these claims of duty and a readiness to act in accordance with them when they are experienced.

Now, the virtuous man would clearly be conscientious if by that term we were only referring to the second aspect, for we do not judge that a man is virtuous if he consistently acts from motives which run counter to his sense of duty. However, to be virtuous a man need not be conscientious in the sense of always being open to the claims of duty. As we have seen in our analysis of direct moral judgments, the experience of duty is not present in spontaneous actions, but is tied to the fact that in conflict situations an agent experiences at least one of two envisioned alternatives as leveling an objective demand against him. However, a virtuous man may frequently escape such conflicts, reacting spontaneously to what others would see as objective demands. Like Kant's deity, he would possess a "frictionless" virtue in which the experience of duty is not present, and he would therefore not be a person of whom conscientiousness, in its double sense, is predicated. The fully conscientious man is a man of conflict, of scruple: to him all problems appear as moral. He too may be exceptional in virtue: his sensitivity to moral conflict is not a moral fault. But the theory that conscientiousness is the essence of virtue would make the man of scruple the man of highest virtue.

We must, then, reject the attempt to equate the meaning of virtue with the attribute of acting from the sense of duty, thus rejecting the attempt to derive a theory of virtue from the realm of direct moral judgments. We must reject such a theory not because the conscientious man fails in virtue, but because a man may be virtuous if he is possessed of some character-attribute which, in shielding him from what others experience as temptation, he reacts spontaneously, without conflict and scruple, to what others would see as being objectively demanded of him.

The second type of theory of virtue is one which seeks to derive our judgments of virtue and vice from our removed moral judgments. According to it, the virtuous man is one who in any given situation acts in accordance with what *we* judge to be the moral demands inherent in that situation. But this theory (and with it our egocentric assumption) shatters upon the fact that we frequently hold a consistently conscientious person to be virtuous even though we deprecate the moral choices which he makes. Furthermore, if we are to judge of his personal goodness, it is insufficient to know that a man acts in accordance with what we find to be the moral demands in the situation which confronts him: we must also know why he in fact acts in this manner.[36] Our judgments of virtue are not independent of our view of the springs of action in a person, but the theory that the virtuous man is the man who performs right actions seeks to avoid inquiry into motives. It is thus not a positive theory of the nature of virtue, but an attempt to deny ultimate significance to that term.[37]

The third type of theory would hold that the meaning of virtue is exhausted in the fact that the virtuous man possesses outstanding actional and dispositional virtues. Now it cannot be denied that the virtuous man possesses virtues, and the vicious man vices, but there is good reason to doubt this additive conception in which virtue becomes the sum of virtues possessed.[38] What often underlies such a conception is the belief that there is a single ideal type of character which represents *the* morally good man. Although this assumption is not uncommon, it is open to two fatal objections.

In the first place we may note that in his actual judgments of personal goodness any one individual may predicate a high degree of goodness of different persons whose virtues are not wholly congruous. Thus, for example, it is possible for one and the same person to hold that the characters of both Socrates and Saint Francis were morally great, though it would be difficult to subsume them under a single pattern of specific virtues. And if we inquire who may be the persons in our immediate environment who afford us the clearest examples of virtue, any one of us may select individuals of the most disparate types. To be sure, each of us is limited by certain stereotypes of the ideal man: the range of our moral appreciation is both culturally and individually restricted. But it is to be noted that when one finds any individual whose evaluation of persons is limited to the consideration of whether or not those persons possess a particular virtue or set of virtues, we distrust his moral discrimination.

In the second place, no person can possess all of the actional and dispositional virtues. Courage and prudence are in essence antagonistic, although not irreconcilable: generosity and a sense of justice (the trait of "rectitude") also tend to conflict. What degree of each will *the* ideal man possess? I submit that it is impossible to frame a conception of an ideal balance of all virtues which would not pale into insignificance beside the full-blooded virtue of an actually good man.

These two reasons are, I believe, sufficient to show the error in thinking that all virtuous men must conform to a single pattern of specific virtues. But there is still a further reason to doubt the additive conception of personal goodness or badness.

A virtuous man need not be wholly without vices, nor an evil man without virtues. The good man's vices do not corrupt his essential goodness, nor in the evil man do virtues redeem. To be sure, we often think that the good man would be better did he not have these vices, and the bad man more vicious without his isolated virtues. Yet this is not always the case. Sometimes the very virtues of a man may be connected with the vices which we regret, and to free him of these vices would be to render him less potent in virtue. (Would the moral character of Socrates truly have been greater if he had been rid of that arrogance which accompanied his humility?) Similarly, the evil which we predicate of a person may not be mitigated by any virtues which we admit him to have. (Is the viciousness of a man who is dominated by cruelty in any manner offset by prudence, liberality, loyalty, or family affection?) It is to a denial of such facts concerning our actual judgments that we would be committed if we were to hold that a judgment of personal goodness or badness is based upon a summing of a man's virtues and vices.

In the same connection we may note that there are *engulfing* virtues and vices. It is no accident that when we call to mind some figure of heroic moral stature we think of him with respect to some virtue which animates and controls his whole being. Similarly, the person whose moral character is corrupt usually furnishes us with an example of how a particular vice distorts the whole of one's moral life. The ideally good man and the vicious man are not, then, to be considered as possessing *all* virtues or all vices: they are more often ennobled or undone through the possession of a single, controlling, pervasive virtue or vice.

If it be objected that one might hold that a man is virtuous because he is the possessor of some particular congeries of virtues (though he need not be the possessor of all), and that virtue simply consists in the possession of these interlocking and significant virtues, while vice consists in the possession of a number of vices, I should answer that this conception of virtue still remains "additive" and still remains unsatisfactory when tested against the actual judgments of moral worth which we make. While no one to my knowledge has consistently espoused such a view, it will perhaps be useful to examine it.

The view would consist in holding that what makes a man virtuous or evil consists in his possession of a number of specific virtues or vices, and that the importance of these (and their influence on his conduct) is what leads us to characterize him as morally good or morally evil. Now, it is of course true (and we shall see why it is true)[39] that a virtuous man possesses virtues and a vicious man possesses vices. However, our present task is that of understanding the judgments which are made on the total character of a person, discovering (if we can) on what grounds such judgments are based. If we were to hold that our judgments were grounded upon seeing that a given man possesses one set of virtues while another man possesses another set, we would also be committed to investigating what vices each possessed, and judging the worth of each in terms of the overbalance of virtue or vice which his character contained. However, in doing this we should be attempting to view his character in isolation from the actual context in which his life was lived: our judgment of his character would not be relative to the situations by which he was confronted, the ideals he espoused, the demands placed upon him by his milieu. Thus, we would still be setting up an archetypal concept of the ideally good or evil man, which would only differ in detail (and not in principle) from that additive conception in which the ideally good man should be in possession of all of the virtues and none of the vices to which man can lay claim. But this conception (apart from all of the previously mentioned objections) is not a conception which can explain the actual grounds of our judgments of a person's moral worth. The specific virtues and vices are themselves relative to types of situation encountered in daily living, and it does not make sense to hold that any particular individual should embody any particular set of these virtues in order to be a morally good man. It is only in Plato's supposedly ideal society that the virtues which a man must possess if he is to be a morally good man can be defined in terms of his place in a social system. In actual life, and in our judgments upon men in actual life, virtue appears as a unitary attribute of character, evidencing itself in specific responses, but not to be identified with any sum of a number of discrete types of response.

We have now seen reason to reject three major types of theory of the nature of personal goodness, or virtue. The first sought to derive it from the agent's conscientiousness; that is, from his direct moral judgments: the second interpreted it according to our own removed judgments of moral rightness or wrongness: the third sought to equate it with a sum of the agent's specific virtues. It is now necessary to offer a positive account of its meaning which will do justice to the following facts: first, that the conscientious man is considered to be virtuous; second, that there is a tendency on our part (although it is not fully justified) to believe that the man whose actions appear to us to be morally right is a virtuous man; third, that there is a connection between virtue and the possession of specific virtues.

It will be possible to avoid some of the confusions into which the analysis of virtue has fallen if we make clear that the term "virtue" does not in fact refer to what we have been calling a character-attribute: it is not, properly speaking, a *part* of a person's character at all. Instead, it is a quality predicated of that character: the quality of being morally good or, in the case of vice, of being morally bad. Whenever we predicate goodness or badness of an entity we regard these qualities as truly descriptive of that entity, but (in Ross' terminology) we do not regard them as constitutive ("natural") parts. So it is here. To speak of a person as virtuous or vicious, as good or evil, as noble or corrupt, is to predicate moral value or disvalue of that person's character as a whole; it is not to assign a specific character-attribute to him.

Now, we have already seen reason to believe that the goodness or badness of a person's character is not merely a question of what specific virtues or vices he possesses, and that it is also not merely a question of what we take to be the rightness or the wrongness of the specific acts which he performs. The ground for our predication of goodness or badness must therefore be some over-all (toti-resultant)[40] property of his character. Such a property might, for example, be the degree of integration of his character-attributes. However, the attempt to interpret predications of moral goodness in terms of such a concept would, I believe, be utterly incompatible with the judgments which we actually make.

A first clue as to the nature of the over-all property of the virtuous man's character is to be found in the already noted fact that we deem the conscientious man virtuous. As we have seen, a conscientious man seeks to do what appears to him to be his duty, and no man who seeks to act in accordance with what he takes to be his duty is deemed wholly lacking in virtue. We may therefore say that the question of what motivates a man to act as he does is relevant to our ascription of moral goodness to him. This I take to be a universally acceptable generalization: he who appears virtuous appears so because of what we take to be a goodness of motives in him.

However, we have already acknowledged that there is a type of "frictionless" virtue, that some men are deemed virtuous even though they acted spontaneously. In such cases it would seem that moral goodness rests not upon the nature of the person's motives, but upon either the habits or the specific virtues which have become ingrained in him. Such a conclusion would, however, be false.

In the first place we must note that although we may attribute a specific virtue to a man when we witness him reacting spontaneously to a situation, and when we recognize that he was not aware of any alternative to his action, these "impulsive" reactions do not provide the basis on which we judge the moral worth of his character as a whole. Such judgments only arise when we view his spontaneous reactions as the products of habits or of specific virtues which to us represent the triumph of a struggle between inclinations and the acknowledgment of objective demands. For example, he who has grown up in surroundings in which he has learned a certain form of mannerly behavior is not praised by us as virtuous because of this behavior, nor do we praise a person who has learned to act in this way merely because he sees that in so doing he will better get along in his society; but he whom we judge to have acquired this behavior through a sensitivity to the needs and interests and feelings of others, is immediately regarded as being in this respect morally good. It is not the habit itself, but the underlying motivation which is responsible for the formation of that habit which is the real object of our judgment of virtue.[41] Thus, even in those cases in which we find that a person has acted on the basis of habit, and not out of a sense of duty, our attribution of virtue or vice rests upon what we take to be the motivation which lies at the root of the action which he performed.

Similarly, we may note that the persons who appear to us to be particularly outstanding exemplars of virtue are usually characterized by what we have termed engulfing dispositional virtues, and those who appear as particularly clear instances of a vicious character possess engulfing vices. Now, as we have seen, a dispositional virtue or vice is itself a motivational force, while an actional virtue or vice may rest upon any of a variety of motives. Thus, if it is true (as I believe it to be) that our predications of moral goodness or badness are more frequently connected with our apprehension of a particular disposition than they are with our apprehension of an actional trait, it would seem that even in cases of a frictionless goodness the motive of the person is relevant to our judgment.

And this point may finally be clinched through an appeal to those cases in which we do in fact pass from the praise of an actional trait to the predication of worth regarding the person's character as a whole. In such cases we assume that the courage, or other trait, springs from a direct response to the demands which the situation contains; if we discover that the source of the courage is a temperamental combativeness or a desire to achieve a particular personal end, we do not pass from the acknowledgment that this act was courageous to the judgment that the man's character as a whole is one which merits moral praise. Similarly, we are only willing to support our condemnation of a man's character when those of his actional traits which appear to us to be vices are acknowledged to rest upon culpable motivation: cowardliness, intemperance, or sloth, remain vices, but an awareness of the factors responsible for them may not lead us to view their possessor as reprehensible. Thus, while we incline to assume that a man is virtuous when we witness some act which exemplifies a specific actional virtue, and we incline to condemn his character because we see that he possesses an actional vice, our judgments undergo modifications or receive support when we inquire into the motivational sources of the act which he performed.

This view represents, of course, an age-old belief which is not likely to be contested, but it is now necessary to show precisely what type of motivation lies at the basis of our predications of moral goodness or badness. It would be correct but unenlightening to say that in the one case we find the motivation to be morally good and in the other morally bad: what is needed is to uncover the common element in the motivation of the conscientious man and the man of spontaneous, frictionless virtue, and to show that this element is precisely what we have in mind when we designate a motive as morally good. Such a common element is to be found in the fact that the morally good man is the man who is seen as being guided by an apprehension of objective demands in the situations which confront him.

When we view a man as conscientious, we believe ourselves to be aware of the demands which he experiences, and we find that he acts on the basis of his apprehension of these demands. We need not agree that he acted rightly, but we see him as a person who has acted in the manner which appears to him to be objectively demanded, or right. Similarly, when we view a man's action as springing from a dispositional virtue, that is, from a sensitivity to a certain type of recurrent demand, we may not hold that he acted rightly, but the objectivity of the demand to which he shows himself to be sensitive leads us to regard him as morally good. And when we see a man acting in a way that to us represents an actional virtue, if we believe his act flows from a direct response to the situation, we view his character as morally good. In all these cases, then, moral goodness of character represents a permeability and responsiveness to objective demands.

Turning to the problem of our condemnations of the moral character of persons, we may once again note the distinction which exists among dispositional vices: some represent an insensitivity to demands which we ourselves see, while others, such as cruelty, represent responses diametrically opposed to those which we believe these demands should call forth. So, too, in our moral condemnations of a person's character as a whole, we distinguish between the person who is *not-good* because he is insensitive to the demands which we believe confront him, and the person who is deemed *vicious* because he is believed to be aware of these demands but does not act in accordance with them.

Now it may of course be claimed that it is illegitimate for us ever to pass moral judgment on the total character of another person, and this claim is not infrequently made today. However, it is not my aim to discuss what judgments we should make, but to understand those which are made; and it cannot be denied that we do praise and condemn persons with respect to their moral character as a whole. Nor can I see any illegitimacy in such judgments *if* we have a right to assume that we can gain some insight into the total character of a person by observing one or more of his actions. However erroneous such judgments may sometimes be, it would be arbitrary and actually contrary to fact if we were to say that we are never able to understand the persistent forms which a person's motivation takes—and this, it will be recalled, is what one has in mind when speaking of a person's character.[42]

The foregoing analysis of the ground of our judgments of the moral goodness or badness of a person's character permits us to answer the three questions which we originally posed. We have already seen why a man who appears to us to be conscientious should also be deemed by us to be virtuous, for his conscientiousness is nothing else than his permeability and responsiveness to moral demands. It is also clear why there should be a connection between the possession of virtues and vices and the fact that a man is deemed morally good or bad: the virtues themselves are responses to recurrent types of demand, and what we view as vices are insensitivities, or failures to respond to demands. Finally, it now becomes clear why there should be at least a modicum of plausibility in the attempt to identify virtue with the consistent performance of right acts: we regard an act as right if it answers to the demands which we see in a situation, and he who always appears to be responsive to the demands which we see will appear as virtuous to us—unless we discover that his action sprang from a source other than a responsiveness to those demands.

In addition to accounting for two of the most usual views of the nature of virtue, and accounting for the spurious plausibility of the other, our analysis of these judgments has two auxiliary advantages which ought not to be overlooked.

First, it provides an explanation of the fact that there are what I have called engulfing virtues and vices, which we identify with the total moral character of the person possessing them. Among these virtues and vices we might cite generosity and humility, cruelty and self-centeredness. In each such case the virtue or vice is a dispositional attribute, a sensitive responsiveness to, or a disregard for, an objective demand. In each such case, also, the type of demand is one which can be evidenced in almost any situation. Therefore, he whose character is formed around such a dispositional attribute, will consistently give evidence of possessing this attribute, and because of it he will appear to us to be virtuous, or to be lacking in virtue, or to be vicious. The fact that he may also possess other attributes of character which we find to be good or to be evil, will not alter our judgment of him if we believe that it is this disposition which is central in his character. Thus it is that he who possesses what appears as an engulfing virtue or vice is judged on the basis of it, and not on the basis of his other virtues or vices, nor on the basis of the specific rightness or wrongness of his individual acts.

The second, and even more important auxiliary advantage which I find in the foregoing analysis of virtue is the fact that according to it the term "virtue" only has adjectival meaning.

To be sure, it is a term which does have a referent, but that referent is not a specific constitutive element within a person's character. Nothing has degraded the meaning of virtue more than the assumption that it refers to something which is a part of the character of some men but not of others. On this basis the man called virtuous must be a rare specimen far superior to the men whom we know. (And so singular a person we should scarcely wish to meet.) But if the concept of virtue truly means what I take it to mean, virtue is simply a more consistent and pervasive sensitivity to those moral demands which each of us often feels and to which we, too, often respond.

v.

BEFORE LEAVING the topic of judgments of moral worth, it will be well to summarize the relations which such judgments bear to the other types of moral judgment with which we were previously concerned.

In the first place, it will be recalled that all of our judgments of moral worth ascribe moral goodness or badness to a person on the basis of some personal attribute which he possesses. Whether or not we speak of an actional or a dispositional virtue or vice, or whether we are judging of a person's character as a whole, what we are affirming is that a particular person possesses an attribute of character which is praiseworthy or blameworthy. It is, of course, through the person's actions that we apprehend his character, but our judgments of worth do not have these actions as their objects; they are judgments which refer to the moral worth of those attributes which the person's actions reveal.

As we have repeatedly noted, the rightness or wrongness of an action which we see a person perform does not serve as the ground for our judgments of moral worth. (For example, we may praise a man's courage and yet hold that a particular courageous act was not the act which he ought to have performed; we may praise a man's generosity and yet believe that his action was not in accord with what he ought to have done; we may even admit the conscientiousness of a person and yet be convinced that the decision which he reached was contrary to the decision which he ought to have reached.) Furthermore, it is also clear that our judgments of moral worth do not serve as the ground for our judgments of rightness and wrongness. Although, as we have seen, a judgment of moral worth may in some cases affect our judgment by saying that the action was not *wholly* wrong, we do not base our judgment of the rightness or wrongness of an action on the moral worth of the trait of character which that action reveals. Thus, there may be conflicts between judgments of obligation and judgments of moral worth, and with these conflicts we shall later deal.[43]

However, it is to be noted that the preceding analyses do not justify the belief that judgments of obligation and judgments of moral worth are totally unrelated ways of viewing human conduct. They do not, for example, justify the view that "the right" and "the praiseworthy" are capable of independent analyses. On the contrary, they lead to the conclusion that the differences between judgments of obligation and judgments of moral worth are to be found in the differences between the objects of these judgments, and are not to be found in any differences in what is affirmed of these objects, nor in any differences between our attitudes toward them. In other words, in making judgments of obligation we are using the same type of predicate in characterizing an action as we are using in characterizing an attribute of character when we predicate moral worth of it; and in both cases our attitudes toward the object which possesses this moral predicate are the same. Thus, the preceding analyses justify the conviction that judgments of obligation and judgments of moral worth constitute a single *genus.*

Finally, it is to be noted that the grounds which have served to render judgments of obligation intelligible have also served to render intelligible the judgments which we make concerning moral worth. Thus, if the preceding analyses have been correct, we have not only found reason to believe that all moral judgments do constitute a single *genus,* but we have also found the characteristic which defines that *genus.* This characteristic is that all moral judgments are grounded in our apprehension of relations of fittingness or unfittingness between the responses of a human being and the demands which inhere in the situation by which he is faced.

CHAPTER

5

THE SOURCES OF MORAL CONTROVERSIES

In the preceding three chapters I have sought to analyze the nature of each of three main types of moral judgment, avoiding any consideration of the content of these judgments, or any discussion of whether there is a standard against which their validity may be assessed. In systematically excluding these problems from the preceding analyses I have wittingly suppressed the dominant issues in philosophical ethics. It is now necessary to allow such issues gradually to arise.

These issues are, of course, the traditional issues regarding the status of moral norms. With such issues every ethical theory must finally be concerned. Whatever other problems have contributed to the main stream of ethical thought, its original source may be traced back to the fact that what seems to one person to be moral or immoral does not, apparently, always seem so to others; yet, when making a moral judgment we feel that we have apprehended a genuine property of the action which we have judged. It is out of this conflict that ethical theory begins, and it is with some systematically grounded position regarding this conflict that it must end.

In the main, two general and opposed positions have usually been adopted concerning this problem, and these may be called the absolutistic and the relativistic views. Ethical theorists have been inclined to compress all other positions into a mold which has been shaped by the issues which most concern these two alternatives, but this seems to me to have been a mistake. Absolutistic normative theories emphasize the fact that in making a moral judgment we feel that we have apprehended a genuine, independent, moral property. However, as we have seen, such theories are faced by an insuperable methodological difficulty: on the one hand, it is impossible to avoid a begging of the question if one attempts to set up a contentual standard without first establishing an area of agreement among all men's moral judgments; on the other hand, it is difficult, if not impossible, to show that all moral judgments do have a common content. It is this methodological difficulty rather than the mere fact that there are conflicts between moral judgments which has lent strength to the alternative, or relativistic, type of position. As has frequently been pointed out, the existence of conflicts does not of itself disprove the contention that there is a universally valid standard against which these opposed judgments may be assessed; rather, it is the lack of any means of validating whatever standard is accepted that provides a cogent reason for doubting the adequacy of the absolutistic view.

However, the traditional forms of the relativistic view are not themselves immune to criticism. Whatever may be the merits or the defects of their specific analyses of other problems, one finds that their discussions of the normative problem are dominated by an urge to deny the existence of a universally valid standard. This, in my opinion, is a shortcoming, since the normative problem exists as a problem whether or not one accepts the view that there is a single universally valid standard for conduct. It is, for example, an inescapable fact that we not only feel that our moral judgments are valid, but that in our controversies with others we seek to win agreement with them. And even when we fail in our attempts to do this, we do not give up the conviction that there are some moral judgments which are more adequate than others, and that there are standards against which such conflicting judgments can be assessed. Since there is such a persisting phenomenon it bears investigation. And since there is a continuing disagreement regarding the explanation of this phenomenon (and regarding other problems concerning moral norms), it would seem to be the part of candor and caution to examine the issue without prior commitments as to what its outcome must be.[1]

If we do not assume that every type of solution to these issues has already been tried, there are several ways in which the problems which are connected with them might be approached. In my opinion there is none which offers as much promise of establishing a generally acceptable conclusion as that which proceeds through analyzing the nature of moral controversies and attempts to locate their sources. Such an approach need not initially be concerned with the specific content of moral controversies; it could treat conflicts between moral judgments merely as instances which serve to reveal what factors are responsible for the differences which one finds. Then, through analyzing the controversies which arise out of such differences, one could determine whether there are in fact any universally accepted general principles which govern whether a moral judgment is accepted as valid or is condemned as invalid. Taken by itself, such a non-contentual approach would, of course, only uncover the standard for what constitutes a *valid* moral judgment; it would not establish a series of specific moral *truths*. However, if one could reach such a universally acknowledged "formal" standard, one could proceed to inquire whether all judgments which were accepted as valid also agreed in their content. If they did, we would have reached a single universally acceptable contentual standard for conduct; and we would have reached it in a methodologically sound fashion. The charge could then no longer be made that the choice of one set of conflicting judgments in preference to another represents a begging of the question: we should have established an area of agreement concerning what constitutes a valid moral judgment, and we would have a justification for our choice.

As the reader will later see, I do not myself believe that it is possible to reach this final goal. Yet, even though I shall fall short of establishing what others seek to maintain, I believe that it is possible to reach important conclusions which lie beyond those which are accepted by most who deny the universal validity of moral standards. And now, following the method which I have proposed, I shall attempt to trace the sources of those conflicts which engender moral controversies. In the following chapter I shall then seek to determine whether there are any general principles which serve to distinguish between valid and invalid moral judgments. When that point has been reached, we shall be in a position to examine the issue of whether one can or cannot say that there is a single universally valid contentual standard against which the conduct of men is to be judged.

As I have suggested, moral controversies arise when we find that the moral judgment of others is apparently not in accord with our own. It strikes one as strange, and somehow as wrong, that another should make a judgment which is different from our own. In moral no less than in intellectual matters there is a feeling that such a discrepancy should be rectified; this feeling persists as long as we do not believe that it is impossible to overcome the conflict involved. And a similar though perhaps less disquieting situation arises when we find that we ourselves, at different times, make discrepant moral judgments. So far as I can see, no new problems arise (and none are eliminated) because of the fact that such judgments are made by the same person, rather than by different persons. The inner debate which characterizes our thought when we find that we have made two apparently conflicting judgments assumes the same general form as that which is exemplified when two persons attempt to resolve their moral controversies. For this reason no distinction will be made between those internal controversies which each of us carries on within himself and those explicit controversies which we carry on with others; in both types of case discrepant judgments engender a consideration of the normative issues of ethics.

However, not all of the discrepant judgments which in fact give rise to moral controversies constitute a single type. It has sometimes been too readily assumed that whenever two persons fail to agree in the specific moral judgments which they make, we are faced by a case in which there is a genuine *disagreement* concerning a moral issue. However, we also find cases in which two persons make conflicting moral judgments, but in which, it turns out, the conflict has arisen solely because of differences in their apprehension of certain matters of fact. In these cases an agreement concerning these matters of fact dissolves the moral controversy. In such cases I shall speak of *disparities* between moral judgments, and not of moral disagreements.

Now, the simplest way to distinguish between disparities and disagreements among moral judgments might seem to be the following: a disparity between moral judgments rests upon differing views of the nature of the non-moral aspects of that which is being judged, while a moral disagreement is present if two persons see all of the non-moral aspects of the situation in the same way, but disagree as to the moral properties which they assign to that which they are judging. However, there also are cases in which we would ordinarily think that a real moral disagreement is present even though the controversy was based upon a differing apprehension of the nature of the object judged. Such cases are of the following form: both disputants may agree as to all of the specific details concerning the nature of an action, but one may view certain aspects of that action as more "important" than others, and they may fall into argument as to which way of viewing the object is the way in which the object ought to be viewed. According to the first mode of distinguishing between "disparities" and "disagreements," such cases would be designated as disparities, since the manner in which the two persons regard the object which they are judging is different: each is, so to speak, seeing it in a different context.[2] However, in such cases the discrepancy between the moral judgments which have been made is not resolved by showing that the persons had differing apprehensions of that which they are judging, nor is there any way in which such conflicts can be resolved by any appeal to further "neutral" facts: the issue is one concerning the way in which this particular action ought to be regarded. Such a conflict, I submit, would usually be termed a moral disagreement. Therefore, I prefer not to distinguish between disparities and disagreements in terms of a distinction between (a) those moral controversies which rest upon differing views of the non-moral aspects of that which is being judged, and (b) those moral controversies which rest solely upon differing moral reactions to objects whose non-moral characteristics are apprehended in precisely the same way by both disputants. Instead, I would designate as a moral disagreement any case in which differing conclusions are reached on a specifically moral issue even though each disputant understands the nature of his opponent's conception of all of the non-moral aspects of that which is being judged. Thus, any cases in which an apparent disagreement is settled when the disputants understand what their opponents take to be the nature of the facts in the case, or any controversy which then becomes a controversy concerning whether one or another view of these facts is empirically the more adequate, would only represent a disparity between moral judgments. On the other hand, any cases in which an argument concerning a specifically moral question persists after each opponent has understood what his opponent takes to be the nature of that which they are judging would be designated by me as a moral disagreement.

If this view of what constitutes a moral disagreement is accepted, it is perfectly possible that there should be various types of moral disagreements, and that their sources and their implications for the establishment of a valid standard for conduct would be quite different. That there are such types seems to me to be true.[3] However, at this point it has only been necessary to point out that not all cases in which moral controversies arise should be taken to represent genuine moral disagreements. Some ultimate disagreements may exist (and, I believe, do exist), but some moral controversies also represent disparities between moral judgments.

In addition to these two main types of discrepant moral judgments, we may note that some moral controversies are also engendered by the fact that the moral judgment of one person does not have a direct counterpart among the moral judgments of another person. For example, an agent may make a judgment regarding the rightness or wrongness of an action in a case in which an observer is not cognizant of any moral demands in the situation which the agent faces; or, conversely, an observer may make a judgment of moral rightness or wrongness in cases in which the agent did not feel that a moral issue was involved. Similarly, it is possible for two persons to be confronted by a single overt action and possess differing moral attitudes toward it when one makes a judgment concerning its rightness or wrongness while the other makes a judgment concerning the moral worth of some trait of the agent's character, or concerning his character as a whole. In both general types of case, the specific moral judgment of one person has no counterpart among the moral judgments of another. I shall speak of all such cases as constituting divergences among moral judgments.

It is with the general problems raised by this threefold classification of moral controversies that I shall initially deal.

i.

AT FIRST GLANCE it would seem that *divergences* among moral judgments should not engender controversies. If a judgment made by one person has no counterpart among the judgments made by another, a mere clarification of this divergence might be supposed to be sufficient to dispel any controversy. And, in fact, this may occur when the divergence rests on the fact that one person has made a judgment of rightness or wrongness while the other has made a judgment of moral worth. As we have seen,[4] these two types of judgment do not concern the same aspects of a given action, and they are therefore logically independent of one another. Further, it is also possible for these judgments to be independent of one another in a psychological sense: the same person may, for example, disapprove of an action and yet praise the trait of character from which it sprang. Therefore, conflicts of this sort cannot be considered to be ultimate: a clear recognition on the part of both persons that they are making moral judgments of differing types should serve to prevent controversy.

Yet this does not always occur. There are cases in which the initial difference between the judgments may engender a real and important controversy. Once having recognized that they have made divergent judgments, two persons might still find cause for dispute with regard to the question of whether one type of judgment ought to take precedence over the other. For example, if one person sees an action as wrong, and the other views it as exemplifying a praiseworthy loyalty, they might argue as to whether its wrongness or the loyalty which it evinced should be the final determinant of one's attitude toward it. In my opinion such controversies do in fact exist, and it seems to me plausible to maintain that there are marked differences between people with respect to their views on this question: the moral attitudes of some persons seem to be most often and most strongly aroused by the apprehension of worthy personal traits, while others seem to be more concerned with what one might term "rectitude," the doing of a right act.[5] And if this is the case, the mere elimination of the original confusion will not ultimately avoid a controversy between them.

However, it is to be noted that when a moral controversy assumes this form we are no longer dealing with a *divergence*, but with a *disagreement*, in moral judgment. For what has occurred is that the two persons are no longer making differing types of judgment: they are contending that one of these types is, in some ultimate sense, more important than the other. Each is holding that while it is possible to view a given action under different aspects, and therefore possible to make different types of moral judgment regarding it, one of these aspects rather than the other ought to be determinative of the moral attitude which one adopts toward the fact that the action was done. Such a difference constitutes a real moral disagreement between them.

With respect to the second type of divergence among moral judgments a different, but roughly parallel, situation obtains. This type of divergence exists when two persons, who are confronted by what is ostensibly the same situation, do not both make moral judgments concerning it. In such cases the persons may both be spectators of the same action, or one may be the agent and the other a spectator, or the same person may find that what he once saw as involving or as not involving a moral issue, he no longer views in the same way.

The mere fact that, in a strict sense, contrary moral judgments have not been made does not lead to an avoidance of puzzlement and controversy. When we find that the moral quality which we believe ourselves to have apprehended is not apparent to others, or when we find others claiming that a moral quality exists where we do not apprehend it, we are no less troubled than we are when another person states that he finds right what we find wrong. Once the divergence in judgment is brought to the forefront of attention, we are led to demand whose judgment is correct.

When faced by such a question we, today, are sometimes tempted to say that the two controversialists are merely seeing the same action from different "points of view." But this is not to settle the question. We are then still impelled to ask which point of view is the one from which the action ought to be viewed. If the answer is given that each is equally correct, the question is of course solved: we must then give up the belief that the moral aspects of an action in any way inhere in the action itself.

However, it appears to me that before most people reach or accept this conclusion they seek to handle these controversies in another way. The conviction that the moral qualities of actions inhere in these actions is sufficiently strong (whether it be justified or not) that they postulate that he who fails to see such a quality cannot really have understood the nature of the act. Conversely, those who find no such qualities in a specific action, but believe them to inhere in other actions, tend to hold that their opponent has read something into the action which does not properly belong to it. In either case, the original *divergence* in moral judgment is treated as a *disparity* between the judgments.

Closer inquiry into such cases will often reveal that in them we are in fact only concerned with simple disparities. The controversy may merely rest upon the fact that those who made the divergent judgments had differing conceptions of the specific nature of that which both were ostensibly judging, and that when each understands the grounds upon which the other's judgment was based, no further controversy of a specifically moral nature will be pursued by them. However, there may also be cases in which no such simple disparity is involved. When each understands what the other took to be the non-moral aspects of the action judged, they may still fall into dispute over whether viewing the action in this way showed a moral insensitivity on the part of one of them, or a hypertrophy of moral squeamishness on the part of the other. Such an argument would constitute a moral disagreement.[6] Whether, in any specific case, a divergence in moral judgment could be said to involve only a disparity in judgment, or whether it must be held to involve a moral disagreement, is a question which would have to be answered by examining the case in detail. However, it is at least safe to say that some controversies which start out as instances of divergences among moral judgments have a tendency to become transformed into either disparities or disagreements. It is therefore not surprising that controversies which rest on the existence of divergences among moral judgments should often have been overlooked: they either do not persist, and they therefore do not become of major theoretical importance for a discussion of the normative problem, or if they persist they assume another form. And now, having noted their existence and the fact that they provide one of the sources of the other types of controversy, we may leave these divergences in order to discuss disparities and disagreements.

We have distinguished between disparities and disagreements on the basis of whether or not a specifically moral controversy persists after each of two persons who makes a conflicting moral judgment has understood what the other takes to be the nature of the object being judged. Now, if all cases of moral controversy represented disparities between moral judgments, the existence of these controversies could not be cited as evidence for the fact that different individuals possess different and incompatible moral convictions. It is only if we find that there are cases of moral disagreements that such a claim could be made. And even if we are faced by such disagreements it is by no means clear just how radical a conclusion should be drawn from them: as we shall see,[7] there are various types of moral disagreement, and the theoretical implications of the various types need not all be the same. However, the issue of whether any moral disagreements do really exist is of such importance that it must be examined here. Regardless, then, of what conclusions must ultimately be drawn, let us examine whether it is plausible to hold that every discrepancy among moral judgments can be said to represent a disparity between these judgments, rather than a moral disagreement.

Unfortunately one cannot decide this question by a direct inspection of conflicting judgments. When two persons make discrepant judgments each not only feels that his judgment is correct, but also feels that it contradicts the judgment of the other: in this respect there is no immediately apparent difference between disparities and disagreements. It is only through inquiry into the manner in which each apprehends the nature of the object concerning which he is judging and through a further inquiry into the extent to which each comprehends upon what basis his opponent is judging, that one can establish whether the conflict represents a moral disagreement. Disparate judgments, we may say, do not bear within themselves an identifying mark of their disparity.

Now, it is obviously impossible for anyone to undertake an inquiry into every single instance of a conflict between moral judgments in the hope of establishing that all such conflicts may be reduced to disparities. Nor is it plausible to maintain that since one can in fact establish the existence of many such disparities one has a right to assume that all conflicts are of this type. Yet, at first glance it would seem equally impossible to show in any specific case that a real disagreement was involved. Now, I should grant that it is difficult, if not impossible, to find any specific case in which we can with assurance say that both disputants had an identical view of every non-moral aspect of that which they were judging and yet reached diverse conclusions regarding its moral quality. While such cases may exist, they are not directly demonstrable.[8] However, it appears to me to be clearly demonstrable that upon occasion two persons may make diametrically opposed assertions concerning a moral issue even after each has understood the nature of what the other takes to be the action concerning which he is judging. In such controversies each may understand why the other judges the action to be right or wrong, and would agree that if he regarded the action from the same point of view as did his opponent, he would form the same moral judgment as did his opponent; but each may argue that the way in which his opponent regards this action is not the way in which it should be regarded. Thus, while cribbing may be regarded as an innocent action by one who sees scholastic success as unimportant,[9] and would be differently regarded by one who attached importance to such success, there is surely a moral question which lies at the root of their discrepant moral judgments and which would be evidenced in any controversy between them: namely, how should this situation be viewed when one makes a moral judgment concerning it? Now, in attempting to answer such a question we are, so to speak, making a "second-order" moral judgment. And it is to be assumed that each of the disputants will in many cases hold that it was his own original moral judgment, rather than that of his opponent, which was made from the point of view from which the action in question should have been judged.[10] Thus, the original difference between their views involves a specifically moral disagreement, and should not be held to be the same type of controversy as is represented by those simple disparities in which an agreement on the nature of certain non-moral properties of that which is judged leads directly to an agreement concerning its specifically moral properties. I therefore would hold that it is necessary to assume that at least some disagreements, as well as some disparities, exist.

If we assume that both sorts of conflict exist, it is important to inquire into their relations and to determine what factors are responsible for each. For example, it is of interest to a normative ethics to know whether some, or all, or none of our moral controversies arise because men possess ultimately different forms of moral consciousness, or whether such controversies represent the intrusion of other variables into the moral judgments which are made. Such questions cannot be answered out of hand. Nor should our answers to them be dictated by any general, pre-accepted theory. Only an investigation of the possible sources of discrepant moral judgments, and of the types of conflict which these engender, will provide adequate grounds for reaching a conclusion. It is therefore to an examination of four such sources, and of their impact upon our moral judgments, that the remainder of this chapter will be devoted. These four sources are: (1) beliefs about matters of fact; (2) emotions; (3) sentiments; and (4) the structure of an individual's personality. As we shall see, each of these may lead, either directly or indirectly, to either disparities or disagreements in moral judgment.

And now, before proceeding to trace the influence of these factors upon the moral judgments of individuals, it will be well to suggest a justification for following what might be considered to be an excessively "individualistic" approach. Such an approach to the problem of conflicts among moral judgments is not the most usual one in contemporary thought. Under the impact of anthropological investigation, attention has been centered upon the varieties of moral codes, and the assumption has been made that disparities and disagreements between the judgments of individuals are wholly attributable to the influence of cultural factors. This assumption is questionable since there appear to be cases in which moral agreement is found in spite of differences in culture, and cases in which moral controversies arise in spite of similarity in culture. And even if it were true that an individual's moral judgments were always a reflection of the codes which are current in his society, the influence of these codes is covert: except on a few occasions, no individual holds that his approval of either a course of conduct or a person is based upon the fact that these are deemed worthy of approval by the other members of his society. His judgments are his own, regardless of how they came to be his. If we are to understand these judgments and compare them with the judgments of other persons we must at the outset inquire into whatever judgmental factors are directly responsible for them. Thus, it is a matter of indifference in the present inquiry whether the disparities and disagreements with which we shall deal are evidenced in the judgments made by the same person on different occasions, by different persons within the same society, or by persons of different societies. Only when we are clear about the factors which limit or determine the moral judgment of any person are we in a position to estimate the role played by culture in fostering moral agreement or difference.

This approach is wholly compatible with the view that cultural differences make a difference in moral judgment. But it proceeds on the assumption that cultural factors—for example, the patterns of institutions, the state of the sciences and the arts, and even the fact that certain religious and moral norms are socially sanctioned—operate upon the moral judgments of individuals in an indirect fashion: they pose moral problems, limit the live alternatives, and play an important part in determining the intellectual apprehension and emotional reactions of individuals. To ascertain in what ways they do this, and to what degree, we would have to possess a comprehensive and reliable body of knowledge in the whole field of social science. But the analysis of moral controversies need not wait upon that day. If there are discriminable factors which always condition the character of moral judgments we may analyze the influence of those factors and leave it to the future to determine in what manner they themselves come to be.

In the following sections I shall therefore in turn consider how each of four factors may so influence our moral judgments as to lead to either disparities or disagreements between them. It is with differences in the apprehension of matters of fact that I shall first be concerned.

ii.

IN CONSIDERING THE WAYS in which differences in the apprehension of matters of fact give rise to conflicting moral judgments, it must not be assumed that we shall be dealing only with disparities, and not with disagreements, between these judgments. While it is true that, in the first instance, all such cases of conflict may be thought to represent only disparities, we have already noted that the controversies which they engender may sometimes reveal that a fundamental disagreement on a specifically moral issue is also involved. It must therefore not be expected that in the present section our attention will be confined to cases of disparities: we shall also be looking for instances in which an examination of what initially appear to be disparities give rise to moral disagreements.

While differences in the apprehension of matters of fact may have consequences for either our judgments of rightness or wrongness or for our judgments of moral worth, the problems involved in these differences are not identical. It will therefore be convenient to deal with each type of case in a separate subsection.

A

There are two obvious and widely recognized ways in which differences in the apprehension of matters of fact may lead to differing judgments concerning the rightness or wrongness of a given action. The first of these relates to differences in the ways in which two persons may apprehend the causal consequences of a particular overt act.

The more obvious form which such a difference may take is that in which two persons hold contrary beliefs as to what results will actually ensue if the act is performed. For example, if a teacher believes that a refusal on the part of all teachers to sign any special loyalty oath will help to maintain academic freedom, his moral judgment regarding what he should do will differ from that of a person who believes that such refusals do not under present circumstances aid, and may hinder, the preservation of free inquiry. Similarly, if two persons in the same or in different societies disagree as to the causal consequences which are involved in any person's committing suicide, it would be natural for them to disagree about the rightness or the wrongness of acts of suicide. This connection between causal beliefs and moral judgments has its theoretical justification in the fact that the actions concerning which we make these judgments include a reference to the consequences to which we expect them to give rise: if the consequences are apprehended as different, the actions which are judged are themselves different.

While this type of influence of causal beliefs on our moral judgments has never been overlooked by ethical theorists, insufficient attention has been devoted to a second point at which the envisioned causal consequences of an action may lead to differences in moral judgment. Such cases are to be found when two persons who do not differ in their judgments concerning the immediate causal consequences of an act nonetheless differ with respect to the range of the consequences which they apprehend the act as having. When one person envisions longer-range consequences as following directly from the act, and the other fails to apprehend any such consequences as being part of the state of affairs to which the act will lead, their moral judgments will thereby be affected: the action concerning which one makes a moral judgment is different from the action as it is seen by the other. When such a situation is recognized to have arisen, we argue as to which of the two ways of apprehending the act is the more justifiable.

Now such controversies are frequently reducible to the first type of case: the question becomes one of whether or not this act really will lead to the further consequences which he who takes the broader view envisions. And such arguments are not always easy to resolve. If the persons concerned should belong to different societies which do not closely resemble one another, an argument of this type is apt to involve questions concerning the validity of the fundamental categories of explanation which are employed in each of the societies.[11] And even when the persons belong to the same society and share a common set of explanatory presuppositions, the argument may involve questions of evidence which are not easily solved; in some cases it may even involve a basic difference regarding the reliance which each person is willing to place upon estimates of what the more remote effects of *any* human action will be. However, in spite of these difficulties, such cases pose no essentially new problems. The disparity which originally involved the fact that one person took a wider view of the consequences of a particular act than did the other remains a simple disparity: the conflict ultimately rests on a difference in views as to what actual effects this act may be expected to bring in its train.

However, there also are cases in which the question of whether a wider or a narrower view of the consequences is the more adequate, involves a moral rather than a purely factual issue. In such cases the conflict of views which originally seemed only to involve a disparity between moral judgments, ultimately involves a moral disagreement. One finds clear expressions of such disagreements in some controversies over whether, or to what extent, good ends can justify evil means. One also finds such disagreements arising when an agent feels obliged to abstain from performing a given act although he acknowledges that an observer might be correct in holding that great benefits to many persons would accrue if the act were performed. In such a case the observer places these benefits in the forefront of attention, while the agent feels that the central moral issue is whether or not this specific act, which he finds inherently wrong, should or should not be performed. When this conflict arises, the question at issue does not concern what the consequences will in fact be: on this both agent and observer agree.

The question is: which view of the situation *ought* to be adopted. Now, in such cases there is no way of settling the question by any appeal to further causal analyses: the agent has already held that in spite of the value of the more remote ends, the action ought not to be performed. And similar cases often arise within our own private moral experience: there come times when, having been judging what we ought to do in terms of long range consequences, we suddenly feel that we have been mortgaging the present to the future; that a halt must be called, and we must decide each issue as it directly presents itself to us; that, in short, it has become wrong to base our moral judgments upon the results of attempts to calculate what a remote and indefinite future may bring.

In my opinion, the ultimacy of these disagreements has been obscured whenever the teleological tradition has been dominant. For if it were true that questions of rightness and wrongness are always to be determined by an appeal to the total consequences which an act may be expected to bring, or will actually bring, then the view which finds an immediate rightness or wrongness to be inherent in an act is but a vestige of a quasi-superstitious conscience. However, the facts of our moral judgments are recalcitrant. No amount of invective, nor any threats that our moral life will be reduced to chaos if we refuse the aid of the utilitarian principle, can coerce us always to accept that view of an act which focusses attention upon its long-run effects. The utilitarian principle is, in effect, a begging of the question which is at issue in these disagreements.

Nor, so far as I can see, is there any escape through that Ideal Utilitarian principle which would have us gather both points of view into a more synoptic judgment, estimating whether "the world as a whole" would be better or worse for our having acted in conformity with what appeared to us immediately right in spite of the fact that the more remote causal consequences of so acting are acknowledged not to be good. Apart from the unclarity of the proposal, and certain other difficulties which it contains,[12] would not he who sees the immediate nature of the act as more relevant to its rightness decide in one way, while his opponent decides in the other? So long as each has already considered the point of view of the other, how does the more synoptic judgment prove that one is right and the other wrong?

The importance of the type of moral disagreements with which we have been dealing will become more apparent as we note other parallel cases and as we later estimate how, if at all, such disagreements may be solved.[13] What is of general interest concerning them is the fact that even though they are grounded in differing apprehensions of a specific moral situation, the issue which divides them is a fundamental moral issue. Thus, in such cases we find that not every difference between two ways of apprehending what are taken to be the same facts is a difference which merely concerns matters of fact.

We have now seen that there are two ways in which differences in the apprehension of the causal consequences of an act lead to conflicts between moral judgments concerning the rightness or wrongness of this act. The first of these ways arises when two persons disagree as to what the actual effects of the act will be; the second arises when they are viewing the act in terms of different contexts, the one seeing its consequences to be wider in scope than the other. We have also seen that in the second type of case the conflict involved might be termed ambipotential: it generates a controversy which either assumes the first form or becomes an example of a moral disagreement. It might therefore be felt that such cases should not have been considered as constituting a separate class. However, if we are to understand the sources of moral controversies, and not merely the forms which they finally assume, it is necessary to take special note of them. In my opinion there are few sources of conflict which are more prevalent.

We turn now to the second major point at which differences in the apprehension of matters of fact lead to differing judgments concerning the rightness or wrongness of a given action. It is to be found when the same overt behavior has different "meanings" for different observers. As in the case of differences regarding the causal consequences of actions, these differences in the interpretations, or meanings, of actions may assume either of two forms. On the one hand, there are those cases in which two observers are judging what are really different actions because they attribute different intentions to the agent; on the other hand they may be judging of different actions because they differ in their apprehension of the situation in which the action is embedded.

As one example of the former type of case we may note that when it is observed that a certain person, present at a social gathering, fails to defend some principle in which we know that he believes, he may either be regarded as evincing moral cowardice or as deferring to certain social amenities. If his conduct is interpreted in the light of these quite different sources, it is not surprising that it should give rise to differing moral judgments, since the object of a judgment of moral rightness or wrongness is always an *action* and not uninterpreted overt behavior. Or, to choose another example, we may note a point admitted by Westermarck[14] and ably illustrated by Duncker,[15] that in different societies a given form of behavior (e.g., the killing of the aged) may spring from very diverse motives, and may be connected with the most different intentions. In all such cases the conflicting judgments which may exist are examples of disparities, not of moral disagreements.

The second type of case in which the same overt behavior has different meanings for two observers arises when the observers hold contrary interpretations of the situation in which the act is performed. For example, if two persons in viewing some act of a third person do not both know that this person stands in a special relation of obligation to another, it will often be the case that an action which he undertakes because of this obligation will be understood and admired by one observer, but not by the other. Similarly, a practice which is seen by the members of one society as an example of licentious behavior might not be so regarded by them were they to understand the religious significance or magical power which those who practice it attribute to it. And here it must again be recalled that the nature of an action can only be understood in terms of the situation in which it is performed: a difference in the interpretations of the nature of the situation implies that the two observers are in reality judging concerning two different actions. To put this now familiar point in a less paradoxical fashion, the observed behavior was in both cases the same, but the behavior interpreted as a morally significant action was different for the two observers. This type of case therefore clearly represents a disparity rather than a disagreement between moral judgments.

However, we must again note that the recognition of a disparity between moral judgments may give rise to a further controversy, and that such controversies sometimes involve a moral disagreement. For example, if in our previous case the original conflict in the judgments of the two observers elicited the fact that one of them had been cognizant of a special obligation on the part of the agent which the other had not known existed, there might still be room for debate as to whether this obligation was or was not the most essential aspect of the situation in which the agent was placed. The two observers might argue as to which of two conflicting sets of demands (both of which each may recognize) is the more stringent. Now, their differences might be interpreted as constituting a primitive, specifically moral disagreement concerning the stringency of one demand as compared to another. However (in some cases at least), it seems to me that their controversy may be said to be susceptible of further analysis. Such an analysis can sometimes be given in terms of differences between the ways in which each "structuralizes" the non-moral aspects of that which he is judging. For example, if one observer focusses attention upon those aspects of the agent's present situation which reach back into the past, seeing the agent's present situation as connected with past obligations, while the other observer focusses attention upon future goods which might be achieved by a specific action undertaken in this situation, their views of which is the more "stringent" obligation will, in fact, vary. And when each attempts to convince the other it will be in terms of which of these two aspects of the agent's situation is seen as being its more "essential" aspect. Each will attempt to adduce an interpretation of the precise conditions under which the prior obligation was assumed, and attempt to weigh the scope of the consequences of fulfilling or not fulfilling this obligation at this precise time; but even if their interpretations of these facts should be the same, their conceptions of the essential nature of the situation in which the agent is placed (and therefore of the "stringency" of these demands) will vary with differences between seeing the present situation as being continuous with those aspects of the past from which the obligation stems, or with seeing the present context as relatively isolated from these past events and intimately attached to the states of affairs which will ensue if the action is performed or neglected. Such a difference in the structuralization of a situation raises the question of how a person *ought* to regard this situation, and is not like a controversy concerning what motive prompted an action nor what causal consequences an action will probably have. To argue which of the ways is, from a moral point of view, the more essential way of viewing that situation, is to argue concerning which is the right, or proper, way in which to decide the moral issue involved. And this is a normative problem.

To what extent, if at all, such moral disagreements may be resolved is not our present problem. However, it is important to point out the inadequacy of one of the ways which may immediately suggest itself as a means of getting rid of such a controversy. On the analogy of those cases in which we wish to clarify and remove discrepancies in our definitions of the nature of an object, we might in this case appeal to the purpose which dictates the adoption of one structuralization of the situation rather than the other. Each of the observers might grant that it would be useful for some purposes to define the essential nature of the situation in one way rather than another, but the question which divides them is how to define it for their common purpose: to decide what is the moral obligation involved.

We shall later have occasion to note the importance of the fact that the moral disagreement which exists in cases of this sort is a disagreement regarding what constitutes the essential nature of a given situation. In the present context it is only necessary to point out that any one of the factors with which this chapter is concerned may influence a person's apprehension of what constitutes the more essential nature of a situation. For example, his views concerning other matters of fact may have an influence; so too may his sentiments. Thus, moral controversies which represent disagreements regarding specifically moral issues *need* not be considered ultimately simple, resting merely on differences in fundamental moral insight. Whether or not they are of this nature will later have to be examined.

B

Having examined the manner in which various types of disagreement concerning matters of fact affect our judgments of the rightness or wrongness of an action, we must now inquire as to the ways in which they affect judgments of moral worth. To do so we must note how it is that we apprehend those aspects of character which we ascribe to persons.

Whether we are considering the nature of a character-attribute or whether we are forming a judgment of a person's character as a whole, we are only in a position to apprehend qualities of character as they are exemplified in a person's reactions to specific situations. Character-attributes and character as a whole are "dispositional" attributes; that is, they are tendencies to act in a certain manner under specific circumstances. Such dispositional attributes can only be recognized if we are cognizant of how the person reacted in at least one concrete situation of the type which evokes this attribute, or else if we are in a position to infer its presence or absence from other attributes which we recognize him to have. It is obvious that we cannot judge the nature of a person's character *in vacuo*.

However, in making a factual judgment of character it is not sufficient for us merely to observe how a person "reacts" to a situation which he faces if by the term reaction were to be meant the type of overt act which he performs. We must understand in what manner he sees that situation; we must see it, so to speak, "through his eyes." Yet, how can we be said to do this unless we already know what he is like, that is, unless we know the very thing which we are trying to discover? To this question, which points out the paradox of much of our knowledge, there is only one answer: here, as elsewhere, we learn in proceeding, relating what we know to what we wish to find out. And if we know nothing of a person, and do not assume him to be like other persons whom we already know, we have no grounds for assuming that we are seeing the situation to which he reacts in the same fashion as does he. But as soon as we know, or think that we know, something about him, we are in a position to judge how the situation appears to him. And it is essential to do so if we are to understand his character.

However, if we are to understand a person's character, either in part or as a whole, we cannot be "identical" with him, seeing the situation to which he reacts precisely as he sees it. In order to understand ourselves or others we must not merely see situations, but must become conscious of the fact that there are various ways in which they can be seen. Self-knowledge demands a division of character, a "psychical distance" from our own behavioral selves; so too in the knowledge of another, we must be equally aware of how a situation appears to him and of how it appears to us or would appear to others. It is only through such contrasts that the structure of a person's character becomes clear.

If the attribution of qualities of character depends upon an awareness of what it is that a person sees in a given situation and what in that situation he fails to see or ignores, it is small wonder that factual disagreements should arise regarding the true nature of a man's character. And since our judgments of moral worth are predicated upon our view of qualities of character, it is natural that moral controversies should develop at this point. These controversies are examples of disparities in moral judgments, rather than being moral disagreements, for they have their source in discrepant apprehensions of matters of fact and disappear when these differences in apprehension themselves disappear.

The forms which such controversies may assume are of two different types. The first is confined to the question of whether or not the agent reacted as he did because he possessed, or failed to possess, a particular attribute of character. Unless both observers can agree as to how the agent himself apprehended the situation which he confronted, they will have no basis for agreement on this point. Further, if they differ as to the alternative ways in which such a situation might be apprehended by others, they will not agree as to what character-attributes the agent's reaction to this situation revealed. Under these circumstances it is obvious that their judgments of moral worth will be likely to conflict.

The second source of disparities between judgments of moral worth lies in what the observers apprehend regarding the situation which the agent confronted. In the first type of case it was assumed that they agreed as to the nature of the situation which the agent really faced, but they differed in their judgments as to the factors which led him to respond as he did. But it is also possible for them to differ regarding the nature of the situation. In such a case, they will differ in their judgments regarding the moral worth of his response. For example, no one expects a very young child to apprehend what is involved in some forms of modesty, nor do we expect him to understand why a person should treat the village idiot with a tolerance not shown toward others: the situation as seen by the child would not contain the same elements which an adult apprehends. Therefore we do not expect a child to see certain virtues, or to condemn all forms of behavior which we hold to be vices. Similarly, among adults, all may not cognize the existence of identical demands when contemplating what is ostensibly one and the same situation. If, in any given case, we fail to see demands which are seen by another, we shall be puzzled as to why he makes the judgment of worth which he does.

Now, even this type of case initially represents a disparity rather than a disagreement in moral judgment, for the conflict in judgments rests upon a difference in the way in which the two observers apprehend the situation faced by the agent. Sometimes such disparities are overcome in the controversy which is likely to ensue, for one observer may lead the other to see the demands which he himself saw. At other times it is *possible* that the controversy reveals that a moral disagreement is ultimately involved: the moral demands seen by one are not apprehended to be moral demands by the other. In such cases the controversy would become focussed upon whether or not specific aspects of character are worthy of praise or of blame. In such cases we would not be dealing with a difference regarding matters of fact, but with a disagreement regarding the worth of a specific character-attribute. Such disagreements (if they exist) may, I believe, be influenced by judgments concerning other matters of fact, but they may also be influenced by the other facts with which we are to be concerned.[16] To these I now turn.

iii.

IN ETHICAL THEORY the terms "emotion" and "emotional" are often used in an extremely broad sense: at times they simply become antonyms of "reason" and "rational." However, for our purposes it will be well to be more precise, and to discriminate the ways in which moral judgments are affected by emotions proper, by sentiments, and by the total organization of a personality, all of which are sometimes considered to be "emotional" factors influencing moral judgments.

In referring to "emotions proper" I am speaking of states such as those in which we feel anger, fear, joy, anxiety, sorrow, loathing, hatred, disgust, impatience, jealousy, contempt, *etc.* No one need be told of the manifold varieties of emotional states, nor reminded of the subtlety of the ways in which they are connected. Nor need we dwell upon the present unsatisfactory state of psychological theory regarding the emotions. Our task is to trace the sources of moral controversies, and we may for this purpose treat the emotions collectively, viewing them as a single type of phenomenon capable of influencing moral judgment. A more detailed analysis of the differences between the ways in which various emotions influence moral judgments would doubtless throw further light upon these controversies; and such an analysis would certainly be of psychological interest. However, in the present state of psychological theory, and in the absence of any general survey of the most obvious ways in which the emotions influence moral judgments, an attempt to make specific and detailed analyses would be premature. Whatever such analyses may in the future reveal, it is essential at this time to try to obtain a broad view of the ways in which any emotion may influence any moral judgment. For this purpose the only distinction between various emotions which it will be necessary to draw is the phenomenological distinction between those which are "objectless," such as euphoric joy or general anxiety, and those which are directly connected with specific objects, as are most states of anger or fear.[17]

It appears to me that there are four different ways in which emotional states may influence moral judgment. In the first three types of case the influence depends upon the capacity of emotions to influence our cognition of that which we morally judge. However, in these three types of case there are differences between the manner in which the emotion influences cognition, and they must therefore be distinguished from one another. As we shall see, the first two types may plausibly be held to give rise only to disparities between moral judgments, while the third may give rise to either disparities or to disagreements.[18]

The first type of case arises because an emotion may exert either a *confusing* or a *distracting* influence upon perception. It has been universally recognized that an emotional state may cause a general "disturbance" in perception, making the person incapable of attending to the actual qualities of the situation which he confronts. And there is no doubt that objectless emotions sometimes give rise to such disturbances in cognition. Under the influence of objectless emotions such as euphoric joy, general anxiety, and generalized fear, the contours of any complex situation may become blurred, its details disregarded, and what is not present may even be apprehended as present. This influence is clear, both in common experience and in psychopathology. And if these emotions are capable of producing such disturbances in perception, their influence will be felt upon moral judgments: the elements between which the relationship of fittingness or unfittingness would ordinarily be perceived may not be apprehended, or if they are apprehended they may not be fixated with any care.

In the case of tied emotions, such as fear of a particular object or anger with a particular object, the effects assume a different form. Any such emotion will have a distracting rather than a confusing influence, for it will lead the person to disregard the situation which he is called upon to apprehend in favor of attending to the emotion-evoking object. While this distracting influence is not enduring, it can at any one time cause an individual not to see relations which, at another time, he as well as others would see.

Now, wherever a controversy arises because of the existence of the confusing or distracting influence of emotions upon cognition, only a disparity, and not a moral disagreement, is involved. If the conflict between the disputants is not settled as soon as it becomes clear to each that the situation as the other saw it was different from the way in which he himself had seen it, their argument will continue as a non-moral argument concerning the real nature of that which was judged: it will not be a specifically moral argument concerning which way a person should (from a moral point of view) have cognized that situation.[19]

The second major way in which emotions may presumably[20] affect moral judgments is to be found in the fact that these emotions may help to structure situations in ways which can influence the judgment which is made. When one element within the situation which we judge is "emotionally charged," our positive or negative attitude toward this element will affect our attitudes toward the other elements which the situation contains. For example, nothing is more difficult than to feel a strong sympathetic emotion toward a specific person, and yet hold it to be just that his claims in a dispute should be denied; nor is it easier to feel a strong revulsion against the use of force in settling a particular dispute, and yet grant that it is morally right that force should be used. Our emotions have valences, and when any one element in a situation arouses an emotion, every other aspect of the situation tends to be lined up as being "for" or "against" this element. Thus the emotion which is directed toward one aspect of the situation tends to structure the situation as a whole. But a moral judgment contains a similar valence of being either "for" or "against." It is therefore difficult to affirm that a course of action which stands opposed to a favored object is morally right, or to find anything morally wrong in that which will undermine or destroy what our emotions have set us against.

There is, I believe, no danger that anyone today will overlook the possibility that there is this structuring effect of emotions upon moral judgments, nor that anyone will be tempted to deny that such an influence may well account for the existence of some moral controversies. However, what is frequently overlooked is the fact that in these cases, no less than in those cases in which an emotion may exert a confusing or a distracting influence upon perception, we think of such influences as being "disturbing" factors in cognition. This being the case, any argument which persists after each of the persons who have made opposed moral assertions has understood that the other has seen the situation in a manner different from that in which he saw it, will become an argument concerning who has apprehended its "real" nature: the argument is not a specifically moral argument at all.[21]

The third way in which emotions may influence our moral judgments lies in the fact that "empathy" is a phenomenon connected with the nature of our individual emotional lives. When we are confronted by a situation involving other persons we may, as a matter of fact, apprehend this situation in terms of its impact upon them. This apprehension is what, in this context, I refer to as "empathy."[22]

Without "empathizing" we would not apprehend most moral situations as we do. Now if, as I believe, our empathic perception bears a relation to the sorts of emotion we are capable of feeling, any difference between the emotions felt by two persons may influence their perception of what any specific situation contains. For example, if there were a person incapable of fellow-feeling he would not understand why another person who was moved by compassion would act as he did. Thus, the moral judgment made by such a person could be expected to be different from the judgment of one who could empathize the compassion which the agent felt. Similarly, if a child has not himself experienced the emotion of modesty, or cannot for any reason empathize it,[23] we should not expect him to make the same moral judgment concerning some actions as do other persons who apprehend the situation as one which will evoke feelings of modesty in the person concerned. As we have seen,[24] judgments of moral worth will vary according to the emotional endowment or experience of different persons; we now see that through the relation between the emotions and the phenomenon of empathic apprehension, the same situation will obtain with respect to the judgments concerning the rightness or wrongness of actions. We may thus say that in so far as our emotional predispositions and our present emotional experience influence what we apprehend as being involved in a situation, they will lead to moral controversies.

However, the controversies which thus arise may be either cases of disparities or of disagreements. In some cases it is true that as soon as one disputant recognizes that his opponent has formed the moral judgment which he did because he apprehended something further in the situation than he himself had seen, he will either change his own judgment or argue whether (as a matter of fact) the situation contained this aspect. Thus, when one person is more sensitive to the feelings of others than is his opponent, their moral judgments may vary; however, the mere indication that a person had been injured by this action may sometimes lead the less sensitive person to change his judgment, or else it may lead him to dispute whether the person involved had really been injured. In other cases, however, it certainly appears to be true that a moral disagreement is involved. The less "empathic" person may grant that he had overlooked or minimized the injury done to the person, but he may still contend that his opponent has overlooked or falsely minimized other demands which the situation contains. Each may then argue as to which, from a moral point of view, is the proper way to regard the situation: should, say, feelings of modesty on the part of a person take precedence over demands which could only be satisfied if these feelings were injured, or should they not? In the familiar moral discussions of "the virgin and the tyrant" (lachrymose as they are) we can see that some persons take opposed stands on such questions. I submit that there also are cases in ordinary life where conflicting judgments concerning the treatment of animals, concerning punishment, and even concerning war and peace show that differences in "empathic" perception lead not only to disparities between moral judgments but may sometimes also show that a moral disagreement is involved.

We have now examined three ways in which emotions may influence moral judgments: first, through the confusing or distracting influence which they introduce into the cognitive situation; second, through their influence in restructuring a situation in which one part of that situation is the object of an emotion;[25] and, third, through their correlation with what we empathically perceive to exist in a particular situation where the feelings of another being are concerned. However, the topic of the relation between emotions and moral judgments is by no means exhausted by these three points of contact. There is a fourth way in which our emotions may exert an influence upon our moral judgments and engender moral controversies. In order to deal with this influence it will be necessary to examine the problem of "the moral emotions."

That there appears to be an essential connection between some moral judgments and the experiencing of an emotion seems to me to be a fact. In such cases we are apt to speak of the emotion as a moral emotion, for example, when we speak of "moral" or "righteous" indignation, or of "moral" admiration. There also are times at which emotions such as anger, contempt, or disgust, seem to be specifically moral in character: they are commingled with moral judgments, and are felt to be essentially connected with the fact that these judgments are made. What differentiates these cases from those which we have previously discussed is the apparent connection between the emotion and the judgment. For example, it seems appropriate that an emotion such as indignation should be felt when we apprehend a blameworthy act; it also seems appropriate that we should admire what we judge to be worthy of praise. On the other hand, it does not seem appropriate that an emotion which is aroused by some isolated, particular component in the situation should lead and direct the judgments which we make. Thus, those cases in which we think (whether rightly or not) that our emotion has been evoked by the specifically moral aspects of an action are cases in which we deem our emotions to be appropriate and morally relevant responses; while if we are forced to admit that the emotion which we feel has been evoked by the presence of any non-moral component in the action, and we believe that it has actually influenced our judgment, we hold it to be a distorting factor. What the nature of these moral emotions may be, and how they are connected with what is asserted by the judgment, must be examined before we attempt to determine how their existence may engender moral controversies.

As is well known, the existence of a connection between moral judgments and the experiencing of "moral" emotions has been differently interpreted by opposing schools of ethical thought. The basic principle of division which may be used in classifying these theories is whether they view such emotions as reactions to the discernment of a moral quality within that which is judged, or whether they interpret the judgment as a by-product of the fact that the emotion was felt. Within each of these general types of view further lines of demarcation may be drawn, but with these we need not here be concerned.

The strength of the first of the alternatives, when compared with the second, lies in the fact that whenever an emotion is commingled with a moral judgment, it does actually appear that the emotion was aroused by the qualities which we apprehended in the action which we judged. To hold that we "first" feel indignation, and that we therefore judge that the action was wrong, seems to distort the nature of our experience.

However, those who grant some sort of "priority" to the emotions can raise a serious objection to the theory that such emotions really are responses to the specifically moral qualities of the action. Their argument can be based upon the fact that any type of emotion which accompanies a moral judgment may also arise when no moral judgment is made; and they can then point out that in the non-moral cases one can presumably explain the appearance of the emotion in purely "natural" (that is, non-moral) terms. They would therefore hold that it seems likely that the same explanation can be given for those cases in which the emotion is apparently aroused by specifically moral characteristics. This possibility can then be strengthened by pointing out that even in non-moral cases, an emotion is *apparently* based upon a prior apprehension of a quality in the object or action. When, for example, we feel fear, we see the object which we fear as being dangerous or threatening; when we feel love, the loved object appears as eminently desirable. In such cases (it is claimed) we know better than to place our faith in appearances:

we know that the presence of the emotion causes the object to take on the appearance which it does. Similarly, this alternative would hold, the apparent primacy of the object in our moral judgments does not prove that the emotion is really a response to a specific moral quality which we have discerned; rather, in spite of appearances, the emotion itself may have caused us to view the object as containing this quality.

While I do not believe that the theory of the emotions which is contained in this answer is adequate,[26] the general purport of the argument is sound. Unless the first alternative can put forward an adequate psychological explanation of the fact that the apprehension of a specifically moral quality can give rise to the same emotions which are aroused when no such quality is present, or unless it can show that the emotions which are involved in the two types of cases are different, it would seem plausible to hold that the so-called moral emotions are evoked by "natural," and not specifically moral, factors.

Now, each of the alternative theories can introduce refinements into the explanations which it offers, and each might possibly take care of all of the objections which could be raised. If they constituted the sole possible alternatives, one would either have to examine such refinements with care, or one would have to decide the issue on general psychological and epistemological grounds. However, it is not true that these two types of alternative theory provide the only ways in which the problem can be solved. Their dominance in ethical thought seems to me to spring from the fact that those who defend each of the positions have prior commitments regarding other problems, and that, in particular, these commitments concern the problem of whether there is or is not a universally valid standard for conduct. If, instead of being bound by either type of theory, we examine those cases in which emotions seem to be essentially connected with moral judgments, a third alternative will be found.

Let us think now only of those cases in which it appears that an emotion is correlated with the fact that we find a person or one of his traits to be morally good or evil, or an action to be morally right or wrong.[27] Such emotional states may be of many kinds—for example, admiration, joy, indignation, anger, disgust, contempt—but, as we have indicated, they are always cases of tied emotions.[28] Now, that to which they appear to be tied is precisely the same relationship that we praise or blame. When, for example, we feel indignation or contempt at the sight of a coward shifting his responsibilities to others, our emotion is directed against him because of an action which we see him perform. And it is this that we also call morally wrong. But our indignation or contempt is not evoked by a recognition that the action was morally wrong. This can be seen from the following fact: which of these two emotions (or what degree of either) we may feel, is apparently a function of the manner in which the responsibility was foisted on others, and of the heaviness of the burden which it placed upon them. Yet such variations do not necessarily affect our judgment of the action's moral wrongness. Similarly, if we see a bully tormenting a child, our indignation appears to be a direct and spontaneous reaction to what we see. In such a case, I find it impossible to assign any "priority" to either our indignation at the bully or to our moral insight that what he did was wrong. And there is no reason to assign priority: what such cases reveal is that the emotion which we feel and the judgment which we make have the same object. What is basic to both is the nature of the situation which we see. Thus, I suggest, one and the same apprehension of an action leads us to *judge* that the action is right or is wrong, and leads us to *feel* admiration, indignation, anger, contempt, or the like. Our emotions are in such cases direct and spontaneous reactions to precisely those aspects of an action which *also* lead us to characterize it as being right or wrong.

This alternative solution of the problem of how moral judgments are related to the emotions which frequently accompany them can be seen to possess the strengths of both alternative positions and the weaknesses of neither. It permits us to hold fast to the phenomenological fact that our emotional reactions to moral situations follow from the properties which we cognize in such situations, and are not the preconditions of making a moral judgment. Yet we are not thereby forced to hold that these emotions differ from other emotions in having as their objects a specifically moral quality; nor are we forced to distort our experience and claim that the particular emotion we felt was a reaction to the single fact that the action was right or was wrong. Thus, the so-called "moral emotions" may be treated "naturalistically": they are simply emotions which are evoked when we contemplate an action in its context, and when our apprehension of these same relations also evokes moral judgment.

This view can be seen to have a further advantage. Not only does each of the other alternatives tend to distort the phenomenological facts, but each would also lead us to expect that every moral judgment should be accompanied by an emotional reaction. Since, however, such a general rule does not hold true, each of these theories would have to provide a subsidiary hypothesis explaining why "moral emotions" are actually experienced in some cases but are not apparently present in others. What seems to be true, and what one would expect on the basis of the present alternative, is that moral apprehension, like non-moral apprehension, is sometimes accompanied by emotion, and sometimes is not. Just as some sights arouse emotions because of the "natural" properties which they possess and we possess, so some actions—because of their "natural" properties and ours—arouse emotions, while others which we see as equally right or wrong do not.

On the basis of the foregoing analysis of the relation between those emotions which are directed toward moral situations as a whole and the moral judgments which are made concerning them, we are now in a position to inquire as to how such emotions are related to moral controversies.

We have seen that there is no necessary connection between variations in the emotions which are felt and the moral judgments which are made: two people apprehending a moral situation may judge identically concerning its rightness or wrongness, but may differ with respect to whether they are emotionally aroused by what they see. And even if both do have some emotional reaction, it does not follow that their reactions need be identical either in kind or degree.[29] At first glance it would therefore seem that variations in moral emotions ought not to engender moral controversies: a moral controversy involves the question of whether an action is right or wrong, or whether a person is to be praised or blamed, and if our emotional reactions vary independently of our praise and blame they ought not to be treated as relevant to this question.

That they ought not to be so treated seems to me clear; however it is equally clear that they sometimes play a large role in moral disputes. Many such controversies concern the shades and degrees of the rightness or wrongness which an action possesses, or the question of just how highly a trait of character, or a person, is to be praised, or how badly to be blamed. Such disputes frequently depend upon the differences between the emotional reactions of different persons, for much of the "flavor" of a moral judgment is contained not in the judgment itself, but is derived from the emotion, or lack of emotion, which accompanies it. He who merely *sees* that a given course of action was wrong, and he who is thoroughly aroused by those of its features which he too sees as wrong, will be likely to fall into controversy concerning the degree of its wrongness.

Thus, the controversies which arise due to differences in the emotional reactions of different individuals to the same situation regarded as a whole are not "substantive" in character: they do not lead to the consequence that what one person finds right another will find wrong. Yet, the qualitative flavor which an emotion lends to the judgment which it accompanies leads to disputes concerning the particular shade and degree of its rightness or wrongness: what one person finds to be a fitting object of moral hatred another may find contemptible, and another merely morally wrong. Thus any assessment of the total range of moral controversy must take these emotional influences into account.

In summary, I should say that the primary reason why it has commonly been held that the emotions play a greater role in fomenting moral controversy than that which we have traced lies in the fact that ethical theories have not been sufficiently clear as to the relation which obtains between the emotions which accompany moral judgments and the judgments themselves.[30] As we have seen, those who have recognized that there are emotions which are essentially connected with moral judgments have been prone to separate these moral emotions from non-moral emotions and have failed to give a plausible psychological account of why moral emotions should arise. The claim that they are responses to our discernment of a specifically moral quality merely notes a connection which sometimes exists, and does not explain why it sometimes exists and sometimes does not. And thus, as a reaction, the psychological theory is born: the emotions are taken to be primary, and moral judgments are interpreted as being merely expressions of them. This theory must then explain why the moral qualities appear to be in the object, and to do so it is led to claim that emotions are aroused by entities independently of the phenomenal qualities which they possess. The only conclusion which such a theory can reach is that a moral quality which appears in the object is the projection of a purely subjective state, and that such states will vary from person to person, depending upon his constitution, his training, and (perhaps) on what he at the moment wills. However, I do not believe that either the phenomenological facts nor the theories of emotion which are at our disposal demand that we accept such a conclusion. Therefore it seems to me clear that emotions need not be considered to be the basis of moral judgments. Nonetheless, as we have now seen, differences in emotion may affect such judgments and may, in a variety of ways, engender moral controversies.

iv.

WE COME NOW to the problem of tracing the influence of sentiments upon moral controversies. As examples of sentiments I would cite the love or hatred of a person, the love of one's country or home, and the love or hatred of a social institution or social class. In all such cases "love" and "hatred" are the polar terms which we naturally use. But a sentiment is not simply a transient emotion of love or of hatred directed toward a person or other object; it is an enduring thing, having its own laws of growth, of transformation, and of extinction. Furthermore, once it has been formed, a sentiment will in large measure control what emotions we feel and what responses we make when a passing situation contains the object of our sentiment, or contains anything connected with this object. And when a sentiment is at its strongest, almost every situation comes to be seen in terms of its relation to that which we love or hate: even an obvious lack of connection is sometimes a connection, as when we become impatient or bored because what we face is not related to the object we love. In whatever fashion one may wish to analyze sentiments, their existence and their force cannot, I believe, be denied. Yet the relative inadequacy of current psychological theory regarding their nature and laws[31] makes it necessary to treat of only the simplest of cases. Among these cases the very simplest which are relevant to the problems of moral controversies are probably those which are to be found when a sentiment influences our judgments of the rightness or wrongness of an action.

The most obvious way in which a sentiment may affect such judgments is when the object of the sentiment either is, or comes to be, included within the situation concerning which we judge. This may occur when a person who is directly involved in the situation is himself the object of the sentiment: when one of the possible alternative courses of conduct bodes well or ill for such a person; or, finally, when through imagination we identify one person in the situation with the object of some sentiment of our own. As an example of the first type we may cite the change which is sometimes effected in our judgment of rightness or wrongness when it is our own child and not, as we had supposed, a neighbor's child who has committed a gross misdemeanor. As an example of the second we may choose our judgment of the rightness or wrongness of alternative courses of conduct when one of these, which would otherwise be seen as being right, is recognized to redound to the detriment of our family; or, to choose another example, those cases in which our judgment is changed because the right act is suddenly seen to bode ill for the nation we love or to aid a nation we hate. Finally, as an example of the third type, we may see how a sense of rightness may be changed when one person comes to identify himself with another, and views the situation as it would appear to him were his own child or his own nation involved. In all three types of case the moral judgment of the individual may be seen to deviate from what it would have been had the moral situation not involved the object of a sentiment. And since it is universally acknowledged that the objects of the sentiments of different individuals are frequently different, such an influence will frequently lead to moral controversies. However, before attempting to say whether such controversies represent disparities or disagreements between the moral judgments which are made, it will be well to describe some slightly more complex cases in which sentiments influence judgments of moral worth.

In tracing the influence of sentiments on judgments of moral worth, it will be essential to bear in mind one of the fundamental characteristics of sentiments. Every sentiment tends to be "enveloping," to extend beyond the point of its original reference and to include all that is connected to this referent. Such a tendency may express itself in either of two ways: intensively or extensively. On the one hand we incline to prize all of the characteristics which are possessed by an object toward which we have a favorable sentiment, and to despise all of the characteristics possessed by the object of an unfavorable sentiment. This tendency of a sentiment to gather into itself all of the qualities of an object, and not remain tied to merely those qualities which were its original source, I shall term its *intensive* enveloping tendency. It is familiarly exemplified in patriotism or in love: when one's nation is the object of a strong sentiment all of its characteristics seem to be favorable, or at least readily defensible; and when one is in love every characteristic of the loved one enters the amalgam of love.[32] However, a sentiment may also grow extensively, may radiate beyond the person or thing which was its original object. For example, the food preferences of a child's hero tend to become his food preferences,[33] and the characteristics of our heroes tend to invest others who possess these characteristics with a value which they might not otherwise have. Even the fact that one of our heroes, or one of our arch-enemies, possesses a certain name—or any other superficial attribute—may lead to some prejudgment of strangers. This radiating effect, which extends beyond the object itself, I shall call the *extensive* enveloping tendency of a sentiment.

The tendency of sentiments to envelop both whatever belongs to and whatever is connected with their objects may influence judgments of moral worth in a variety of ways. But before we proceed to analyze these influences we must take cognizance of one often neglected fact: a sentiment itself often develops upon the basis of a judgment of moral worth. The small boy's hero often becomes a hero to him because of the courage, or unfailing sportsmanship, or patriotic self-sacrifice which he shows. To the manly strength of the hero, tawdry fiction usually adds a reserve of moral power, which is expected to evoke hero-worship; and one can see in the movies that a rich girl is only a heroine if beneath her glamor she possesses a core of folksy virtue. In spite of their sentimental mawkishness, there is a continuity between these cases and what even the most sophisticated person demands in his hero: he who is judged to be a hero must possess characteristics which are judged to have outstanding moral worth. And it is these characteristics which, more often than not, are the sources for the growing sentiment of love for those who appear as heroes to us. Thus, in its formation, a sentiment is not necessarily blind to the moral qualities of a person.

Of course, sentiments may also develop due to other causes. The sentiment of love for our children does not have its source in the moral qualities of the child, nor does our hatred for a person who has offended our ego always rest upon the moral quality of that offense. It is only important to note that, contrary to widely held notions, the influence of our sentiments upon our judgments of moral worth need not be an alien influence: sentiments themselves may develop out of, and be reinforced by, such judgments.

If we turn now to trace the influence which existing sentiments may exert upon judgments of moral worth, we immediately note that any such influence is held to be a disturbing factor. When, for example, we are called upon to make a moral judgment concerning the character of a person to whom we are bound by a sentiment of love or of hatred, we usually attempt to discount any influence of our sentiment upon our judgment and to deny that such an influence exists. In such cases, as in the cases of judgments of the rightness or wrongness of conduct, we feel that a sentiment has no place. But though we seek to adopt the point of view of an impartial spectator, the influence of a sentiment is not easily circumvented.

Some of the ways in which the intensive enveloping tendency of a sentiment influences our judgments of moral worth may here be traced. First, any person who is the object of a strong sentiment will of course possess many characteristics which have nothing to do with the origin of our sentiment. Yet the sentiment will tend to make us see all such qualities as praiseworthy or blameworthy, and to judge his character as a whole as being morally good or evil. Thus, our attachment to our own children leads us to attribute to them both moral and non-moral qualities which they do not possess. Second, due to public recognition of certain moral qualities as the fitting basis for the development of a sentiment, we may even be led to explain our sentiments in moral terms, praising or blaming persons in order to justify the strong non-moral attraction or repulsion which we feel. (For example, those who are moralistically inclined will claim a special virtue for children in order to justify their love for them, and the poetry of youth seems always to find that prostitutes embody the wisdom and goodness of the Earth-Mother.) Third, the glaring absence of a certain trait in our heroes may, when our sentiments are sufficiently strong, even cause us to denigrate the virtues which they fail to possess. And in some cases a sentiment may even lead to a fallacious conversion of a proposition: to the anti-Semite not only are all Jews bad, but all who are bad become Jews; to the hero-worshipper not only are all traits of the hero good, but what the hero lacks cannot be good. In such ways, then, the force of the intensive enveloping tendencies of a sentiment lead us to moral judgments which, without the sentiment, we would never have made.

The extensive enveloping tendency of a sentiment also influences our judgments of moral worth. Although it operates in less devious ways, some of its effects seem to me to be of wider significance, and of more permanent influence, than any effects of the intensive sort. One of these effects is to be found in the fact that the existence of a sentiment toward a person who possesses a certain virtue or vice makes us more sensitive to its presence or absence in others: we find ourselves looking in all men for the particular traits of character which the objects of our love or of our hatred possess. If I am not mistaken, much (though not all) of that moral education which proceeds through example depends upon the existence of a prior sentiment toward the person who sets that example.

The second, and perhaps most drastic form in which the extensive, radiating effects of sentiments exert an influence upon our judgments of moral worth appears to me to lie in the fact that they play an important role in determining the order of precedence among the virtues which we recognize, and among the types of character which we extol. When, for example, we develop a sentiment for a person who possesses certain salient virtues, and when by the extensive enveloping tendency of this sentiment others who also possess this virtue thereby (as well as through their own merits) come to be the objects of positive sentiments, a pattern is built up in which these virtues, shared by those whom we reverence and love, seem to us to be of paramount importance. We are not as a result necessarily blinded to the quite different virtues of others; yet the worth of these virtues may never shine quite so brightly for us.[34] The growth of a homogeneous cluster of sentiments thus canalizes our sense of moral value: we tend to become more fixed in our conception of a hierarchy among the virtues. And so too with the vices: the vice which for each of us stands at the lowest point of the pit is most often that vice which has been embodied in one whom we have intimately known and hated, or it is a vice which has undone the object of a love, or threatens to undo us ourselves.[35] Only the growth of wider ranging sentiments can check this canalization, and we do not always possess the imaginative sympathy which is required for this growth to take place. Thus, sentiments not only affect our judgments of moral worth from case to case: due to their extensive tendency they play a role in moral education, and they also have a pervasive influence on the order of precedence which we find among virtues and vices.

If all of the preceding remarks are true, it is readily seen that variations between the sentiments of different individuals, and variations between the sentiments most generously fostered in different cultures will lead to conflicts among moral judgments.

Whether such conflicts represent disparities between moral judgments, or whether they are cases of moral disagreements, is a problem which must now be faced.

The answer to this problem is of a type already familiar to us: while such conflicts originally represent disparities between moral judgments, the controversies which they engender often become transformed into moral disagreements. That they are first to be considered as examples of disparities should be clear. We have noted how the existence of a sentiment affects the apprehension of an object, tending to envelop all of the qualities of that object, and radiating beyond it to any characteristics or persons connected with it. Under these circumstances two persons who view what is ostensibly one and the same situation will not see it as possessing identical characteristics if their sentiments differ. Whether in such cases the sentiment changes the appearance of the specific characteristics of the object, or whether it merely introduces differences in emphasis upon different aspects of the situation, or whether it does both, is not a problem with which we need here be concerned: so long as one of these types of change occurs, that which is apprehended by the two observers will be different. The conflict between their moral judgments will therefore apparently be a case of a disparity.

However, when the influence of a sentiment upon a moral judgment is once noted, it may engender a controversy concerning the appropriateness of viewing the situation as it appears when affected by this sentiment. At first glance it would seem as if this question should always be solved in favor of that judgment which remained unaffected by any sentiment: as I have noted, we incline to believe that a moral judgment should be free of any "emotional" factor, and should be of the type which would be made by any "impartial spectator." Yet I have also noted the fact that in its origin and its growth a sentiment may (though it need not) be fostered by the discernment of a moral quality. Therefore he who would admit that his moral judgment had in part been determined by a sentiment, could claim that such a sentiment was not a distorting factor in his judgment; that it was itself dependent upon a prior moral apprehension which any impartial spectator should share. And he could further argue that a failure to feel love or hatred toward the object of his sentiment bespeaks a blindness to the very qualities which the action in question possessed. Thus, for example, in a controversy as to whether a given action was right or was wrong two persons might agree that a third person, whom one reveres, would have acted in one way and not the other: for the one this constitutes evidence that the action is right, for the other it does not. While one of the disputants could argue that only a reverence for this person made the act seem right, the other could answer that the person was worthy of reverence and emulation, and that the failure of the other to be aware of this fact is of a piece with his judgment that the action in question was wrong. Such an argument clearly constitutes a disagreement between moral judgments. And considering the extent to which we are influenced by the moral decisions of those toward whom we feel either love or hatred, the occurrence of such disagreements is by no means rare.

v.

HAVING ANALYZED the relations of emotions and sentiments to moral judgments, it is now necessary to examine how the latter may be affected by the total structure of an individual's personality.

In my opinion it is important to examine this question since there are few popular ethical generalizations which are more widely held than that which states that our moral judgments are the products of the sort of people we are. This generalization would, of course, be a truism were it not interpreted in a special sense. The special sense in which it is usually taken is that individuals differ with respect to the patterns of their personality, and that because of these differences the moral judgments of different individuals conflict.

That there are conflicts among the moral judgments of different individuals is a fact which has never been questioned. In the preceding sections I have attempted to find the sources of such conflicts in differences in the ways in which specific situations are apprehended and in the influence of emotions and sentiments upon the moral judgments which any two individuals may make. Our present problem is to see whether, in addition to these factors, there is any influence which may be said to be due to the "personality" of the person who makes the moral judgment.

In examining this question one must be clear as to what is meant by the factor of "personality." As we have seen,[36] the term personality may be taken to refer to all of the persisting attributes of a person, including not only the characteristic forms of his motivation, but his interests, endowments, sentiments, and temperament. Now, if we are to hold that the moral judgments of an individual are the products of all of these factors combined, we shall certainly not have said anything enlightening. Such an "explanation" of conflicts between moral judgments would merely consist in repeating the fact that differing individuals do make different moral judgments. What is actually involved is, instead, the belief that the over-all structure, or organization, of an individual's personality is the function of one or more "hidden" attributes of his nature, and that it is these attributes which govern the moral judgments which he makes. It is then contended that these "hidden" attributes are not identical in all individuals, and that the moral judgments of different individuals will therefore conflict.

With the contention that there are (or may be) such "hidden" attributes I have no quarrel. If we are to explain the significant differences between the personalities of any two individuals, and the consistency of their individual responses to varying situations of the most diverse types, it would seem necessary to postulate some fundamental differences in their natures. Whatever may be the shortcomings of the uses to which terms such as "introverted" and "extroverted," "aggressive" and "submissive," "constricted," "compulsive," or "uncontrolled," have been put, it does remain true that some individuals manifest these characteristics in much of their behavior, and that there are significant relationships between that behavior and their general intellectual and emotional life. This unity of pattern within any one individual, and the diversity of pattern between individuals, makes it legitimate to assume that there are (or may be) covert persisting factors responsible for the sort of personality which each individual displays. What the nature of such factors may be, and what may be their genesis, is an open question. It is also an open question as to whether it is possible to classify individuals according to a few major types of personality-pattern. For the purposes of the present discussion these questions need not be answered; it need only be assumed that individuals do in fact show a significant unity or pattern in the modes of their thought, their feeling, and their expression, and that this pattern is not the same for all. Our problem is whether those factors which are responsible for such a pattern do influence moral judgments, and if so in what way. It will be my contention that such factors do exert an influence over the moral judgments which any individual makes, but that, so far as the *content* of these judgments is concerned, this influence is indirect, rather than direct.[37]

In contrasting a direct and an indirect influence of a personality-factor on the content of a moral judgment I have reference to the difference between saying, on the one hand, that what we affirm or deny in making a moral judgment is a product of the basic, controlling trait of our natures, and saying, on the other, that what we affirm or deny depends upon how the situation appears to us to be structured. The second alternative does not exclude the possibility that the way in which a situation appears to be structured may often be partly determined by the basic, controlling trait of our natures and in such a case there will be an indirect influence of this trait on the moral judgment. It might even be claimed that how such a situation appears to be structured is *always in part* determined by such a trait, or that it is *sometimes wholly* determined by such a trait. But even if either of these two more extreme claims were to be accepted (and I myself find no grounds for accepting them), the position which would be adopted would be different from holding that what a moral judgment affirms or denies is the direct product of the controlling trait of our personality. What the latter thesis involves is the interpretation of moral judgments as being direct "projections" of those factors which are responsible for the over-all structure of our personality. Of course, this thesis is not intrinsically inconceivable. For example, it might be the case that whenever a situation arises in which we find that our wishes are incompatible with one another, our dominant wish takes on the aspect of being a superior, "external" demand, and in that case what seems to be morally demanded is merely a projection of whatever factor in our personality makes this wish stronger than another. This general type of thesis has often been held, although it has usually been stated in more complicated forms.

However, although it is conceivable that our moral judgments might be explained in this way, it is by no means plausible to hold that this is the explanation which is most in accord with any of the facts which a survey of moral judgments can supply.[38] For example, on the basis of this hypothesis it would be difficult to explain why there is as much diversity in the moral judgments of any single individual as we in fact find; or why among his judgments there seem to be nuances which apparently depend upon the precise nature of the situation which he confronts: if our moral judgments were projections of our dominant traits, the judgments of any one individual would, I submit, tend to be more uniform than they are. Further, the moral judgment of highly diverse sorts of persons could not be expected to converge as frequently as they in fact do.[39] Finally, if the thesis were true it would be difficult to explain why two persons who are similar in their basic personality would ever agree in their moral judgments if the action which they judge is recognized to be likely to affect their basic interests differently. The fact that all of these possibilities are actualized in some cases, although not in all, seems to provide evidence against any simple explanation of moral disagreements in terms of a projection of the personality-factors of those who make these judgments.

And, in fact, one can readily accommodate all the data which seem to demonstrate the influence of differences in personality upon our moral judgments if one merely postulates that such differences may be reflected in differences in the ways in which persons structure the situations which they confront. When a situation may readily be structured in two or more ways, a difference between basic personality factors may be reflected in differing ways of structuring that situation. For example, we do not expect a markedly "outgoing" personality to be as cognizant of how an action will affect the feelings of others as a person of another temperament may be; consequently, that aspect of a situation which concerns the feelings of others will be less in the forefront of his attention than it will be for others. In such cases the conflict in judgments follows from personality differences, but it follows indirectly, and not directly, from them.

Whether the influence of factors of personality is an indirect rather than a direct influence is a question of theoretical importance. If, as I have claimed, the influence is indirect, then all such cases may constitute examples of disparities between moral judgments, rather than being cases of moral disagreements. To be sure, in this case as well as in those which have been previously noted, what at first appear to be simple disparities may, upon investigation, turn out to be cases of moral disagreement: each individual may claim that his way of viewing the situation is more adequate to its nature than is the way in which the other person views it. While it could of course be true that this more ultimate controversy is itself engendered by the differences between the two personalities, the influence of such a personality factor would still be indirect: it would operate through its impact on the way in which two persons come to see the nature of the situation which both confront. Under these circumstances we cannot directly explain the content of specific moral judgments in terms of the personality of the person making them. On the contrary, each moral judgment would have to be interpreted in terms of the nature of the situation which is apprehended. The influence of personality on moral judgments then becomes a question of tracing to what extent, and in what ways, this influence operates on the manner in which different individuals apprehend what is objectively one situation. If I am not mistaken, one could not easily defend the view that basic personality-factors are in themselves sufficient to give every situation whatever structure an individual apprehends it to have. Thus, the supposedly obvious truth that our moral judgments are the products of our individual natures loses its spurious plausibility, and gives rise to a genuine psychological question: to what extent, and in what ways, do personality-factors structure our apprehension of life-situations and thus indirectly lead to moral controversies?

In my opinion, any attempt to answer this question would involve a consideration of differences in what might be called the emotional constitution of different persons. For example, whatever attribute of a personality we choose as possibly being a basic factor in the personality will have some relation to emotional control, to the feelings of selfhood, and to the stability or lability of sentiments.[40] It is for this reason that the influence of personality upon moral judgments is usually classified as being an "emotional" influence. Because of this classification it might be thought that my previous insistence upon the indirect, rather than the direct, influence of personality-factors on moral judgments has missed the basic point at issue. It might, in short, be argued that through its influence upon an individual's emotions and sentiments his basic trait of personality would *directly* affect the content of his moral judgments; that it would not have to operate through its influence upon his apprehension of the situation. But such a contention would be false. In the first place, it seems doubtful whether any basic personality factor directly and of itself engenders a particular emotion or sentiment; instead, it seems more plausible to hold that such a factor merely controls the duration, expression, and total impact of the emotions or sentiments. Therefore the content of moral judgments is not likely to be *directly* affected by such a factor. In the second place, even if this were not true, we have already seen that, in some cases, the influence of emotions and sentiments upon moral judgments is exerted through the ways in which they affect our apprehension of the situations in which we stand. Therefore, regardless of the influence of personality upon emotions and sentiments, this influence would, in some cases, only operate indirectly on the judgments we make. In my opinion it is therefore perfectly clear that however great may be the influence of personality differences upon moral controversies, this influence cannot be claimed to be *the* factor which is determinative of the content of the judgments which we make.

However, it is essential to note that although the content of an individual's moral judgments is surely not in all cases (if in any) directly determined by the basic structure of his personality, there seem to be marked differences in the extent to which various individuals find that the situations which they apprehend contain moral demands. Some persons find many more situations to be morally significant than do others, and to them other persons appear to be morally obtuse. On the other hand, they themselves appear to others as being tortuously finikin in all that concerns moral judgments. Whatever may be the genesis of such differences in moral "sensibility," experience seems to show that these differences are tied to the other persisting attributes of the individual. He who evinces what seems to others to be an excessive moral scrupulosity is not likely to perform any task in an easy and uncomplicated way. This can scarcely be held to follow from the fact that his spontaneity is inhibited by his moral discernment, for in many such persons one finds that the processes of thought, the interpretation of the motives of another, and even the ordering of the details of life, reflect the same niceties and indirections as the search for a moral issue in all of the events which he views. Similarly, those who seem to others to be morally obtuse also frequently manifest traits and attitudes which reflect a failure to attend to any but the most obvious among the features of the situations they confront. Thus, there seem to be personality-factors which differentiate individuals with respect to the extent to which they view a situation as containing a moral demand. Such factors do not determine *what* demand they may see, but only the extent to which they attempt to structure a situation in such a way as to make it contain *some* demand, or the extent to which they respond to all situations without first examining how these might appear if their own interests were not affected by them.

Now it is obvious that if there are personality-factors which lead differing individuals to differing degrees of moral sensibility, such factors will result in controversies. These controversies will initially represent divergences in moral judgments. However, we may again note that any such divergence may become transformed into a moral disagreement. In the cases before us this occurs when each individual insists that he is seeing the situation as it really is, and that the other mode of apprehending what it contains has been influenced by a personal idiosyncrasy. In short, each would claim that what he sees is what an impartial spectator would see.

How, if at all, such a controversy might be solved is not our present problem. However, it is here necessary to point out that the existence of such controversies has sometimes been taken to suggest that there is no common denominator in the moral judgments which different people make. If each person appears convinced that what he sees is what an impartial spectator would see (or approximates this), might not their disagreement arise due to the fact that the moral consciousness of each was fundamentally different from that of the other? The difference here in question would *not* be a difference in the content of specific moral judgments: men might reach opposed conclusions concerning the rightness or wrongness of a particular act, or of the praiseworthiness or blameworthiness of particular attributes of character, and yet be said to possess a similar type of experience which could be denominated "moral experience." Ultimate differences in moral consciousness would only exist if either of two conditions were to be fulfilled: first, if there were some persons who do not seem to possess what we term moral experience; or, second, if some persons were led to form diametrically opposed judgments of rightness or wrongness, praiseworthiness or blameworthiness, in *all* cases in which we and they could be presumed to have precisely the same view of the non-moral properties of that which was being judged.[41] Neither of these conditions seems to me to be fulfilled by the evidence at our disposal. While this evidence cannot, in the nature of the case, be conclusive, there are certain facts which strongly militate against holding such a view.

In the first place we may note that in every society there exist some standards of right and wrong conduct, and some standards of moral worth. In every society, therefore, a large group of persons do have some form of moral experience, judging some acts to be right and others wrong, and holding to some standards of moral worth. What the genesis of such judgments and standards may be, and what may be their specific content, is not the point at issue here; their existence is of itself sufficient to show that some form of moral experience is to be found among some of the members of all societies.

In the second place we may note that within any particular society the specific standards of what constitutes right and wrong conduct, and of what constitutes moral worth, are extremely widespread. Even those who rebel against these standards accept more from them than they know, or would readily acknowledge. This may be explained solely in terms of "social conditioning," or solely in terms of the individual's sense of what is fitting in this social milieu, or, better, in terms of both together; but however it is to be explained it shows the extent to which moral experience spreads through the whole of any community.

In the third place we may note that even where we might expect to find a total absence of moral judgment, among the outcasts and criminals in a society, we do not find a complete moral "blindness." In our own society, for example, the evidence seems to show that moral concepts possess significance for even "the hardened criminal." While a criminal may or may not see his own crime as an act of wrongdoing, and while many of his other moral judgments may also seem to us to be distorted, there always seem to be at least a few areas within which he shows a moral consciousness similar to our own.

Finally we may note the fact that we expect all persons who are endowed with other human capacities to be able to draw moral distinctions. The persistence of this expectation suggests, although it does not prove, that if there are persons incapable of moral discrimination they are few in number. And when we note that we do not expect animals, infants, the mentally retarded, or the insane, to apprehend the distinction between right and wrong, it becomes evident that we assume a correlation between other faculties and the recognition of moral meanings. Such an assumption seems to me to be so well supported by empirical data, and so consistent with any plausible theory of the nature of moral judgments, that I see no warrant for the belief that there are in fact persons who differ from ourselves in the sole respect of failing to be cognizant of moral distinctions.

The second possibility which we have to consider is that different persons may all draw moral distinctions, but that the meaning of such distinctions is fundamentally different for each. With respect to this possibility the evidence is, in my opinion, less conclusive. Yet I believe it sufficient for us to hold that there is probably no fundamental, irreducible heterogeneity in the moral experience of different persons, whether they be members of the same or of different societies.

The issue here, I repeat, is not one with respect to variations in the specific content of particular moral judgments made by different persons. Concerning the fact of such variation there is, I think, little doubt, although the degree of variability which is present is open to dispute. In the preceding sections we have traced the sources of such variations and we shall in the next chapter weigh the problem of how far the disputes which they engender may be resolved. However, these disputes cannot be resolved unless it is in fact true that all persons share a common moral experience to which each person may have recourse in assessing the claims which others make.

There appear to me to be two independent lines of argument which could establish the existence of a homogeneous moral consciousness. The first would consist in showing that we can understand and sympathetically appreciate the morality of the specific prescriptions and proscriptions of the codes of conduct of different individuals and of all different cultures when we understand the beliefs and the conditions of life under which these people live, and when we note how, from case to case, emotions, sentiments, and the like, may influence specific moral judgments. At the present time the evidence that we can do so is insufficient to warrant a positive conclusion: much of the presumed moral conduct of people in our own and other cultures is still opaque to us. Yet it is not too much to say that we often come upon instances of apparent moral judgment which we suddenly come to understand, however alien to us the specific content of such a judgment may be. We also find that some of the apparently irreducible heterogeneity of the moral consciousness of different peoples disappears when we see that what we had assumed to be moral issues were merely non-moral customs in a community different from our own. Such instances of a penetration of apparent diversity to a common core of moral experience are sufficiently frequent to lead to a hope, if not a belief, that the diversity of content in various moral codes is not a reflection of a diversity of moral experience but a mask which conceals a common moral consciousness.

The second form of argument which might establish the basic homogeneity of men's moral experience is of a positive nature. It would consist in the attempt to show that all men share the same type of moral experience through an analysis of the nature of that experience. If such an analysis were adequate to the cases upon which it was based, and if it could be seen to apply not only to those cases but to all others which might be cited, then there would be ground for a justified belief that all men share the same type of moral experience. It is of course the aim of this book to give precisely such an analysis. With what success it may be said to do so, and what justification it provides for a belief in the uniformity of men's moral consciousness, is a question which the reader alone can decide.

CHAPTER

6

THE RESOLUTION OF MORAL CONTROVERSIES

Now that we have traced the sources of moral controversies we are in a position to estimate to what extent, and by what means, they may be satisfactorily resolved.

The problem of the resolution of moral controversies has been accorded little attention in the history of ethical thought.[1] On the one hand, those theories which have attempted to demonstrate that there is a universally valid standard for conduct have generally employed arguments which made it unimportant to investigate whether there is agreement among the moral assertions of different persons; on the basis of their arguments, the existence of irreconcilable conflicts between moral judgments is ultimately irrelevant to the question of whether there is such a standard. It is therefore not surprising that these theories have contained no more than hints and suggestions as to how, if at all, moral controversies may be resolved. On the other hand, one might expect that those persons who take the opposed position, denying that there is a universally valid standard for conduct, would examine moral controversies with care. However, this has not generally been the case. Those among them who have been cautious enough to recognize that the existence of contradictory moral assertions does not *of itself* prove that there is no universally valid standard for conduct, have used these contradictions in an indirect way. They have first sought directly to disprove their opponents' claims, and have substituted what seemed to them to be a more adequate alternative theory of moral judgment. Integral to such theories there have always been epistemological, psychological, or sociological assumptions. By means of these assumptions they have sought to explain why contradictory moral assertions are made. Thus, they have been primarily concerned to use the existence of conflicting moral judgments as confirmatory evidence for the truth of assumptions which they had antecedently adopted. However satisfactory this method of argumentation may in other respects be, it can scarcely be said to have involved a free and candid appraisal of the means by which, or the extent to which, moral controversies can be resolved.

In the preceding chapter, however, we have traced the sources of moral controversies and have gathered results which are, in my opinion, not wholly consonant with the assumptions of the most usual types of relativistic theory. Some of the points at which our results pose problems for these types of theory may be briefly designated. In the first place, moral judgments were not found to be based upon "emotions": the so-called moral emotions were held to be concomitants of moral judgments, and not their sources. In the second place, the effects of emotions, of sentiments, or of the structure of personality were seen to operate upon moral judgments in a variety of ways, and the theoretical implications of these various forms of influence was not in all cases the same. Therefore, no all-embracing generalization which attempts to explain moral judgments in terms of "non-cognitive" factors will suffice to explain the bases of the moral judgments which we actually make. In the third place, the role of belief concerning matters of fact was accorded far more influence upon moral judgments than it is accorded by most forms of relativistic theory. While no single one of these three results of our preceding analysis need be denied by every relativistic theory, it seems to be the case that all current forms of relativism tend to deny one or another of them. For example, while Westermarck could stress the role of belief no less than do I, his theory runs counter to what I take to be the evidence concerning the first and second propositions; and while Stevenson need not (and does not) deny the first and second propositions, the role which he assigns to beliefs concerning matters of fact in influencing moral judgments is assuredly not the same direct role which I have suggested it plays. And even if no one of the three propositions should be denied by a relativistic theory, the general tenor of the preceding analysis runs directly counter to what relativism seeks to maintain: in every aspect of the preceding analysis we have found that the dominant influence upon moral judgments is the influence of the cognitive structure of that which is being morally judged; it is not the influence of "subjective" states of emotion, sentiment, or personality which are projected on otherwise neutral objects. The close correlation between moral judgments and the cognitive structure of a moral situation is, I should say, the result which most clearly emerges when we consider the nature and sources of moral controversies.

However, it is obvious that the preceding analysis can give no support to the absolutistic position. While there is a similarity between our results and the absolutist's insistence that moral judgments are not projections of subjective states, but are responses to the moral demands which a person cognizes, absolutist theories treat moral judgments as being simpler phenomena than anything which the preceding analysis permits one to hold. The assumption that there is a specifically moral property resident in that which is morally judged, and that this property is independent of how any person may perceive that which he judges, is not borne out by our analysis. Such a view would lead to a too simple interpretation of the sources of moral controversies, for it would incline us to say that differences in belief about matters of fact, differences in emotion, in sentiments, or in the total organization of personality, merely mask the moral property which is really there. We, however, have seen that a moral judgment varies concomitantly with the way in which a situation is cognized; that variations in belief, and in emotions, sentiments, or personality, do not merely screen out a resident moral characteristic, but help order and organize that which we see, and therefore that which we morally judge. Human variability in belief, in emotion, in the objects of sentiments, or in personality, are therefore not (from our point of view) irrelevant to the issue of whether there is or is not a single, absolute, *discoverable* standard against which conduct is to be judged. This most general of the normative issues of ethics then becomes one of finding some standard by means of which these morally relevant cognitions are to be assessed.

Now, if we are to reach a solution concerning this issue, we cannot find the clue to it within our preceding analyses. While they have shown that a moral judgment is a response to what is cognized in a situation, they have not set up a standard by means of which it can be decided that what one individual has cognized is more adequate from the moral point of view than what has been cognized by another.

To be sure, if all moral controversies were in fact examples of simple disparities between moral judgments, this problem would be widely admitted to have a ready solution. It is usually held that there are universally accepted criteria by means of which it is possible (in principle) to show that one view of a situation is more adequate than another. If this is true, and if it were also true that all moral controversies represent simple disparities, it would be possible to solve these controversies in an acceptable fashion by means of purely factual evidence. However, as we have seen, even those controversies which originally seem to involve only disparities between moral judgments sometimes evidence the existence of a real moral disagreement: the issue does not remain one of what are the facts in this case, but raises the problem as to which of two morally relevant sets of facts is the more significant for reaching a moral decision.[2] Thus, even if we were in possession of criteria which would enable us to dissolve those controversies which represent simple disparities between moral judgments, we would not be in a position to claim that we could solve all moral controversies by means of them: we should still be forced to examine the problem of how we can justify the belief that one moral judgment represents a morally more adequate view of what is involved in a specific action or a specific trait of character than does another judgment which conflicts with it. The attempt to show how we may justify our acceptance of one moral judgment, and how we may justify our rejection of another, is the crucial problem of the present chapter. Unless such justifications can be offered it is impossible to say that moral controversies can be satisfactorily solved.

In the following appraisal of the means by which and the extent to which moral controversies may be satisfactorily resolved we shall not, of course, attempt to gather quantitative estimates of those cases in which moral controversies reach a conclusion which is mutually acceptable to all parties concerned, nor shall we sample the methods of argumentation which are used when this result is obtained. Not only would such a task be impossible of fulfillment; it would also be pointless. To ask whether a controversy is soluble is not identical with asking whether it has been resolved to the satisfaction of all those who are parties to it. As has often been pointed out (generally with the aid of an analogy to mathematics), the fact that one party to a dispute fails to acknowledge that he has been mistaken does not exculpate him from error: a controversy may legitimately be claimed to be soluble even when no actual agreement is reached.[3] However, this is only a legitimate claim if one can show that one of the conflicting judgments is an *invalid* judgment. Therefore the first step in appraising whether there is any solution to moral controversies consists in determining whether there are any general principles by means of which one can justifiably distinguish between valid and invalid moral judgments.

This problem, it may be noted, constitutes a basic issue for any theory which deals with normative ethics, and is not solely characteristic of the present approach. As we shall see, almost every ethical theory has at least tacitly assumed that some moral assertions represent valid moral judgments, while others do not. However, it is characteristic of those who have denied that there is a universally valid standard for conduct to gloss over the necessity for making any such distinction; in general it may be said that they have tended to take every moral assertion at its face value. This escape from the problem is unjustifiable. *No one* takes every moral assertion at its face value; we are (at the least) forced to distinguish between an assertion which represents a "genuine" moral judgment and one which is merely masquerading as such.[4] Under these circumstances it is necessary for anyone who utilizes contradictory moral assertions in support of his denial of a universally valid standard for conduct, to be prepared to defend the proposition that each of the assertions which he cites has an equal claim to be considered as valid. On the other hand, those who have affirmed a universally valid standard for conduct have been equally guilty of neglecting to consider with care what constitutes a valid moral judgment. They have tended to estimate the validity of each moral judgment in terms of whether what it asserts agrees or disagrees with the standard they espouse. This too is unjustifiable. As we have repeatedly pointed out, an appeal to such a contentual standard of validity begs the question which is raised by the existence of conflicting moral assertions; far from solving the controversy, it leaves us with precisely the same conflict as that with which we began: each of the opponents would regard his own assertion as true, and would therefore regard his own judgment as valid, and any judgment which asserted its contradictory he would denominate invalid. If, then, we are to be able to *justify* a claim that certain moral judgments are invalid, we must do so on grounds other than that they contradict what we are willing to affirm. At least one such ground can be found in differences between the conditions under which valid and invalid moral judgments are formed.[5]

A consideration of these conditions is often avoided because of our chariness of whatever may be thought to border upon "the genetic fallacy." It is also easy to overlook the significance which we actually attach to these conditions because of the manner in which, in their initial stages, moral controversies are usually carried on. When two persons find that their judgments conflict, each seeks means of convincing the other that what he has asserted is true. Not only will he attempt to indicate to the other what he finds to be praiseworthy or blameworthy in the object; he may use a variety of devices to extort at least a verbal agreement from him. Thus, in their initial stages, moral controversies are apt to be solely concerned with the content of the opposed assertions, and moral judgments tend to be considered as valid or invalid in so far as they agree or disagree with the judgments which we ourselves have formed. However, in spite of all attempts to educe agreement, it is frequently true that disagreements persist. It is then that we seek to distinguish between valid and invalid moral judgments in some other way. It is here, I submit, that the first of what I shall term the principles of moral judgment becomes manifest. Instead of asserting and reasserting the same moral proposition, we attempt to show that our opponent has failed to concur because extraneous factors have interfered with his judgment. By this means we seek to prove that his judgment cannot be considered to be valid, not because of what it asserts, but because of how it came to be formed.

This mode of argument (which we all constantly use) would be fallacious if it depended upon the mere fact that we can find psychological causes for our opponent's judgment: we cannot fail to acknowledge that our own judgments must have their own causes as well. To be acceptable, the argument must be based upon some general principle which permits us to distinguish between those causes which lead to valid moral judgments and those causes which lead to invalid moral judgments. To find any such principal may (at best) appear to be a hopeless task. Nor does the task become easier when we recognize that such a principle must be *universally* accepted if we are to be able to justify our view that any specific judgment is invalid: were our opponent to reject this principle we would have no ground for holding that it was his judgment, and not ours, which had been invalidly reached. Therefore, it is only if we can demonstrate that there is a universal acceptance of at least one principle which serves to distinguish valid from invalid moral judgments that we can discount any moral judgment on the basis of the causes which contributed to its formation.

Now, there are, in my opinion, certain universally accepted principles of moral judgment, and the first of these has to do with the sources of valid, as distinguished from invalid, moral judgments. It is with this principle that the following section will be concerned.

i.

IN ORDER to avoid misunderstanding, it should again be noted that the acceptance of any principle does not in itself guarantee that this principle will, in practice, be successfully applied. It cannot be assumed that the existence of unresolved moral controversies disproves our contention that there are universally accepted principles of moral judgment: it is perfectly possible for a person to accept a particular standard of validity, and to claim that his thought conforms to this standard, even though it does not. And this, as we shall see, actually occurs with respect to moral judgments. It is for this reason that the question of whether a moral controversy is soluble is not identical with the question as to whether a solution acceptable to both parties has been—or will be—actually reached.[6] In speaking of a "satisfactory" resolution of moral controversies in what follows, I shall therefore be denoting those cases (if any) in which a controversy is "in principle" soluble, rather than confining my discussion to those cases in which actual controversy disappears.

Precedents for dealing with the problems of solubility in this manner are easily found. In controversies concerning many specific matters of fact, and in controversies which are concerned with whether or not an hypothesis has been verified, we do not identify the solubility of the problem with whether it has been solved to the satisfaction of all parties concerned. We believe that granted adequate evidence a solution can be reached; but we do not necessarily assume that if such evidence were available to all individuals they would accept it as binding and would actually reach an agreement. We know that in any factual dispute there may be reasons why one or both persons will fail properly to apply the available evidence to the case at hand. Nonetheless we believe in the solubility of factual disputes because we believe that all men actually do share some common standards of evidence and inference; that, granted sufficient evidence, their final failures to reach a mutually satisfactory conclusion rest not upon a difference in their standards, but upon a failure to apply the standards which both in fact accept. It would of course be difficult to formulate the precise nature of such standards, and perhaps equally difficult to justify the assumption that they are universally shared. However, this is not our present problem. I wish to avoid it not because it is irrelevant to ethics (for it is not), but merely because of its extreme difficulty.[7] Its relevance to ethics can be seen when one considers how many moral controversies represent what I have termed disparities in moral judgment: cases in which the controversy is rooted, and remains rooted, in a controversy concerning matters of fact. However, since there appears to be universal (or almost universal) agreement among ethical theorists that controversies of this sort are in principle soluble,[8] it may be legitimate to by-pass this formidable problem, confining the following discussion to those moral controversies which represent genuine moral disagreements. Our problem is, then, that of determining whether there are any universally accepted principles of moral judgment which can serve as ground for the claim that moral disagreements may be satisfactorily resolved. As we have seen, the first step to take toward a solution of this problem is to determine whether there is any such principle which can serve to distinguish valid from invalid moral judgments in terms of the respective conditions under which they are formed. I believe that there is such a principle, and I shall designate it as "the principle of the primacy of the facts."

The principle of the primacy of the facts may be stated as follows: *To be valid, the predication of a moral quality must arise as a direct response to the apprehension of the non-moral properties which the object which is praised or blamed actually possesses.* This statement, it will be noted, involves two considerations. In the first place, it states that no moral judgment is valid unless it springs directly from an apprehension of the non-moral properties (including, of course, relational properties) of that which is said to be right or wrong, good or bad. In the second place, it states that no moral judgment is valid if it is based upon a false cognition of the relevant[9] non-moral aspects of an action. It will be convenient to begin the discussion of this principle with its second aspect.

That we do only consider a moral judgment to be valid if it is based upon a true cognition of the relevant non-moral aspects of what is being judged can most readily be seen in the extent to which questions concerning matters of fact enter into moral controversies. Whenever a controversy arises regarding the rightness or wrongness of conduct, or regarding a judgment of moral worth, both disputants will claim to found their moral judgments on a true view of the facts relating to the action or the person judged. If either disputant can be shown that he possesses an erroneous view of these facts, he will admit his moral judgment to have been erroneously grounded. While he may go to considerable lengths to support his original moral judgment, we do not find a disputant in a moral controversy rejecting every appeal to matters-of-fact as being morally irrelevant. On the contrary, we find that the most usual way of attempting to cling to a moral judgment is to insist that the facts are really as one has seen them, or, failing that, to admit that while one's original apprehension of these facts had been faulty there are other facts which lead to the same moral conclusion. The very lengths to which we feel impelled to go to defend our view of the facts in any moral controversy, and the extent to which such controversies involve us in disputes concerning purely factual matters, seem to me to show that we regard a true cognition of the non-moral aspects of that which we judge to be a necessary condition of a valid, or binding, moral judgment.

This being the case, it would be strange if this aspect of our principle were not to be acknowledged by almost every ethical theory. And it is indeed difficult to find any clear-cut exceptions. One can find great diversity in regard to what constitute those non-moral aspects of an action which are relevant to moral judgments; however, once these aspects are specified, every theory seems to acknowledge that they must be correctly cognized if a valid moral judgment is to be made. The universality of the agreement on this point is, I believe, so obvious that the matter need not be pursued further: we may take it as a fact that a moral judgment is only considered to be valid when it is acknowledged that the person making that judgment has truly cognized the nature of whatever non-moral aspects of an action are thought to be relevant to the judgment. However, in order to see why there should be such universal agreement on this point, we must consider the other aspect of that principle of validity which I have termed the principle of the primacy of the facts.

It will be recalled that the principle states that, to be valid, the predication of a moral quality must arise as a direct response to the apprehension of the non-moral properties which the object which is praised or blamed actually possesses. Therefore it is now necessary to show that in assessing the validity of a moral judgment we do actually use the criterion of whether it sprang directly from the apprehension of the non-moral aspects of that which is judged, rather than from any other source. It is this thesis (which will doubtless seem at first glance to be extremely perverse) that lies at the heart of the principle of the primacy of the facts, and which we must now defend.

Before attempting to show that it is in fact true that we use this as a criterion of validity in both moral controversies and in ethical theory, I should like to render my thesis more plausible by calling to the reader's attention that this same criterion actually is used to discriminate between "genuine" moral judgments and those assertions which seem to represent moral judgments because they contain the same terms, but which we dismiss as being "spurious" or discount as "derivative."

By a "spurious" moral judgment I refer to assertions which purport to represent a moral judgment, and externally appear to do so, but which are asserted only because their assertion will serve some ulterior end. Such would be those cases in which a man makes a moral assertion under duress, or those cases in which he makes a moral assertion for the sake of gaining power over another[10] or for the sake of having others esteem him. I know of no one who, in daily experience, would consider such assertions to be moral judgments, though what is asserted is, in itself, indistinguishable from what is asserted when one actually judges a given action or trait of character to be worthy of praise or of blame. To call such assertions *spurious* moral judgments is not to use too strong a term.

By a "derivative" moral assertion I refer to assertions whose source lies in the fact that others have made the same assertions. Examples of this sort may belong to two quite different classes: those which are taken over by habit, and repeated by rote on every occasion in which they may seem to be appropriate, and those which are made because the person takes them on the authority of an individual or institution which he regards with moral respect. I know of no moral theorist who would consider these derivative judgments as being on a par with "original" moral judgments, and who would not wish to penetrate beyond them to examine the original moral judgments upon which they were based. Even though such assertions are not made with any ulterior end in view, and are not masquerading as something which they are not, and even when they are made on the basis of a prior moral judgment which is taken as justifying them, these derivative assertions cannot be considered as being as relevant to the problems of ethics as are the judgments from which they presumably came.

I believe it to be clear that the distinction which we draw between "genuine" moral judgments and either spurious or derived moral judgments rests on the fact that the former are taken to be direct responses to what a person apprehends in the objects which he confronts, while the latter are not. Having discovered that a moral assertion has been made under duress or that it has been made for an extraneous, calculated end, we not only do not consider it to be valid, but we refuse to regard it as a moral judgment at all. With respect to derivative moral judgments we are only slightly less severe. The fact that many persons may agree in the moral assertions which they make is a fact that loses its impressiveness if we find that these assertions are merely repetitions of one another. To be sure, such repetitions are often cited by those who agree with particular moral assertions, but when these assertions are challenged they are forced to show that the source of the agreement is not to be found merely in habit, nor merely in authority, but lies in the fact that all who agree have originally done so on the basis of an original and independent moral judgment which, in case after case, finds itself further confirmed. It is in this sense that we discount derivative moral judgments; it is not they, but their originals, which provide evidence that a given moral proposition is to be accepted. Thus, both spurious and derivative moral judgments are contrasted with "genuine" moral judgments; neither the spurious nor the derivative are held to be invalid, but are, rather, discounted as not constituting genuine moral judgments with which moral theory must deal.

We may now turn to the application of this aspect of our principle to the problem of when a moral judgment is to be considered as valid, and when it is to be considered invalid. What I am concerned to show is that when we do not discredit a moral assertion as being either spurious or derivative, but acknowledge it to be a genuine moral judgment, we nonetheless consider it to be invalid if its source can be traced to anything other than the person's apprehension of the properties of that which he asserts to be worthy of praise or of blame. And if it be asked what other sources such a judgment may have, we may cite pride, sympathy, and concealed self-interest, to mention only three.

Let us take the case of concealed self-interest. We have already seen that if a moral assertion is explicitly designed to further one's own interest any person who recognizes this motive as its sole source will not consider it to be a moral judgment at all. We shall now see that if it is believed that such an assertion was not made for this reason, but that it nonetheless did have self-interest as its concealed source, it is not considered to be a *valid* moral judgment. To see the initial plausibility of this statement one need merely recall the extent to which moral theorists have used the ideal of "the impartial spectator" as a means of criticizing moral judgments which arise out of self-interest. However, the usual formulations of this criterion of validity are not as clear as one might wish; they tend in fact to confuse, or to identify, the *impartiality* of "the impartial spectator" with the *universality* of the judgments which such a spectator would make.[11] Though these two aspects of the ideal of the impartial spectator may certainly be said to parallel each other, it may also be important to keep them distinct. I find this to be the case. I shall therefore, for the present, confine attention to that aspect of the ideal of the impartial spectator which is suggested by the use of such terms as "impartial," "unbiassed," "disinterested," and the like,[12] attempting to show that the principle of the primacy of the facts underlies our acceptance of this ideal.

When we object to a moral judgment because it springs from a concealed self-interest, and is therefore out of line with what an "impartial spectator" would affirm, it is not in fact the element of self-interest which leads us to discount it. This can be seen when we note that the ideal of "the impartial spectator" is also frequently used to criticize those judgments in which an individual unduly neglects to consider his own interests in forming a judgment of what is right or is wrong. The basis on which we reject judgments which spring from a concealed self-interest is, rather, the fact that these judgments are not responses to what the situation itself is held to demand: we reject such judgments when we believe that they have been distorted by a failure to consider one's self no less than we reject them when we believe that they have been distorted by too great an interest in self.[13] In my opinion the ideal of impartiality may be said to represent the attempt to appeal to what the situation itself demands.

The same point may be made with reference to sympathy. There are cases in which we willingly admit that a moral judgment is valid when a precondition of its having been made is that there has been a feeling of sympathy on the part of the person making it. However, the form of "sympathy" which is then involved is, I submit, considered as an essential element in the perception of what a situation contains: for example, that a person is suffering. In this sense of the term "sympathy," we are actually referring to that mode of perception which is also commonly denominated by the no less ambiguous term "empathy." While it is true that the person would not have made the judgment which he did were it not for the "sympathy" which he felt, we do not consider such a feeling of sympathy to have distorted the nature of the situation which he has judged: without such a feeling he would not have been able to perceive this morally relevant aspect of the situation concerning which he was judging. On the other hand, there are cases in which what is also denominated by the term "sympathy" is held to invalidate a moral judgment. In these cases, however, the "sympathy" which is present is an essentially different phenomenon: it is not a mode of perception, but an emotional reaction to that which is perceived. Such an emotion, like any other emotion, may distort the nature of a situation by focussing the whole of one's attention on the suffering which is being experienced, and making it difficult to apprehend clearly, if at all, what other relations obtain within the situation which evokes the moral judgment. However praiseworthy a sympathetic nature may be, this second form of "sympathy" may easily distort the nature of that which the sympathetic person is seeking to judge, and it is for this reason that we consider a judgment which is affected by sympathy, taken in this sense of the word, as not binding or valid.[14] The distinction between this rejection of "sympathy" and the acceptance of "sympathy" of the first type is, I submit, most easily understood in the following way: in the first case the affectivity which is involved is a precondition of grasping what a situation contains; in the second case it distorts this cognition. And to test this contention one need only note that if one were to try to explain the reason for our acceptance of the first form of sympathy, and our rejection of the second, in distinctively *moral* terms, one would come out with a conclusion directly contrary to fact: we do not consider an empathic perception of suffering as a distinctively moral virtue, but we do consider the capacity to feel the suffering of another as our own as a moral virtue, yet it is the first type of sympathy, and not the second, which we consider to be a precondition of a valid moral judgment, and it is the second which we reject as leading to invalid moral judgments.

The foregoing discussions of self-interest and of sympathy are obviously related to the way in which the ideal of "the impartial spectator" has often been used in the history of moral theory. This ideal has, I believe, been either explicitly or implicitly present in almost every ethical theory.[15] In fact, in an important recent article, Roderick Firth has claimed that the meaning of the term "right" is to be defined in terms of the reactions of an "ideal observer," and he defines the characteristics of such an observer in a way which, as he recognizes, is surely not dissimilar to the way in which "the impartial spectator" was conceived in traditional ethical theory.[16] While his treatment of these characteristics is both more discriminating and more detailed than that of any of his predecessors, neither he nor they seek to find a common ground for our insistence that a valid moral judgment should not only be based upon an adequate cognition of all of the non-moral (but morally relevant) aspects of that which is being judged,[17] but that the judge should also be disinterested, dispassionate, and normal.[18] Such a common ground, I have attempted to show, is to be found in the principle of the primacy of the facts: the disinterestedness, dispassionateness, and normality of the "impartial spectator" (or "ideal observer") is a function of the fact that only he who is conceded to have these attributes will be acknowledged to be a person whose moral judgments are based upon the non-moral relationships that are "really" contained within the situation which is being judged.

Having now seen that the appeal to the ideal of "the impartial spectator" is but one facet of the principle of the primacy of the facts, it only remains for us to note that this principle is indispensable even for those ethical theories which attempt to draw a sharp line of demarcation between moral and "natural" (non-moral) predicates. One would, perhaps, not expect this to be the case, for our principle states that a moral judgment is only valid if it is derived from a true and adequate cognition of the *non-moral* aspects of that which is being judged. Yet, as we shall now see, even those who would completely reject what is called "the naturalistic fallacy" (insisting that moral predicates are different from all "natural" predicates) not only can accept our principle, but must do so.

As is well known, a theory which is "non-naturalistic" in the sense that it draws a sharp line between moral and non-moral predicates may either be a "cognitive" or a "non-cognitive" ethical theory. A cognitive theory of this type would hold that moral predicates refer to non-natural properties which truly qualify certain entities, while a non-cognitive theory would hold that moral predicates do not refer to any properties of the object, but express a state of feeling (or the like) concerning the objects to which these predicates ostensibly refer. It is my contention that both types of theory not only may accept the principle of the primacy of the facts, but that both actually need it in order to render an adequate account of moral judgments.

Let us first examine this contention with respect to cognitive theories of this type. So far as I know, all such theories have acknowledged that there is an asymmetrical relation between the characteristics to which non-moral predicates refer, and the characteristics to which we refer when we use a specifically moral term. Moral characteristics are not held to be independent of the "natural," or purely descriptive, attributes of an object, nor of the "natural" relations in which that object stands; on the other hand, the "natural" characteristics of an object are held to be independent of whatever moral attributes it may possess, and also to be independent of whatever moral relations it enters into or leaves. This asymmetry is, perhaps, best expressed in Ross' terminology, where he characterizes the moral attributes as being "consequential," while the non-moral attributes are the "constitutive" attributes of an entity.[19] This does not, of course, mean that Ross (or any other person believing in a non-naturalistic cognitive theory) would hold that moral attributes do not genuinely belong to the entities of which they are predicated; all that the distinction involves is the acknowledgment that "value [or, I might add, any similar moral predicate] seems quite definitely to be based on certain other qualities of its possessors, and not the other qualities on value."[20] But this acknowledgment entails that the principle of the primacy of the facts must be accepted as at least a negative criterion of validity: no judgment concerning a moral quality will be valid if he who makes it has falsely apprehended the non-moral qualities of the object which he is judging.[21] To show, however, that it also affords a positive criterion, and that even a non-naturalistic theory must hold a moral judgment to be *derived* from a cognition of these non-moral aspects, would seem to be more difficult.

Let us, however, examine what it is that a cognitive theory of this type must maintain. If it admits that a moral property is distinct from all non-moral properties, and that it depends upon their presence and particular relationships (which is what has already been admitted), then any moral judgment which predicated a moral property of an entity on any basis other than a true view of the non-moral properties of this entity would have been invalidly grounded. It might affirm the same proposition through another (valid) judgment, and might be held to have stated a moral truth, but it could not be claimed to have *established* this truth. In short, once a cognitive theory admits that the moral qualities of an action, or of any other entity, depend upon the nature of its constitutive properties, the adequacy of the cognition of these properties is not merely a negative criterion of the validity of the moral judgment, but must also be acknowledged to be its foundation. To be sure, it may be claimed that in the moral judgment there is *also* the discernment of a further non-natural quality, but whatever is said on this score does not alter the fact that "before" such a quality can be discerned one must have apprehended the non-moral aspects of the entity to which it attaches. Thus, I submit, even a cognitive theory of moral judgments which draws a sharp line between moral and non-moral predicates will also be forced to acknowledge the principle of the primacy of the facts as a means of testing the validity (though not the truth) of moral judgments.

When we now turn to those non-cognitive theories which draw a sharp distinction between moral and non-moral predicates, a similar situation obtains. However, non-cognitive theories hold that moral predicates do not refer to properties which reside in the entities of which they are predicated, and our argument must therefore take a different form.

It is the essence of non-cognitive theories that they interpret moral judgments as containing some element which goes beyond the mere cognition of *any* of the properties which are genuine characteristics of the entity which is judged. This non-cognitive increment is, of course, variously conceived; in all non-cognitive theories, however, it is held to reside in some affective or attitudinal factor which is, in some sense, an addendum to the perception of the non-moral properties of the object. This being the case, it would seem that such theories would not accept the principle with which we are here concerned. Their rejection of this principle might be expected to hinge upon two points: first, that it is not meaningful to attempt to set up any general principle of validity for moral judgments unless this principle is itself to be found in some affective or attitudinal factor; second, that the affective or attitudinal addendum which characterizes a moral judgment, distinguishing it from non-moral judgments, precludes one from saying that a valid moral judgment is based upon the cognition of the non-moral properties of that which is being morally judged. For the sake of convenience in exposition, let us begin by considering whether the first of these anticipated rejoinders would really lead a non-cognitive theory to reject the principle of the primacy of the facts.

As I have already pointed out, no ethical theory, of whatever persuasion, can deny the fact that we do *believe* that certain moral judgments are valid, and that we *believe* that others are not. And since I am here solely concerned with the principles upon which we attempt to distinguish between valid and invalid moral judgments, the fact that non-cognitive theories deny that moral judgments may be designated as "valid" and "invalid" in the sense attached to these terms by cognitive theorists, is wholly immaterial to my argument.[22] So long as it is admitted by a non-cognitive theory that we do actually believe that some moral judgments are valid, while others are not, the problem of determining what principles (if any) determine this distinction remains a legitimate problem.

Now it might be thought that if a non-cognitive theory were correct, such principles would have to be sought in some affective or attitudinal factor in the person drawing the distinction, and not in any principle such as that of the primacy of the facts. But even this conclusion would be false. We are here concerned—let me repeat—with the distinction which any person draws between valid and invalid moral judgments. Whatever may be the psychological causes which lead him to say that judgment *A* is valid while judgment *B* is not, these causes are not the basis upon which *he* seeks to justify his distinction. Therefore, even if one or another typical non-cognitive ethical theory were true, it would not be essential that the same analysis should be given of the distinction between valid and invalid moral judgments as is given of the significance of the predicates contained in such judgments. And it would, in fact, be wholly unwarranted to claim that the principle which we use to justify our contention that one moral judgment is valid and another is not, is the fact that we have a particular affective or attitudinal relationship to that which is asserted by these judgments, or toward the fact that these judgments were made. On the contrary, if any one can convince us that this has been the actual basis upon which we have estimated the validity of a moral judgment, we give up our claim. Thus, while it *might* be true that the actual discriminations which we make between valid and invalid moral judgments represent the influence of affective or attitudinal factors, it cannot be claimed that we *believe* that the validity of a moral judgment is a function of the feelings or attitudes which we have toward what it asserts or toward the fact that it was made. Thus, so far as our *beliefs* are concerned, even a non-cognitive theory can, I submit, accept the principle of the primacy of the facts as the standard which we use in estimating the validity of a moral judgment; and I should add that it must accept this principle if it is to be consistent with the data of our criticism of moral judgments.

We now turn to what might appear to be a more basic reason why a non-cognitive theory might be expected to reject the principle of the primacy of the facts. It was stated that a moral judgment must be based upon the apprehension of the non-moral qualities of that which is judged if the judgment is to be considered valid; yet, a non-cognitive theory considers a moral predicate as the expression of an affective or attitudinal increment to a cognitive judgment, and might therefore be expected to deny that the application of a moral predicate to any entity is based upon the cognition of its non-moral aspects. Yet we must again note that the principle of the primacy of the facts refers to a standard which we use in estimating the validity of a moral judgment, and therefore has reference to our *beliefs* concerning the relation of moral to non-moral predicates. Now, from the point of view of our *beliefs* concerning this relationship it seems to me that a non-cognitive theory must give precisely the same sort of priority to the non-moral predicates as does a cognitive theory. Even if it were true that the proper causal analysis of our use of moral predicates would lead us to hold that these predicates merely express an affective or attitudinal increment to our non-moral judgments, this would not entail that we *believe* this to be their relation to cognition. And, in fact, such is not our belief. When we say that an action is "wrong" we think that this predicate attaches to the action because of its particular characteristics, and not because of our feelings or attitude toward it. To be sure, we do not think this predicate characterizes the action in precisely the *same* way as do its non-moral characteristics; but this, as we have seen, is a point also admitted by those cognitive theories which draw a sharp line of demarcation between moral and non-moral predicates. The non-cognitive increment—whether it be an increment contributed by "the moral sense" or whether it be an imperative increment, as Stevenson, for example, would hold—is based upon what we *believe* the nature of the object to be, and it fluctuates as our beliefs concerning the object fluctuate.[23] Thus, whatever may be held to be the true causal analysis of the fact that we have predicated a moral quality of an object, the directly experienced relationship between our moral judgment and our beliefs about the "natural" qualities of the object judged is an asymmetrical relation in which these beliefs are taken as the ground for predicating a moral quality of the object. And this, let it be recalled, is all that I have attempted to prove.

If, as I have claimed, it is true that the principle of the primacy of the facts is a standard which we use (and which all ethical theories must acknowledge that we use) as a basis for distinguishing between valid and invalid moral judgments, it should be possible to solve at least some moral disagreements by the employment of this standard. And this would remain true even if a non-cognitive ethical theory were correct; we should then find that even though moral predicates did not in fact refer to any properties characterizing objects independently of our feelings or attitudes toward them, we could still solve some of the moral controversies which beset us. How this could occur we shall later see; meanwhile it is necessary to turn to the second principle which we employ in estimating the validity of a moral judgment. This principle I shall refer to as *the principle of universality*.

ii.

ONE OF the most persistent problems in the history of ethics has been the question of whether moral judgments are strictly analogous to judgments which assert non-moral propositions. In the present section I shall be dealing with one significant point at which there appears to be a similarity between them. This similarity lies in the fact that a moral judgment, like any other judgment, purports to assert a proposition which is true. As I shall show, this fact provides us with one of the principles by means of which we distinguish between valid and invalid moral judgments.

However, it is important to warn the reader that to say that each moral judgment purports (i.e., puts forth the claim) to being considered a true assertion is not to say that such a claim is ultimately justified. In what follows, I shall not be dealing with the traditional problem of moral truth: neither with the general question of whether moral judgments, when properly interpreted, must necessarily be either true or false, nor (if this be affirmatively answered) with the further question of whether a particular moral proposition is or is not true. If one wished to solve the first question one would have to go beyond the phenomenological similarity between moral and non-moral judgments and deal with the problem in terms of some wider psychological or epistemological theory; and if one wished to solve the second question one would have to do so on the basis of an adequately grounded normative ethics. However, my present purpose is that of determining by what means we discriminate between valid and invalid moral judgments, and for this purpose a merely phenomenological inquiry will suffice. It will be my contention that the fact that a moral judgment purports to assert a true proposition (whether it "really" does so or not) provides us with one of the principles by means of which this discrimination is actually made.

I believe that if anyone examines his own moral judgments he cannot doubt that at the time at which he makes them he is attempting to assert something which he regards as true. When one says "that would be wrong," or "he ought to do that," or "that was a courageous thing to have done," one means to say that a moral quality truly belongs to that of which it is predicated. And when we examine the moral assertions of others we do not doubt that they too meant to make true statements, no matter how disinclined we are to believe that these statements really are true. It may then be said that all moral judgments purport to be true assertions in the sense that each such judgment is interpreted by the person who makes it as stating something more than the fact that *he* finds this action to be praiseworthy or blameworthy. In other words, a moral judgment makes the claim that a particular moral predicate really characterizes that of which it is predicated; it purports to be a correct judgment, and not merely a judgment which is correct when interpreted as the expression of a single, limited point of view.

If this were not the case it would be difficult to understand how moral controversies arise: if each person who disagreed with another were to interpret both his own judgment and that of the other as expressions of differing points of view, both judgments could be true, and there would be no occasion for controversy.[24] It is only because each interprets the judgment of the other as the attempt to speak of the same action which he himself is judging, and because each sees that the other is attributing a different moral quality to it, that they become embroiled in a controversy. Similarly, if this were not the case, it would be difficult to understand why we are troubled by the inconsistencies between our own past and present moral judgments, whether these be only concerned with our own past actions or whether they are judgments concerning the actions of others. Unless we assume that a moral judgment expresses the belief that a moral quality really characterizes the action of which it was predicated, and does not merely represent how a given action appeared to a person at a given time, there would be no reason to hold that our two judgments had contradicted one another. But the fact of the matter is that we interpret at least our present judgment as an assertion about the object judged, and not merely as the expression of the way in which we, under present conditions, view that action. That this is the case can be illustrated in many ways: for example by the strength of our inclination to deny that we have really contradicted ourselves. When challenged by the fact that we have apparently made contradictory moral assertions, we use every means at our disposal to prove that the action which we had previously judged was different in significant respects from that action which we now are judging. This we may attempt to do by arguing that we now know more about the motives which gave rise to it, or about the situation in which it was embedded, or that we now better see the nature of the consequences to which it might have been expected to lead. In short, we attempt to show that our conflicting judgments represent a disparity between two moral judgments, and not a real disagreement. Where we find ourselves really contradicting what we formerly asserted, we are troubled and we seek to resolve the contradiction; but we do not do so by averring that *every* moral judgment (our own present moral judgment included) merely represents what is seen from the specific "point of view" from which that judgment was made.

This point is of sufficient importance to warrant one further remark which may serve to fend off a possible misinterpretation. It may be the case—and I believe that it often is the case—that when I say "I ought to do this" I may not be willing to assert that everyone ought to do this sort of thing; nor need I be willing to assert that I ought, under all circumstances, to act in this same manner. It may be that I would only be willing to hold that anyone like me, placed under precisely these circumstances, ought so to act. But such a proviso, whether it be explicit or implicit, refers to the conditions under which the act is obligatory, and not to the conditions under which the judgment is made. Similarly, we may acknowledge that an action which is right at one time, or under one set of cultural circumstances, would be wrong at another; but in such cases the circumstances to which the rightness or wrongness of the action is relative are those circumstances which help to define the nature of the action, and are not the circumstances under which the judgment of that action was made. In short, each moral judgment purports to be true or false independently of the point of view from which it is made.

To be sure, there are ethical theories which deny that any such claim is legitimate, and which seek to explain its presence by a combination of psychological and epistemological considerations. Such theories may be defined as "relativistic" theories, since they insist that the proper analysis of any moral judgment will contain a reference to the particular time, place, or circumstances under which it was made, or to the nature of the person making it.[25] Without entering into the question of whether their final position is or is not true, it is obvious that their analysis of the truth-value of moral judgments does not coincide with what we believe is the truth-value of such a judgment at the time at which we make it. This discrepancy they would not deny. What then leads them to hold that theirs is the proper analysis of such judgments?

There are, of course, many such reasons, and they will vary from one relativist to another. However, there is one reason which is frequently encountered in popular discussions of ethical theory, and which sometimes seems to be shared by philosophers who treat of the issue. Since this reason can be discussed without transcending the phenomenological limits which I have set for our comparison of moral and non-moral judgments, it may be useful to show that it, taken by itself, lacks cogency. At the very least, the following considerations will explain why antirelativists have claimed that a relativistic analysis of moral propositions involves an *ignoratio elenchi.*

The argument which I wish to examine proceeds by assuming that even non-moral assertions must be analyzed in relativistic terms, and then applies the same sort of relativistic analysis to moral assertions. For example, it is held that when I say "this paper is white" my assertion, when properly analyzed, means "Under the conditions now obtaining what I call 'this paper' appears 'white' to me." And if this be a proper analysis of such a non-moral assertion it should be clear (it is argued) that the assertion "that was wrong" is to be interpreted as meaning "Under the conditions now obtaining what I regard as 'that action' appears 'wrong' to me."

Now, I do not wish to argue that a relativistic analysis of either moral or non-moral assertions cannot be upheld; but I do wish to point out that the relativist analysis of *non*-moral assertions involves precisely the same problems as does the similar analysis of moral assertions. This being the case, it cannot be taken as providing an obvious justification for the latter. As I shall point out, the only reason why this has not been universally acknowledged is that the relativist analysis of non-moral judgments does not so glaringly exemplify a distortion of our ordinary meanings as does a relativist analysis of moral judgments: what is an identical problem is more easily overlooked in the one case than it is in the other.

Let us first see how the matter stands with respect to moral judgments.

It seems obvious to popular thought that when a person makes a moral judgment he is merely asserting what appears to him to be right or wrong. That what he asserts to be right or wrong is what appears to him to be right or wrong cannot be denied.[26] But from this it does not follow that what he means to assert is the fact that something *appears to him* to be right or wrong. The assertion that a given action *is* right or wrong is a normative, moral assertion; the assertion that an action *appears to me* to be right or wrong is an assertion which describes a particular psychological event. It is because of this difference between the normative and non-normative characters of the two assertions that the opponent of the relativist thesis usually regards this form of the thesis as springing from a stupid or wilful confusion.

Now let us turn to the relativistic analysis of *non*-moral judgments. If I say "This paper is white" I am asserting something different from what I assert when I say "this paper appears white to me under the conditions which now obtain." The first purports to be a statement about a material object, the second is a statement about what I am aware of when I look at what I term that object; thus the meaning of the two statements is not the same. That this difference between the meanings of the two statements should have been so frequently overlooked in epistemological discussions seems to me to have been unfortunate. However, it is easy to see why it is less recognizable than is the similar distinction between the meaning of a moral judgment and the meaning of the assertion that a moral quality appears to me to characterize an object: in the latter case, as I have indicated, one, but not both, of the statements is normative, while in the former case there is not this difference between the statements.

Now, as I have said, I do not wish to argue that an epistemological theory which would analyze the statement "this paper is white" into statements of the form "this paper appears white to me" (or "appears white to persons of a particular nature under particular circumstances") is necessarily a false epistemology. Nor, do I wish to argue that a relativist analysis of moral judgments is necessarily false. I have merely wished to indicate that neither form of relativist analysis can claim to establish its position on the basis of a phenomenological account of the meaning of moral or perceptual judgments, but must on other grounds deny that these meanings conform to what a proper analysis of their "real" meanings would reveal. Since this is no less true of non-moral judgments than it is of moral judgments, one cannot uphold relativism in ethics by an appeal to the obvious "truth" of the relativity of perceptual judgments.

If this be granted, we are now in a position to state a second principle which is used in determining the validity of a moral judgment. Such a principle, we have seen, must be based upon some universally present characteristic of moral judgments, and the assertoric, non-relativistic nature of moral judgments supplies such a characteristic. The principle may then be stated as follows: *To be valid, a moral judgment must make an assertion which is not restricted by a reference to the conditions under which the judgment was made.* This principle may be termed "the principle of universality" since what it involves is the claim of each moral judgment to being universally acknowledged as true.

The "universality" here in question is not, of course, a universality of agreement among all persons making moral judgments; to decide that a judgment is valid on the grounds of the agreement of others would be to put the question of the truth of a judgment ahead of the question of its validity—a procedure which we have already found reason to reject. Rather, the "universality" involved in our principle is the *claim* to a universal acknowledgment which every moral judgment must make if it is to be taken seriously in a moral controversy. When such a claim is present, we cannot justifiably dismiss the judgment as false merely because it asserts what we are unwilling to assert; thus, the question of the validity of a moral judgment cannot be decided in terms of the truth-value assigned to that judgment.

However, it is now easy for us to see why this obvious point should have been consistently neglected in the history of ethical thought. The reason lies in the fact that *every* moral judgment purports to be true. Such a claim to universal acknowledgment tends to confine the attention of those who are concerned with moral controversies to the contradictory or non-contradictory character of what is asserted by different moral judgments, and thus immediately raises the problem of moral "truth." However, having recognized the methodological difficulties in this procedure, and having been willing to consider moral judgments in terms of their structural properties rather than their specific content, we are in a position to approach moral controversies in a different way. We shall now examine how the fact that every moral judgment purports to make an assertion which is true, irrespective of the point of view from which it was made, provides us with a universally acknowledged principle which is operative in solving moral controversies.

Let us first examine those cases in which we find that one of our present moral judgments contradicts a moral judgment which we had previously made. By following out the dialectical process which in some such cases ensues, we shall be in a position to see how the principle of universality operates at a number of different points in moral controversies. I ask the reader only to remember that I am here choosing to follow what happens in some cases, but not in all; I am taking the ideally persistent case of a moral contradiction, and not assuming that every case runs through the full gamut of the stages which I shall trace.

It is obvious that we frequently find that one of our present moral judgments seems to contradict a moral judgment which we had previously made. Such an occurrence may arise in a number of different forms. For example, I may find that my judgment of the past behavior of another person is no longer identical with what it formerly had been, or that my judgment concerning my own past behavior runs counter to the direct moral judgment which I had previously made.[27] In all such cases it is the present judgment which is felt to merit credence, since every judgment which we make seems to us to be true when we make it. We are therefore tempted to hold that it must be our past judgment which was mistaken. We do not justify this weighting of our present judgment merely because it came later in time, for that would conflict with our feeling that it really asserts a true proposition, and does not merely assert what now appears to us to be true. Nor can we be satisfied that we should accept our present judgment as true merely because we now think it to be true, for we can readily recall that we also thought that our earlier judgment had been a true judgment. Thus when we are troubled by the contradiction (and it is only with such cases that I am concerned) we do not decide the question in terms of belief. What we do, as I have already suggested, is attempt to show that the object of our two judgments was only apparently the same object, that we now have a more adequate view of the real nature of the action, and of the situation in which it was embedded. Thus we seek to nullify our conviction that a real disagreement in judgments was involved, reducing the case to one of a disparity between two moral judgments. And since we believe that our present view of the facts is the more adequate view, we feel that our present moral judgment is true. In this way we not only overcome the troublesomeness of being aware of a contradiction between two of our moral judgments, but we can escape the necessity for undermining the credence attached to that judgment which we presently make.

This happy solution is often more available when we are considering contradictions between two of our own moral judgments than it is when the contradiction lies between what we assert and what another person asserts. And it is easy to see why this should be so. When we are arguing with another, he can force us to be explicit as to precisely what discrepancy is involved between his view of the situation and ours; and he can then challenge our assumption that it is our view which is factually correct. Furthermore, when we argue with another, and when we are forced to be more explicit concerning the disparity than we are likely to be when we reason only with ourselves, it may turn out that what seemed to be merely a disparity transforms itself into a real moral disagreement.[28] But if we are honest with ourselves we can see that many of the contradictions between our past and present judgments represent disparities of this type: we have not come by new information since our original judgment, but we have changed our view as to which of two structuralizations of the situation was morally more adequate. Such discrepancies leave us with a genuine problem to face: if we admit that the conflict between our own two judgments arises out of a conflict between two ways of regarding the same action, we must ask which of the ways of regarding that action is the more justifiable. It is at this point that the principle of the primacy of the facts will not, in itself, provide us with guidance;[29] we must appeal to the principle of universality in an attempt to reach a justifiable solution.

What shall I do when I recognize that when I regard an action from one point of view it appears to be right, but when I regard it from another point of view it appears to be wrong? How can I decide from which point of view it *should be* regarded? What I shall of course be inclined to do is to hold that the way in which

I now regard it is the correct way, and that I was previously mistaken. However, I am bound to recall that I had also believed my previous judgment to have been correct. If I cannot find that there is a simple disparity between the two judgments, but that the apparent disparity concerns the question of which structuralization of the situation serves as the more adequate basis for a moral judgment, I attempt to find the cause of my former view of that situation in the specific conditions which obtained at the time and place at which my judgment was made. For example, I will hold that I saw one aspect of the situation as being more relevant to a moral judgment than was the other aspect because at that time I was "romantic" or "idealistic" or believed that all human action should be directed toward the alleviation of human suffering, etc., etc. In other words, I seek to relativize my past judgment by explaining it as springing from a particular point of view.

Our belief in the truth of the judgments which we now make is so strong a belief that we are apt to overlook the lack of cogency in such an argument, but a moment of unbiassed reflection will reveal it. If I can relativize my past judgment by pointing out the causes from which it sprang, I should also admit that my present judgment has its causes: I am no longer "romantic" and "idealistic," but am "realistic," and that too expresses a present point of view. Thus, such a causal argument begs the question at issue. In using it I am using the principle of universality, which is based upon the assertoric character of moral judgments, but I am using this principle in a theoretically indefensible manner.

We must now ask in what other manner this principle can be used. The answer lies in the appeal to consistency which it justifies us in making. Yet, as we shall now see, an appeal to consistency may, in one of its forms, lead to precisely the same begging of the question at issue.

That we do appeal to consistency in attempting to defend one moral judgment against another seems to be plain. It is also plain that such an appeal would not be made were it not for the assertoric character of moral judgments. We are unwilling to hold that both of two contradictory moral judgments can be true. When we find such contradictions we appeal to other moral judgments in an attempt to show that the judgment which we now accept is consistent with them.

However, this form of the appeal to consistency also begs the normative question which it is attempting to solve. We cannot claim that one of our judgments is false merely because it does not seem to comport with our other moral judgments; for all that we have established, it may be the case that it is these judgments which are false, and the judgment opposed to them which is true. And if to this possibility it be objected that some principle of mental economy prevents us from viewing a whole series of moral judgments as false, I should point out two facts: first, it is quite possible that no such principle is in all cases stronger than the feeling which we possess that a particular judgment *is* true; and, second, cases of "moral conversion" seem to show that it in fact sometimes happens that a whole coherent mass of past moral judgments is discarded under the pressure of what appears to be a new moral insight, discovered (perhaps) in a single case. Thus, the attempt to establish the truth of one of two conflicting moral judgments by an appeal to its consistency with what is asserted in other moral judgments constitutes a question-begging procedure.

In spite of the fact that this procedure is theoretically indefensible, it is worth noting that we not only do in fact often use it, but that on the basis of it we sometimes cast aside a present judgment of whose truth we had previously been convinced. Therefore, in spite of its obvious circularity, it would seem necessary to examine this form of the appeal to consistency with some care. As a starting point, it will be well to inquire what might be meant by the "consistency" of two or more moral assertions.

We use the test of consistency (whatever it may be) when we wish to show that one moral assertion, rather than another, must be accepted. We attempt to show this by showing that it is "consistent" with other moral assertions, concerning other actions,[30] and thus that it must be accepted. Now, the "consistency" to which we here appeal must be something stronger than mere non-contradiction.[31] The assertion which I wish to impugn cannot, strictly speaking, be claimed to contradict assertions concerning the rightness or wrongness of other actions. What I aim to show is that one of the two competing assertions accords with the principles implicit within other moral assertions which I still willingly accept, while the opposed assertion does not.

In such an attempt there are obvious pitfalls. In the first place the principles implicit within these other assertions may not—in the light of my new moral judgment—seem to be the ultimate moral principles which I am willing to accept. Therefore the judgment which follows from those principles is not necessarily to be regarded as asserting a true moral proposition.[32] In the second place, it is always possible to argue that the action which I am judging is significantly different in its moral aspects from the actions with which my other moral judgments have been concerned, and therefore that the assertion which seems best to comport with these judgments need not be taken to be true.

Yet, in spite of these (and other) difficulties, it seems undeniable that we do use some criterion of consistency in attempting to solve moral controversies, and that we do so both when we are arguing with ourselves and when we are arguing with others. I submit that the criterion we use is not that of the consistency between *what* is asserted in one moral judgment and what is asserted in others, but a consistency in the "*method*" by which each was reached. In other words, while we cannot directly determine that one rather than another of two moral assertions is *true* by means of an appeal to the test of consistency, we can use this test as a means of impugning the *validity* of one of the two judgments.

In order to show how the criterion of consistency is thus used, let us examine the case of what occurs when I recognize that two of my own moral judgments contradict each other, and when this contradiction represents a real shift in the manner in which I have regarded a situation and cannot be resolved into a simple disparity between my two judgments. In such cases I may at first attempt to solve the conflict by an appeal to the consistency of my present judgment with what I had in past cases asserted, and what others, too, have asserted. And this use of the test of consistency may well satisfy me—*if* I find support for the judgment which I presently believe in those judgments to which I appeal. However, if it is my present judgment which seems to conflict with the wider area of judgments to which I have made appeal, I will speedily recognize the circularity inherent in this form of the consistency test. What I then do is utilize the test of consistency in another form. I ask myself whether I am really willing to commit myself to that view which I now hold to be a true moral appraisal of that which I am judging. To ask this question is to ask whether I am willing to accept the implications of affirming the truth of this judgment. But what are these implications? They are of two kinds. In the first place, the acceptance of the truth of my present judgment carries implications concerning the truth or falsehood of other judgments. For example, I am committed to holding that what I had previously asserted had been false, and that if I were ever to assert it again when faced by the same action performed in the same situation, it would also be false. However, it would not necessarily imply that I must accept any particular moral assertions concerning any other actions (or any similar action performed under other circumstances), for this would only follow if I also accepted the conclusion that an extreme form of perceptual intuitionism is mistaken. If this further premise were not introduced, I could not deduce any conclusions concerning the rightness or wrongness of other, somewhat different, actions from the judgment made regarding this action.[33] Thus, all that is implied concerning the truth or falsity of other moral assertions is restricted to assertions concerning this particular action, and concerning any other action which I am willing to acknowledge to be identical with it in all morally relevant respects. This, of course, is a trivial implication. However, there is a second type of implication which is involved in applying the test of consistency to our acceptance of the truth of a moral judgment, and this use of consistency springs from the principle of universality.

The principle of universality states that, to be valid, a moral judgment must make an assertion which is not restricted by any reference to the time at which, conditions under which, or point of view from which it was made. Because of the acceptance of this principle, whatever point of view one adopts in making what one takes to be a true moral judgment must be a point of view which is also to be adopted in making other moral judgments. Thus, for example, when I am struck by the fact that a disagreement between two of my judgments arose because I had previously been "romantic" or "idealistic," and had placed certain concerns in the foreground of attention, and I find that from my present point of view the focus in which I view situations is a different one, the acceptance of my present judgment as true commits me to viewing other actions from the same point of view if I am to regard these judgments as valid. I can then only defend my present judgment by a willingness to accept the point of view from which it was made as being the point of view from which all moral judgments ought to be made; thus my interpretation of these judgments is not restricted by interpreting them as being merely true from one among a number of possible points of view. What they assert is binding because this assertion is what one sees to be true when one adopts the perspective which it is proper to adopt in making any moral judgment.

This mode of solving a moral controversy by means of the acceptance of the principle of universality (which we do, I submit, all acknowledge as binding in moral argument) avoids the question-begging character of other appeals to "consistency." Yet it enables us to understand why consistency among an individual's moral judgments has always been considered as essential to the defense of any moral judgment which has been challenged. While it recognizes that every moral judgment is made under certain conditions, and from a specific point of view, and while it admits that whenever a moral judgment is made there may be (and probably are) causes operative upon that person other than the bare facts with which he is faced, it does not thereby relativize these judgments. On the contrary, it accepts them as *valid* so long as they spring from the point of view which a person consistently shows that he is willing to adopt as being the point of view from which the morality of an action ought to be judged. What it rejects as invalid is a shift in point of view which is not accompanied by a denial of the truth of an assertion which was made from the previous point of view. Thus, in our own inner arguments we use the test of consistency to see whether we are willing to adopt the point of view from which we have made the judgment whose truth we wish to affirm. If we are willing to hold to this point of view, judging other cases from it, we can find no reason to impugn the truth of our judgment: from what we take to be a proper moral point of view, the assertion need not be qualified or restricted. But what we are apt to find (when we are honest with ourselves) is that we are unwilling to commit ourselves to a single point of view, that we vacillate as the conditions under which we make moral judgments themselves change. When this is recognized we have relativized our judgments, and we cannot find within ourselves a standard for validity, and therefore a means of establishing moral truth.

It is at this point that we tend to appeal to what an "impartial spectator" would judge. In such an appeal we are attempting to neutralize all points of view and all special restrictive conditions applicable to the act of moral judgment. In this form "the impartial spectator" is not merely the disinterested observer, free of bias and partiality, but is a ghostly spectator of the human scene who judges the morality of actions without himself possessing moral conviction. It is this *Unding* who has brought down contumely on the ideal of the impartial spectator. Thus, while we do have the right (as we have seen) to appeal to the ideal of the impartial spectator in judging of matters of fact, we have no right to appeal to this ideal in order to escape from specifically moral contradictions. Every moral judgment is made from a specific point of view, under concrete circumstances, and contains an element of moral involvement. Therefore we must abide by the only test of consistency which we have: a willingness to be consistent in the point of view from which we have made that moral judgment which we now take to be true. As we shall see, this form of consistency is related to the third principle which I shall discuss, the principle of the ultimacy of moral judgments. However, it will be well before we proceed to attempt to make more plausible the view that the consistency by means of which we attempt to establish the validity of a moral judgment is not through showing a consistency between what various judgments assert, but a consistency in the moral attitude which we are willing to adopt in making any moral assertion.

In this connection it is to be noted that this test permits us to discard a whole mass of past judgments in favor of our present judgment no less than it permits us to reject the present judgment. In short, it is perfectly compatible with the fact that "moral conversions" do occur. If one sees that the whole of one's past moral judgments could only be regarded as true from a specific point of view, and if one becomes convinced in a single case that this point of view is itself morally wrong, then all of one's past judgments are neutralized; the moral attitude embodied in the present moral judgment then comes to serve as the attitude with which all other judgments must be consistent, for the judgment that this attitude is the morally right attitude is itself accepted as a true moral judgment. However, moral conversions do not usually arise in this saltatory form. It is probably more common to find that a person has come to make a series of moral judgments which represent the adoption of a different point of view from that which he had previously taken, and that after a gradual increment in the number of these cases, none of which he rejects, he suddenly discovers that he has not always been adopting a single point of view from which to judge actions; he then reverses his earlier judgments in order to maintain consistency with the attitude he finds to be present in these scattered judgments whose truth he finds himself unable to deny. Thus we may say that in moral conversions, as well as in other cases, the resolution of a conflict between two of our moral judgments may be achieved through an appeal to consistency, but that we can only legitimately use this appeal to establish the *validity* of one of these judgments. The truth of what it asserts cannot be thus established. However, its claim to truth can be undermined; this claim *is* undermined if it becomes apparent to us that the point of view from which the judgment was made is not a point of view which we are willing to adopt in all cases.

If it be thought that we do not in fact proceed in any such way in attempting to resolve moral controversies, let me remind the reader that I do not claim that we always in fact proceed in this way. It is natural to seek to suport the truth of what we assert by pointing out that it coheres with what is asserted by other judgments, whether these be our own or those of others;

but I need not point out again that such a procedure is not only unjustifiable, but runs counter to those instances in which a present judgment is accepted and previous judgments—though greater in number—are rejected. And I should contend that this is not only the way in which we must defend our final acceptances and rejections of conflicting judgments, but that it is also a way which is not infrequently used. In case this be doubted let me point out the strong similarity between what I have argued and what can be seen when we attempt to decide which of two conflicting *non*-moral judgments is true.

When inconsistencies arise between two of our own non-moral judgments we always attempt to decide the issue by an appeal to the consistency of one of these judgments with the other judgments which we have made. And we are always inclined to do so by the simple means of comparing whether one of these judgments is more consistent with the others with respect to what it actually asserts. And in most cases this seems to suffice. But if the inconsistent judgment none the less continues to put forth a strong claim, or if for any other reason we are troubled by the doubt that perhaps all of our previous assertions may themselves not have been true, we appeal to the *method* by which we had reached those judgments whose truth we find ourselves incapable of doubting: that judgment which represents the use of this method we take as valid, and accept what it asserts as true, and we discredit the way in which we had reached our contradictory judgment, thereby undermining its claim to truth.

But now we must ask what it would actually mean to discredit the "method" which underlies a particular moral judgment. Such a "method" would refer to the means by which we had reached our moral judgment. In the first instance this "method" would then be our response to the nature of the facts in the case which we were judging, and this would, of course, throw us back to the principle of the primacy of the facts. However, in the cases with which we are here concerned this principle does not, in itself, offer guidance, since these cases involve moral disagreements, and not simple disparities in moral judgment. It is here that we must use the criterion of a consistent commitment to that point of view which seems in other instances to be sound; and it is on this basis that the issue is to be decided. In the realm of non-moral truth the analogue would then be the means by which we would decide between two alternative methods (if such there be) of reaching truth in factual matters. If we were (or are) faced by such a dilemma, as some anthropologists and some theologians have seemed to assume, we can only justify our decision by attempting to show that we have consistently followed that method which seemed to enable us best to understand those matters of fact which we were least able to deny. Such a commitment to consistency in method is, I submit, demanded by our ideal of what constitutes a valid method of arriving at factual truth. It is also a strict analogue of what it is that we do in attempting to discriminate between valid and invalid modes of moral judgment.

Having traced the forms of inner argument over moral truth as far as we can, we must now illustrate how the same principles are applicable to moral controversies which involve different persons. In these cases it is not to be expected that we shall find an equal number of instances in which an acceptable resolution of the controversy is reached—for it is certainly the case that in our own deliberations we wish not to rest until we have reached a solution[34]—but the methods of attempting to solve such controversies are precisely the same.

Let us then directly start with a real moral disagreement—one in which every attempt to show that there is only a disparity between the two judgments has already failed. For example, let one disputant claim that *X* has a moral obligation to place the interest of his family above that of his country when he is faced by a specific choice, and let the other deny it. How, we are to ask, is the matter to be settled; how can the principle of universality be used in this argument after any appeal to the principle of the primacy of the facts has broken down?

What frequently happens is, of course, that each disputant may attempt to make an appeal to the authority of others in order to prove that his judgment is correct and his opponent's is not. Such an appeal presupposes an acceptance of one form of the criterion of consistency: we are troubled by the contradiction between what is asserted by the two judgments and wish to show that what is asserted by the judgment which we make concords with what is asserted by the judgments of others. However, such an appeal does not, in itself, settle any moral issue. In the first place it is usually possible for both of the disputants to find others whose judgments seem to agree with theirs. In the second place it is always possible to accept the judgments which are cited, but to deny that the cases with which they were concerned were really similar to the specific case under dispute. In the third place it is possible to be so convinced of the truth of one's present judgment that one is willing to reject as authoritative those judgments of others which one had previously been willing to accept. Thus, the appeal to the authority of the moral judgments of others poses exactly the same problems which we have found to obtain when we examined the attempt to support one of our own present judgments through an appeal to the other judgments which we had previously made: the criterion of consistency cannot settle the issue so long as the consistency involved is the agreement of what is asserted in one case with what has been asserted in other cases.

However, the appeal to the judgment of another may take a different form: instead of appealing to the authority of past judgments we may agree to lay the facts before an "impartial spectator," who will decide our dispute merely in the light of the particular case at hand. This, of course, obviates the first two difficulties in the appeal to authority, but it does not obviate the third. While we may have antecedently agreed that this person was not, to our knowledge, partial in the dispute, and that he was not antecedently committed to any particular point of view from which these facts should be judged, it is still possible for the person whose judgment was denied to hold that the neutral observer was wrong. The confirmation which his opponent was granted would not settle the issue for him; it merely showed (what he doubtless had prior reason to believe) that his opponent was not alone in disagreeing with his moral judgment. While he may have undertaken to act in accordance with whatever course the third person believed to be morally right, and he may feel bound by this undertaking, he need not believe that the controversy has been satisfactorily settled; he may still claim that his original judgment represented the morally adequate response to the situation. In fact, this feeling may be so strong that he will in fact feel obligated to break his pledge to abide by the judgment of the impartial spectator and will act as he originally saw it right to act.

However, there is a point at which an appeal to a neutral party is often genuinely effective (as well as being theoretically defensible) in an attempt to resolve a moral controversy. This point is reached when the neutral observer is asked to judge not the truth of a moral assertion but the consistency of the person in making this assertion. The neutral observer (or, for that matter, one of the disputants) can attempt to analyze the particular point of view from which one of the judgments has been made, and can attempt to show, through a variety of cases, to what further judgments a consistent adherence to this point of view would lead. In doing so, it is of course necessary not only to have clearly exposed the particular point of view from which the judgment was made, but to find essentially similar cases against which to test the consistency with which this point of view will be willingly maintained. It is because the latter task is one of considerable difficulty that moral discussions so frequently involve hypothetical cases, and moralists are so inclined to pile agony upon agony in the cases which they cite: an hypothetical case is more likely to be granted to be essentially similar to the actual case under discussion than any other actual case is likely to be, and the agonizing circumstances are introduced in order to extort a judgment which will show that the original point of view has been abandoned. By this means, it appears to me, many moral controversies come to be resolved. And even when no actual resolution is forthcoming, it frequently becomes clear from a man's other actions and judgments that he has not been consistent in adhering to the point of view from which his disputed judgment was made. When this occurs, we may with reason say that his original judgment was invalid, since it sprang from a point of view which he himself is unwilling consistently to maintain. By such means the criterion of consistency, which rests upon the principle of universality, may justifiably be used as a basis for claiming that a specific moral judgment is invalid. However, as we have already noted, this use of the criterion of consistency does not itself permit us to say that any set of judgments springing from a point of view which is consistently maintained is either invalid or untrue.

We must now examine this problem. I shall do so by stating what I take to be a third universally acknowledged principle concerning the validity of moral judgments.

iii.

THE THIRD of the principles of moral judgments I shall term the principle of ultimacy. It may be stated as follows: *Any moral judgment which is believed to be valid is incorrigible, and any incorrigible moral judgment must be acknowledged to be binding upon thought and upon action.* This principle is obviously more complex than the two which we have thus far discussed, and it may even seem to overstep the limits which I have set to this discussion, for it touches upon the province of traditional normative ethics. That it does not overstep these limits can only become clear as we proceed. However, to obviate difficulties for the reader it will be well to note two points at which it differs from the principles previously discussed.

It is first to be noted that this principle presupposes the others, rather than being independent of them. This is apparent in the fact that it is stated that a moral judgment which is considered as valid (and which therefore is held to conform to the first two principles) is "incorrigible"; it is not stated that the principle of ultimacy can itself afford a criterion for determining that any particular judgment is or is not valid. Why I nonetheless list this principle with the others, as a principle of validity, will only become clear as we proceed.

In the second place it is to be noted that the principle of ultimacy asserts that any "incorrigible" moral judgment must be acknowledged to be binding upon thought and upon action. This might be considered to mark a departure from our previously set limits for discussion, for it would seem that the principle constitutes a normative precept for action rather than being a principle which serves to discriminate between valid and invalid moral judgments. *However*, the reader will note that I have employed—and wish to underline—the phrase "must be *acknowledged* to be binding." What this aspect of the principle then holds is that a moral judgment which seeks to correct what is admitted to be a valid moral judgment (and is therefore incorrigible) is itself an invalid moral judgment. Thus, though there may be some normative precepts concerning action which may be entailed by this aspect of our principle, the principle itself will here only be applied to what might be called "second-order" moral judgments, that is, to those moral judgments which concern what it is right for a person to do when he has made a specific moral judgment whose validity has not been impugned. That there are such "second-order" judgments, and that they play an important role among our other moral judgments will also become clearer as we proceed.

Let us now examine what is meant by saying that a moral judgment which is believed to be valid is "incorrigible." This statement may immediately encounter the objection that since I have held that every moral judgment appears to be valid to the person who makes it, at the time at which he makes it, *every* moral judgment will be incorrigible. To such an objection, however, there is a ready answer: it is only the case that a moral judgment appears as incorrigible so long as it is still believed to be a valid moral judgment. And this, of course, is in accord with the facts concerning moral judgments. Two such facts are particularly worthy of notice: first, that when we attempt to correct a moral judgment made by another we seek to show that his judgment has violated either the principle of the primacy of the facts or the principle of universality; second, whenever another seeks to correct a moral judgment which we have made, and when he fails to convince us that our judgment has violated either of these two principles, we insist that his claim to have made a true moral assertion carries no more weight than does our contrary conviction that it is he who is in error. Each of these facts merits attention, but I shall deal with them in reverse order.

It is never easy to accept the conclusion that any moral controversy may ultimately reach an impasse, and that both of two contradictory judgments are incorrigible. The reason this is so, however, is merely one further illustration of the already noted fact that each moral judgment seems to be both valid and true to the person who makes it at the time at which it is made. Convinced as we are of the validity of our own judgments, and therefore of the truth of what they assert, we cannot help but believe that our opponent must ultimately grant the truth of those assertions. And this inclination is assuredly fostered in those cases in which we find that others make judgments which also assert that which we have asserted. When we are thus among the majority (at least among the majority of those whose judgments we choose to consult) we can easily find terms with which we think we can explain our opponent's error: we may characterize him as being morally blind, morally perverse, or even a moral imbecile; we may blame his lack of moral education, the unfortunate conditions of his early life, or the limited moral enlightenment of the community in which he was reared. All such "explanations," however, fail to show that *he* is in error, and that it is in fact our assertion which is true. Nor, if we are placed among a minority, can we show that those assertions which are made by the majority are false, explaining them in terms of the vested interests of that majority, the stupidity of most people, their hidden resentments, or their eagerness to share a majority view. And if it should happen that we are alone in our moral conviction regarding any matter, the incorrigibility of a moral judgment may be pressed home: search as we can, we may find no error in our judgment; prodded as we may be by a desire to conform, the assertion may remain our conviction; and it is then that we realize that not only is our own judgment incorrigible, but the judgments of others are also incorrigible. They are incorrigible; yet we cannot give up seeking to correct them!

But there is, of course, a way to correct them: we need merely show that they were invalid. For if we can convince ourselves that they were invalid we can dismiss them; and if we can also force our opponent to acknowledge their invalidity, we will actually have corrected them. But this, let us recall, is precisely what the principle of ultimacy states: every moral judgment which is believed to be valid is incorrigible so long as it is believed to be valid. We have corrected the judgment by undermining our opponent's belief in the validity of that judgment. And this brings us to a consideration of the other fact which I have selected as worthy of special notice.

I have stated (and we have just seen) that moral assertions are incorrigible unless they can be shown to rest upon judgments which violate universally accepted principles as to what constitutes a valid moral judgment. Now, we have seen that there are at least two such principles: the principle of the primacy of the facts and the principle of universality. That the principle of the primacy of facts leads to the corrigibility of moral assertions is easily seen. When two persons make contradictory moral assertions and one can convince the other that the latter has a false view of the facts, the assertion of the other is undermined. Similarly, it follows from the principle of universality that we can correct moral judgments through using a test of consistency, and thus moral judgments are corrigible in so far as they can be shown to be invalid on the basis of our opponent's unwillingness to adhere to the point of view from which these judgments were made.

However, there is one point at which the principle of the ultimacy of moral judgments collides with the principle of universality in a way in which it does not not collide with the principle of the primacy of facts. The principle of the primacy of the facts merely states our conviction as to how a moral judgment should be formed, and does not state how it should be interpreted; but the principle of universality demands that we should not deny the assertoric character of moral judgments. Now, if we are not to undermine the assertoric character of a moral judgment by restricting it to the point of view from which it was made, we have difficulty in interpreting our own judgments as binding upon thought and upon action. The difficulty is not, of course, a logical one: there is no inconsistency between the two principles. And so long as I am only concerned with interpreting my own moral judgments there is no psychological difficulty in accepting both principles: if I am willing consistently to hold to the same point of view in all of my moral judgments, this strengthens rather than weakens my feeling that they are binding upon me. However, when I consider the moral judgments of those who consistently make judgments different from my own, it is psychologically difficult to adhere to both principles. On the one hand, one is then tempted to deny that the judgments of others should be binding upon their thought and action because one feels so strongly the assertoric claims of one's own judgments. Thus, much of the force of moral dogmatism arises out of an emphasis upon the principle of universality, to the neglect of the principle of ultimacy. (However, this principle is none the less accepted by the dogmatist when he is concerned only with his own judgments.) On the other hand, the fact that one wishes firmly to hold to the principle of ultimacy for one's self tempts one to deny the assertoric claims of *all* moral judgments in order to cling to the incorrigibility of one's own. Thus, much of the force of moral scepticism rests upon a thorough acceptance of the incorrigibility of one's own moral judgments, even though this may involve a disregard of the principle of universality. (However, even the sceptic may feel the need for consistency within the sphere of his own judgments.)

In spite of this psychological opposition of the two principles when there is a conflict between our judgments and the judgments of others, it would be a mistake to yield to the temptation of discarding one in favor of the other. As we have noted, the two principles are not only logically compatible but both are accepted (and each tends to reinforce the other) when we are considering only our own judgments. Therefore I shall later attempt to point out another way in which this psychological conflict not only should be, but is, overcome.

Let us now turn our attention to the second facet of the principle of ultimacy: that any incorrigible moral judgment is binding upon thought and upon action.

To say that any incorrigible moral judgment is binding upon *action* is, of course, to refer to direct moral judgments only: it is these judgments, and these alone, which contain the reflexive element of a demand upon the agent himself. However, it will be well to postpone a consideration of this aspect of our principle (an aspect which is identical with one of the problems of a traditional normative ethics) until we have examined what it signifies to say that an incorrigible moral judgment is binding upon *thought*.

To speak of *any* judgment as "binding upon thought" signifies that such a judgment has a hold over one, that what it asserts is believed. Whether it ought to be believed, whether it ought to be considered as binding, is not a question which can be answered merely by pointing out that it does or does not accord with other judgments which the same person, or other persons, have made. As we have already seen, one cannot decide that it ought or ought not to be considered as binding on these grounds: it may always be that the other judgments with which it does or does not accord are themselves judgments which ought not to be binding. The only question which we can solve is, therefore, not whether it ought to be binding, but whether it in fact *is* binding: whether it is "accepted" or "believed." Now, if any judgment appears incorrigible, it appears binding: until we have grounds for rejecting it, it maintains its hold over us. What may constitute such grounds in the field of non-moral judgments is not our present concern; but we have seen that in the case of moral judgments these grounds must be that the judgment is recognized to have been invalid. It is rejected not because of what it asserts, but *either* because it flouts the principle which we accept as definitive of the "proper" source for all moral judgments *or* because it fails to conform to that which any moral judgment must "properly" claim.[35] Thus, so long as a moral judgment appears valid to a person, he finds that it is binding upon his thought: he cannot reject it, he cannot fail to accept it, it cannot but be believed.

This we can see in all types of moral judgments, whether they be direct or removed judgments of rightness or wrongness, or whether they be judgments of moral worth. For example, when I make a direct moral judgment concerning whether it is right or wrong for me to act in a certain manner under the circumstances now confronting me, my query is answered when I apprehend this situation as demanding that I do this rather than that. And such a judgment appears to me valid; I cannot doubt it; it is something which I find myself forced to believe.[36]

Now, precisely the same situation obtains with respect to both removed moral judgments of rightness or wrongness and judgments of moral worth. When we view the action of another and find it to have been right or wrong, or to have exhibited character attributes which are praiseworthy or blameworthy, we cannot doubt that what appears as right or wrong or as praiseworthy or blameworthy, really does possess these characteristics: we do not speak the language of "appearing," but of "being." To be sure, when we find that our judgment contravenes the judgment of another, we may sometimes become puzzled, but our most usual reaction is merely to deny that which he has affirmed. Now all this we have already seen. And we have also seen that, when there is a conflict between judgments, these judgments are only considered corrigible in so far as they are held to have violated one or both of the principles of validity with which we have been concerned. But when they are not thus corrigible what results? What results is that no amount of argument, invective, or bluster makes us any the less sure that we are right; and the more we are threatened for our judgment, the more certain we feel that our opponent has illicitly sought to take advantage of us. Our judgment of the moral property of that which we judge is as inexpungeable a datum of our experience as the fact that we see one line as longer than another, or one surface as blue rather than red, that what we taste tastes salty rather than sweet, or that what we smell is not a fragrance but a stench.

So long as a moral judgment appears to us to be valid—so long, that is, as we still apprehend the facts in the situation in the same way, and our judgment is not undercut by a recognition that what we assert can only be asserted from our own present idiosyncratic point of view—we cannot free ourselves of the belief that what it asserts is true. We cannot free ourselves of this belief because we can find no reason to doubt it. Thus even those who accept one or another theory which would deny that any moral judgment can be said to be true, cannot, in spite of their theory, rid themselves of the belief that their own moral judgments *are* true. Now, this belief does not bind them to accept an alternative theory: the bindingness with which we are concerned need not embrace the whole realm of our beliefs. It does, however, elicit assent; it cannot be argued out of existence. For example, whether we like or dislike a moral conclusion which we reach, our preference does not directly influence that conclusion.[37] And no matter how inconsistent such a conclusion may be with other moral judgments which we have made, we cannot abandon this judgment until we can actually see that it was invalidly reached. Similarly, and more importantly, the fact that our judgment conflicts with a judgment made by another does not suffice to weaken assent. In those cases in which we admire the other person, an awareness of the conflict will suffice to make us doubt the validity of our judgment, but it is only if we first see that the judgment is invalid that it loses its power to compel. And this power is lost because we can turn our attention from what it asserts to what underlay its formation. But if it remains valid we are apt to remark of the conflict, "Even he (the man we admire) might be mistaken." And where we do not already have grounds for admiration of the moral qualities of our opponent we feel sure that it is he who is mistaken, and resent as unwarranted his attempt to deny that which appears to us as being as clear as the hand before our face.

This has, of course, a strict analogue in our perceptual judgments. When I am aware of a particular shape or color or of an object moving, I cannot doubt that I "really" see that which I am seeing. No matter how many contradictions are evoked by my acceptance of this datum, the datum is a real datum which is not thereby changed. Conflicts may cause me to inquire why it is that I see what I see, and thus may turn my attention from what I see to the question of why I see it as I do. And this may modify the further assertions which I had been inclined to make on the basis of that which I saw. However, in most (if not, as I believe, in all such cases) this does not directly change the characteristics which I see: to know that one line is really not longer than the other, or that one motion is not really swifter than another, does not directly change the appearances.[38] They remain as they are, and no one can argue us out of them. No theory can lead me to deny that I saw them; it can only limit the assertions which I am willing to make on the basis of what I then saw, and it does this by shifting the attention from *what* was seen to *why* it was actually seen.

Thus, we cannot argue a man out of his moral convictions; what is seen as right or wrong is not changed by argument. What an argument can succeed in doing is not a matter of directly changing our moral judgments, but it can loosen their hold on our thought by shifting attention to the conditions under which they were formed; and when it appears that these conditions were such as to make the judgment unacceptable to us (i.e., invalid) we stop basing any further assertion upon it.

This being what is meant by the fact that any moral judgment is binding upon *thought* so long as it is considered to be a valid moral judgment, we must now turn to what it means to say that any such judgment is binding upon action.

As I have already pointed out, this problem does not arise with respect to any moral judgments save those which are to be classified as direct moral judgments. When, for example, I judge that an act done by another was wrong, the demands which I see are directed against him, not against me. I am bound to think what he did was wrong, or—if his action is a contemplated, not yet realized, action—that it would be wrong; but I am not bound thereby to act at all. And, obviously, if the apprehended wrongness of his action leads me to feel that I ought to rectify what he has done, or if the apprehended wrongness of what he contemplates doing leads me to affirm that I will not act in a similar way in a similar situation, the judgment which I am making is a direct moral judgment: it merely happens to be based upon a prior removed judgment, and is not identical with the latter. Similarly, when I judge that a particular act was a courageous or cowardly thing to have done, my judgment of the character of the agent who performed it does not, in itself, bind me to any specific action in the situation in which I am presently placed.

However, when we make a direct moral judgment, that which we judge is the rightness or wrongness of setting ourselves to perform one action rather than another. In such a situation we see that one proposed line of conduct would be right, the other wrong. And this seeing of an action as right or as wrong is—as we have noted—an inexpungeable fact: so long as we have no ground for doubting the validity of our judgment we must give assent to that which we find ourselves discerning. But in such a case what we see is that *we* ought to do this, and ought not to do that; it is our contemplated action which is discerned as right or wrong, and thus we feel ourselves not merely bound to accept our own judgment but to act as we think we ought to act.

Now it is certainly possible that we will not in fact act as we feel that we ought. To speak of a moral judgment as binding upon action is not to say that it will lead to action. It is merely to say that in a direct moral judgment we cannot see an action as right and not feel obligated to do it, nor see an action as wrong and not feel obligated to shun it. And if for any reason we fail to do what we see that we ought to do, we are troubled by "conscience," which, in this sense of the word, is merely the feeling of ourselves as having been bound.

Now, just as we can divert our attention from any moral belief which we hold about another, shifting our concern to the conditions which led to this belief, so we can assuage our "conscience" by a retrospective invalidation of that which led us to judge as we judged. But at the time of our judgment, when we consider our judgment valid, the contemplated action appears as right or as wrong, and as binding upon us. To act contrary to this appearance is possible, other pressures upon us being what they are, but the bindingness loses none of its force, and the sense of wrongdoing persists so long as the judgment cannot itself be invalidated.

Thus, to prove to another that what he feels obligated to do is not, in fact, what he ought to do is impossible until one has shown him that his judgment is invalid. And this, of course, is what we attempt to do when we seek to dissuade a person from acting in the way in which he believes it to be right to act.

Now, suppose that we fail to convince him, suppose that his judgment that he ought so to act remains unshaken in spite of our attempts to make him see that his view of the facts in the case is an incorrect view; or suppose that he has reached his decision because of factors which he himself would admit to invalidate that judgment. What then do we say of his action? It would seem that we are caught in a dilemma. To say that he ought to act as he believes that he ought, is to recognize that his own moral judgment is binding upon his action; but at the same time it is also to recognize that we consider it right for him to do what we believe to be wrong. Conversely, to say that he ought not to do what he believes to be right, but should instead do what we believe to be right, is to deny that an agent's own direct moral judgment defines the nature of his obligation to act in one way rather than another. If we decide for one of these solutions against the other, our decision might be based on either of two contentions. First, it might be based upon the conviction that when there is a conflict between a direct and a removed moral judgment, one rather than the other of these types is always to be given precedence.[39] However, this solution cannot be consistently maintained, since when we ourselves make direct moral judgments we are unwilling to accept the judgment of another as more authoritative than our own merely because it represented a removed moral judgment; and, contrariwise, when we make a judgment concerning the action of another we are unwilling to hold that what he discerns is more truly characteristic of the moral nature of the situation which is judged than is what we discern. Thus, we cannot consistently apply the view that the type of judgment which is made is determinative of whether that judgment is correct. Second, we might attempt to hold that what a person should do is defined by what is objectively right for him to do, regardless of whether that which is right is discerned through a direct or through a removed moral judgment. However, this is not to settle the issue, since the point in dispute is precisely that of determining which is the objectively right action.

The method by means of which one can escape from this classic dilemma must be of another sort, and it is, I am sure, already apparent to the reader: it consists in applying the standard of the ultimacy of a moral judgment to the judgment which the agent makes, as well as to our own judgment. If we disregard *what* is asserted by any specific moral judgment, and consider only how a man ought to act when he feels that a particular course of conduct (whatever it may be) is binding upon him, we find that we are willing to say that he ought to act as he believes that he ought. We may criticize the basis for his feeling that he ought to act in this way; but to do so is to attempt to show that his judgment was invalid. Once we recognize that he has acted in the way in which he believes that it would be right to act, we do not make the further criticism, claiming that he ought to have acted in another way. This fact is, I believe, recognized in one form or another by all moralists, and it is simply a recognition of what I have termed the principle of ultimacy.

It should now be clear why I have classed the principle of ultimacy among the principles of validity, even though it does not itself afford a criterion for the *correction* of "first-order" moral judgments. By a first-order moral judgment I here refer to those cases in which we apprehend a specific action as right or as wrong, or in which we make a judgment of moral worth concerning a trait of character or a person. By a second-order moral judgment I here refer to those judgments of rightness or wrongness which we make when we recognize that the agent himself has made a specific judgment of rightness or wrongness.[40] The objects of our first and second order judgments are ostensibly the same: the rightness or wrongness involved in this specific action. But in fact they are different. The object of the one is the rightness or wrongness of this man's setting himself to do this rather than that, and does not raise the question of what demands he himself sees the situation as containing. The object of the other is the rightness or wrongness of his having set himself to do that which he believed to be right or wrong. Now the principle of ultimacy is a principle of validity which can serve to correct our second-order judgments, showing them to be valid or invalid. It entails that any judgment concerning the rightness or wrongness of a specific action is an invalid judgment if it has neglected to consider the judgment which the agent himself made in that situation.

Now, I should expect that some might deny that this is a universally accepted principle; they might wish to deny that we must take into account what the agent himself judged when we make our own moral judgments concerning the rightness or wrongness of an action. However, I believe that this objection rests on a misunderstanding. I have definitely not contended that we should affirm that what the agent apprehends as right or as wrong *is* right or wrong. His judgment, or even his failure to make any moral judgment, is not binding upon us: our first-order judgment is not changed by his first-order judgment. However, there is a distinction between saying *X* would have been the right action for him to take, had he not thought it wrong, and saying *X* was the right action for him to take, regardless of the fact that he thought it wrong. It is the second type of statement (and not the first) which is declared invalid by the principle of ultimacy. And it is to be noted that I may affirm the first statement without overthrowing my own judgment that a contrary action, *Y*, was the "objectively" right action which he should have seen to be right. However, the principle of ultimacy demands that I can only substantiate the latter claim if I can find adequate grounds for saying that his judgment was invalid because it was based upon a false view of the facts, or violated the condition of universality.

I do not believe that it will be contended that this solution of our dilemma runs counter to the actual judgments which men make. However, there are those who would give another explanation of the facts, and while not disagreeing with the outcome of our analysis would reach it in another way. They would be inclined to say that we may legitimately claim that the agent's judgment was in fact mistaken, and that what he set himself to do was "objectively" wrong; but they would then go on to say that his action was not blameworthy (or might even be praiseworthy) because he set himself to do the "subjectively" right thing. Such a solution seems to me to rest upon a distortion of the meaning of the term "right," when used in a moral sense; and this distortion seems to me to have been introduced into ethical theorizing in the interest of escaping from what is merely "subjectively" right to what is "objectively" right. Yet those who seek to make this escape fail to show how we may pass from the former to the latter. Unless the judgment can be shown to have been an invalid judgment, what it asserts to be true is no less likely to be true than what we assert. Furthermore it is not the case, as they would seem to have us believe, that we are praising the character of the agent for having done what he saw to be right. In such cases it is precisely upon his character that our blame often falls: that he saw this as right often seems to us to indicate a blameworthiness of character. Nor do we split our judgment, adversely judging his character in so far as it led to his seeing this as right and judging his character favorably in so far as he acted on what he saw as right, and (be it noted) also judging the action itself to have been wrong. It seems scarcely likely that this splintering of our judgment occurs. Would it not be more plausible to say that when we contemplate his action, recognizing that he felt certain demands levelled against him by the situation he confronted, we are simply making a removed moral judgment of a type different from our own first-order moral judgment concerning that situation; are we not viewing the situation as he saw it, and saying that if this were also the way in which we saw it (which we already know it is not) this action would be a right action? And when we say this we are faced with the task of showing that the way in which we apprehend the situation is the correct way, and the way in which he sees it is the incorrect way. We are thus forced to show that his judgment is an invalid judgment. Thus we are thrown back upon the other two principles in order to establish the truth of our assertion. And thus the principle of ultimacy is consonant with those second-order judgments which we make concerning the rightness of acting according to what is "subjectively" right.

We see, then, that while the principle of ultimacy rests upon both of the prior principles of validity, it sets a limit to what may be achieved through an application of the second of these. The principle of universality is employed to resolve moral controversies which cannot be resolved by an appeal to matters of fact, and this, as we have indicated, it may upon occasion achieve. However, there come points at which this criterion fails to provide a solution to the controversy. When this occurs the principle of ultimacy forbids us to transcend the limits of the subjectively right; it precludes us from justifying the belief (though not of course from actually believing) that what we hold to be objectively right *is* right.

iv.

WE ARE NOW in a position to draw together our argument, estimating to what extent moral controversies may be satisfactorily resolved. The preceding sections of this chapter have already suggested the general nature of a solution to this problem, but it remains to relate our discussion of the principles of validity to our discussion of the various factors which, through their influence upon moral judgments, engender the controversies with which we are concerned. In so doing, we shall also have occasion to see in what ways the three principles of validity are related to one another.

It will be recalled that some moral controversies represent simple disparities in moral judgment. It is generally held that all such simple disparities can be satisfactorily resolved. This confidence rests upon the assumption that one can (in principle) settle disputes concerning matters of fact. However, it does not rest upon this alone. In order to hold that simple disparities between moral judgments can be satisfactorily resolved, one must not only assume that purely factual disagreements are capable of resolution, but one must also hold that a valid moral judgment is based upon a correct apprehension of the non-moral characteristics of that which is being judged. If one did not make the latter assumption, contradictory moral properties could still be validly predicated of an action after a merely factual contradiction concerning its nature had been overcome. Thus, in so far as one accepts the generally held belief that simple disparities between moral judgments can be satisfactorily resolved, one must also accept one of the aspects of the principle of the primacy of the facts.

I know of no moralist who denies that these simple disparities between moral judgments can be resolved. And I suspect that if such a denial were to be made it would rest on the contention that it is impossible (even in principle) to settle all factual disputes.[41] While no one (I should think) would be tempted to hold that disparities between two moral judgments are *in all cases* incapable of being resolved, the actual persistence of some of these controversies might tempt one to hold that there are some simple disparities which cannot (even in principle) be overcome. And there is, in fact, a means by which we can distinguish between two general classes of disparities among moral judgments, classifying them by virtue of the sources from which they arose. On the one hand there would be those cases in which the different views of the facts in the case would be based upon differing states of knowledge, or upon differing antecedent beliefs which are relevant to the judgment of the nature of this action; on the other hand there would be those cases in which the different views of the facts were caused by the effects of, say, emotions or sentiments. While moralists generally claim that disparities of both types may be resolved, it would be theoretically possible to hold that disparities of the one type were soluble while those of the other were not. It will therefore be prudent to examine each separately.

As examples of disparities which rest directly upon differing states of knowledge, or upon differing antecedent beliefs, we may cite such cases as the following: instances in which two persons hold differing views as to the causal consequences of an action or of the motives of an agent, instances in which they have differing views as to the situation in which the action is performed, or in which they interpret the same overt behavior in terms of different "meanings."[42] In attempting to resolve disparities of this type we appeal directly to other factual judgments which are considered relevant to the facts in dispute. For example, we try to determine how probable it was that certain causal consequences would ensue if the action were performed, or we attempt to determine the motives of the agent from other information concerning him, or we attempt to determine the "meaning" attached to a certain overt form of behavior in the society in which it was performed. And it would seem to me unlikely that anyone would hold that disparities of this type are not in principle capable of resolution.

The situation is somewhat different with respect to those cases in which the source of a disparity is traced to the effects of emotions or sentiments upon our view of those facts which serve as the bases for our moral judgments.[43] If we are to claim that these disparities are in principle capable of resolution we must make the assumption that while emotions and sentiments may distort our apprehension of facts there is some means by which this distorting influence can be overcome. The belief that we can overcome the effects of emotions and sentiments might take the form of holding that some of our cognitions are unaffected by them, or it might take the form of holding that even if all cognition is influenced in some degree by emotions or by sentiments there is some way of neutralizing their impact and arriving at an accurate view of the facts in the case. Now, it would be possible to doubt that either of these means of escape from the emotions and sentiments is open to us, and if this were doubted it might be denied that this type of disparity between moral judgments is capable of being satisfactorily resolved.

Now, I do not believe that any moralist has ever held this position, and there is good reason why none should have attempted to do so. Apart from certain other difficulties, the position would end by denying that we have any way of escaping the impact of emotions and sentiments upon our factual judgments; however, the very distinction which was originally drawn between those disparities which spring from antecedent factual disagreements and those which spring from the influence of emotions or sentiments, is a distinction which could not be maintained if the conclusion were true. Thus, either all disparities must be considered to be in principle incapable of resolution (with all that *this* entails for our non-moral cognition) or none can be claimed to be so.

However, it is of interest to note that we may, in practice, actually attempt to resolve the two different types of simple disparity in different ways. Our ordinary empirical criteria of truth are the usual means by which we attempt to settle disputes which spring directly from differing states of knowledge or differing antecedent beliefs. But when we think that the source of the disparity can be traced to the influence of an emotion or a sentiment we may introduce the principle of universality into our consideration of the judgment which was made. We do this by attempting to show that the moral judgment of one or of both of the disputants must be interpreted in terms of the specific point of view from which it was made, for what was seen as the non-moral nature of the action was dependent upon the experiencing of a specific emotion, or the possession of a particular sentiment, at the time at which that judgment was made.

The fact that such an appeal to the principle of universality is used in attempting to solve simple disparities between moral judgments shows that this principle is closely related to the principle of the primacy of the facts. Actually, in one of the aspects of each, these principles are in practice complementary: a moral judgment which is based upon a correct view of the non-moral properties of the object would not be relative to the point of view from which it was made, and a moral judgment which is not restricted to the point of view from which these facts are seen, is presumably based upon a correct view of the nature of these facts. However, though the two principles are in this respect complementary, they are not to be identified with one another, since each contains an element which the other lacks. The principle of the primacy of the facts asserts that a valid moral judgment is a direct response to the apprehended nature of these facts, and the principle of universality says nothing concerning this. On the other hand, the principle of universality goes beyond the principle of the primacy of the facts in stating how our moral judgments must be interpreted if they are to receive recognition as valid moral judgments, while the principle of the primacy of the facts says nothing concerning the necessary assertoric character of moral judgments. It might, of course, still be the case that one of these principles was a corollary of the other, and this possibility I do not seek to deny.[44] For our purposes, however, this would be immaterial, so long as it is granted that each of the two principles contains an element which the other does not contain, and that each is therefore distinct from the other.

Regardless of the manner in which these two principles are related, it is worth noting that they can only be used in this complementary fashion when we are dealing with simple disparities between moral judgments. As we have seen, when what apparently are disparities become transformed into moral disagreements, or when moral disagreements arise from any other source, the principle of the primacy of the facts cannot be used to settle the issue. It was only our present purpose to note that in the case of disparities between moral judgments, the ensuing controversy is generally considered to be soluble, and its solubility rests upon the fact that we accept these principles. Which one of the two principles we are apt to use in settling a particular controversy depends upon whether we initially believe that the disparity springs directly from differences in factual belief, or whether we interpret these differences as themselves being due to the effects of emotions or sentiments.[45]

Let us now turn to examine whether those controversies which involve actual moral disagreements, and not mere disparities, can also be said to be capable of being satisfactorily resolved. At this crucial point we should proceed with great care, and I wish to avoid making any blanket assertions about what either is or "must be" the case. This is all the more important since not all moral disagreements are of one type.

On the basis of the preceding discussion of the sources of moral controversies it seems to me clear that there are three different types of moral disagreements. In the first type of case what appear to be disparities or divergences between moral judgments become transformed into moral disagreements when the question arises as to which of two ways of regarding an action is morally more adequate. In such cases we find that two persons reach different moral conclusions regarding a specific action because they have differing views of what, from a moral point of view, is the more adequate way of regarding the relation between an action and the situation in which it is embedded. Their controversy does not concern the existence of the demands which each sees, but concerns the question of which of the alternative ways of regarding that action is the way in which it ought to be regarded by one who is to assess its rightness or wrongness or its moral worth. In the second type of case, two individuals may agree as to the rightness or wrongness of an action, or as to the praiseworthiness or blameworthiness of two traits of character or persons, but may differ regarding the degree of rightness or wrongness, or of worth, which are to be assigned. In the third type of case the disagreement arises because one person fails to find either the same or any moral quality in a specific action which another holds to be present in this action, even though both may (so far as we can tell) have precisely the same view of all of the non-moral properties and relationships of the action judged.

Now, it has been usual for moralists to regard only this third type of case as a real instance of a moral disagreement, for they have been less concerned with the problems of estimating the extent to which specific moral controversies can be resolved than with stating whether or not there is a universally valid contentual standard for conduct. For this same reason they have also been inclined to discuss the question of whether there are any such disagreements in terms of whether there are any persons who, upon all occasions, show that they disagree with the moral judgments which others make. Our present concern with specific moral controversies is, then, different from the approach which they take. It will only be later, after estimating the extent to which specific moral disagreements may be resolved, that we shall be in a position to state to what extent it is plausible to hold that there are or are not such all-pervasive moral disagreements.

With respect to the existence of disagreements of the third type (in which two persons have an identical view of all of the non-moral properties and relationships of that which they judge, and yet form conflicting moral judgments), I should admit that it is not possible to establish their existence by a direct examination of the judgments which are made. It would always be possible to hold that the two individuals do in fact have different views of the non-moral properties of that which they judge. However, the fact that we can always give this alternative explanation of the controversy does not prove that it is the best explanation; and the fact that we may be inclined to accept it does not prove it to be correct. (It could be that our inclination to apply it to all cases springs from its compatibility with our feeling that whatever moral assertions we make must be true.) But if we examine the question indirectly, through noting the sources out of which moral controversies apparently arise, there is no reason to doubt that some controversies represent disagreements of this type. This point is of sufficient importance to be worth further consideration before we proceed.

If, as I have argued, some moral controversies seem to spring from differences in the "emotional sensitivities" of different persons, it would be likely that we should find that there are some disagreements of this third type. I see no reason to hold that a person who manifests cruelty in his actions must be oblivious of the suffering which his actions cause others, nor that he merely disregards the wrongness of inflicting such suffering because he is so conscious of other aspects of the action which he performs. If, as seems to be the case, his enjoyment rests in witnessing or imagining the suffering he inflicts, it would seem implausible to deny that he really disagrees with those who view his action as wrong. To this it may of course be answered that his enjoyment really rests upon flouting his own "moral sense," in rising above it, or acting contrary to it, and thus it might be said that he too feels the same demands which we feel. However, this is not to banish a real disagreement: the disagreement then becomes even more fundamental, for it rests upon a difference between those persons who feel bound to act in accordance with the objective demands which they experience, and those in whom there is a subjective demand to override and violate at least some of these demands.

I have also cited cases in which differences in "emotional sensitivities" may be taken to affect our judgments of moral worth. In these cases too it seems to me plausible to hold that two persons may agree in their views of the non-moral facts concerning a trait of character or a person, and may also be regarding the object they judge in the same way, but that one may be responsive to certain types of demand in recurring situations, and find this character-attribute morally praiseworthy, while the other may not. In these cases, too, we should have examples of specific moral disagreements of the third type.

However, it should be noted that the examples which I have chosen do not represent disagreements between two removed moral judgments: the first example involved a disagreement between a direct and a removed moral judgment, the second involved two judgments of moral worth. I am unwilling to state that in removed moral judgments of rightness and wrongness disagreements of the third type also arise. Where only removed moral judgments are involved, it seems to me equally plausible to hold that the disagreements are based either upon differing structuralizations of that which is judged or that they involve differences in the degrees of rightness or wrongness which are assigned to the action.[46] However, the fact that the third type of disagreements may not arise in removed moral judgments need not lead us to say that they are not present in the other cases, and that they do not exist.

Since the reader may still find it difficult to accept the thesis that there are moral disagreements of this third type, I should like to point out that I have nowhere contended that any person who is similar to other human beings in the non-moral judgments he makes will be *totally* devoid of a "responsiveness," or "emotional sensitivity," to those demands which others feel as moral demands. I should not wish to be thought as arguing that, as a matter of fact, there are any persons who are under all circumstances indifferent to the suffering of others: for example, that a man who does not in a specific case feel that it is his duty to relieve the suffering that he deliberately caused will never, in any case, feel an obligation to relieve suffering, whether he has caused it or not. I have merely wished to state that he may, in some instances, not feel the same restraints which others feel, and will not make the same judgments which they make. Such differences may then be held to be due to differences in the degree of his "emotional sensitivity" to the types of demand which others experience, rather than to a total insensitivity on his part to these demands. Thus, a disagreement might be present in one case while in another case both would make precisely the same judgments of rightness or wrongness or of worth.

In order to show that there almost certainly are instances of specific disagreements based upon differences in "emotional sensitivity," I shall take two examples other than cruelty. *First*, consider the case of the effects of sympathy. Those who would say that "If we all ate at the same table, no one would go hungry" have an important truth on their side: the weakness of our imaginations would no longer enable us to forget those whom it is convenient not to help. But is there any reason to assume that all who ate at that table would feel under the same compulsion to share and share alike? We do not, for example, assume that when a parent recognizes that children like affection, he inevitably feels under obligation to give his children this affection, nor to give them it equally. We may believe that he is wrong in not feeling these obligations, but if we do so it may be because our sympathy is stronger and wider in what it embraces than is his. I see no apriori reason to claim that such is not an adequate explanation, and that every disagreement between parents as to what is the duty of each must really be based upon a disparity between what they take to be the needs of their children or upon a different view of which is the most important set of needs, their children's immediate needs for affection or some other demands placed upon them. Does it not in some cases seem that parents differ in their responsiveness to the needs of their children, and that these differences are based upon differences in the strength of their sympathy? Such cases, I submit, engender controversies between parents as to what, in a specific case, the duty of one of them may be. *Second*, consider the strength of self-regarding and other-regarding impulses. In some cases it seems to be true that when one individual praises a specific act as generous, another may insist that there must have been a concealed self-interest behind the act. Such an insistence does not of course mean that the sceptic himself is under all circumstances incapable of either generous action or of acknowledging the existence of some generous acts. However, it does suggest that there are degrees in the extent to which persons are sensitive to those situations which call forth generosity, and in the case of an act of great magnanimity the degree may transcend the power of a person to feel: in such cases he could only make the act intelligible by means of some other explanation of its source. Now, this would not of course mean that in this specific case any controversy which arose between them would be an example of a moral disagreement: it would in fact be an example of a simple disparity between their judgments. However, if there be differences of this magnitude, is it not plausible to contend that such differences would reflect themselves in some discrepancies among direct and removed moral judgments and some discrepancies among judgments of moral worth?

These considerations seem to me to be sufficient to show that it is likely that moral controversies concerning specific cases sometimes involve disagreements which are attributable to differences in the "emotional sensitivity" of different persons. It is with such specific controversies, and not with ultimate normative generalizations, that I am here concerned. I shall now discuss whether, by the use of the principles of valid moral judgment, controversies which represent each of the three types of disagreement may be satisfactorily resolved.

Regarding the first type of case (in which an apparent disparity or a divergence in moral judgments can be seen to involve a moral disagreement), I have already indicated that the principle of the primacy of the facts is of no help in attempting to resolve the controversy, since such a controversy involves a difference between two opinions as to which of two equally possible ways of regarding the same set of facts is *morally* more adequate. As we have seen, such differences cannot be settled by appealing to factual judgments of "a higher order," nor can they (without circularity) be settled by an appeal to the truth of one ethical system rather than another.[47] However, while the principle of the primacy of the facts fails to provide any means of settling such a dispute, the principle of universality is applicable.

As our very statement of the disagreement suggests, the question at issue is whether one point of view regarding a set of facts is morally more adequate than is another. Since the principle of universality states that a moral judgment can only be considered valid if it is not restricted by the point of view from which it was made, the possibility of applying the test of consistency to each of the conflicting judgments is immediately suggested. And it is, in fact, in this manner that we do actually proceed. To be sure, as I have pointed out, we are inclined to use the ideal of consistency in a theoretically indefensible manner, testing the consistency of what is asserted with what is asserted in other moral judgments. While this may suffice to resolve the controversy *in practice*, if it fails to resolve it in practice it also fails to resolve it *in principle*. It is when such a failure ensues that we must use the test of consistency in the other fashion: testing to see whether each person is willing to be consistent in adopting the point of view from which he has made the specific judgment which has been challenged.

Now, it seems to me to be the case that in some instances this application of the principle of universality will actually resolve some moral disagreements. For example, the use of this test may sometimes reveal to a person that his judgment had actually been formed under the influence of a sentiment, which caused him to structure the situation in one way rather than another. And even if he would fail to admit this (which is not always the case), it sometimes becomes clear to an outsider that this particular judgment was not in fact made from the same point of view as the other judgments which the person has made, and which are still accepted by him. If this becomes apparent, the observer will rightfully conclude that the disagreement has been resolved, even though the actual controversy has not been settled.[48]

However, it would be a mistake to assume that *all* such disagreements can in principle be resolved by means of this use of the test of consistency. In fact, it appears to me that there is empirical evidence which is sufficient to suggest that such will not be the case. We have seen that there may well be basic personality factors which differ from individual to individual, and which may, in part, be responsible for the ways in which different individuals structure certain recurring types of situation.[49] If this empirical generalization is accepted, then it cannot be assumed that all such disagreements will disappear when the test of consistency is applied. For example, if it were the case that some individuals were wholly consistent in structuring all situations in terms of the impact of an action upon their own interests (which I do not believe is true), the test of consistency could not resolve the moral disagreements which would arise between them and individuals who possessed other-regarding impulses. Any such disagreements which may exist would not only have to be admitted to be in principle insoluble, but it would also be the case (as we shall see) that the principle of ultimacy would demand of us that we acknowledge as incorrigible that judgment which stands opposed to our own.

However, before discussing this thesis, which involves a radical departure from a major tradition in ethical theory, let us turn to the second type of moral disagreement in order to see to what extent controversies of this type may be satisfactorily resolved.

This second, or comparative, type of disagreement, it will be recalled, consists in those cases in which two persons agree concerning the rightness or wrongness of two actions (or concerning the praiseworthiness or blameworthiness of two traits of character or persons), but disagree in their estimates of the degree of praise or blame to be assigned to each. In some of these cases, it will be recalled, the disagreement appears to be rooted in differences between "the moral emotions" which the two persons felt with respect to the objects of their praise or blame. Where this is acknowledged, the disagreement is in principle soluble through a *joint* appeal to the principles of universality and of the primacy of the facts.[50] This joint appeal to the two principles is used to substantiate the conviction that the degree of moral emotion which is felt may vary independently of the degree of rightness or wrongness (or of moral worth) to be assigned to that which evokes the emotion.[51] The principle of the primacy of the facts is relevant to the establishment of this conviction since a valid moral judgment must be a direct response to a correct apprehension of that which is being morally judged. If the existence of the emotion, or its strength, were to depend upon any "subjective" factors, such as one's present bodily state or one's past experience with this type of action, the moral judgment would be invalid in so far as the praise or blame which it involves were to be equated with the strength of that emotion. However, it would be possible to answer that the emotion was not in this case related to bodily states, past experience, or the like, but was a direct response to the qualities apprehended in that which was judged. Therefore, this argument must be supplemented by an appeal to the principle of universality, and the test of consistency must be used. It must be asked whether the person will in all cases be willing to equate the degree of moral rightness or wrongness of an action (or praiseworthiness or blameworthiness of a person or trait) with the degree of "moral emotion" aroused in him by such an action. I submit that no one will in fact agree to, and adhere to, such an equation. However, it is to be noted that this appeal to the principle of universality cannot in such cases be used independently of the appeal to the principle of the primacy of the facts; this is why I speak of these principles as here being jointly used. We cannot resolve such a controversy merely by appealing to the principle of universality since it would always be possible for a person to say (if he failed to acknowledge the principle of the primacy of the facts) that a moral judgment was merely a reflection of the emotion which he felt. If this were to be maintained he could maintain that whenever he made a moral judgment he was being consistent in assigning a specific degree of worth to an action or trait or person on the basis of the emotion he felt.

Of course, no one argues this way. That they do not argue in this way suports my contention that both the principle of the primacy of the facts and the principle of universality are universally accepted. And the fact that they are universally accepted is the reason why no one will hold that moral comparisons may legitimately be based upon the degree of emotion which is felt when the object is judged. Thus, we all acknowledge that moral controversies which arise concerning comparative degrees of rightness or wrongness are not in principle insoluble *if* they have their source in differing degrees of moral emotion, however difficult it may be in practice to resolve the actual controversies which arise in this way. The judgments, we hold, *should not* be affected by the strength of the emotions which accompany them.

However, controversies concerning the degree of rightness or wrongness (or praiseworthiness and blameworthiness) may not have their sources in differences between the degrees of emotion which they arouse. They may, for example, also spring from the effects of sentiments (for example, when a man finds an act either particularly reprehensible, or almost excusable, because it was done by his own child) or from the effects of the basic structure of personality (for example, when a person is more sensitive to the demands which underlie certain virtues, and is relatively unmoved by those which underlie other virtues, while his opponent is conversely affected.) In those cases in which it is the sentiments which have this effect we of course apply the principle of the primacy of the facts, sometimes also using its complement which the principle of universality involves.[52] All such cases, I have already argued, may be said to be in principle soluble, though the extent to which an actual agreement can be reached will vary from case to case. However, when a controversy over comparative merit springs from differences in personality we can only rely upon the principle of universality. As we have previously seen,[53] these controversies are in principle soluble when the test of consistency can effect a resolution; when this test fails, the controversy cannot be solved.

This "sceptical" conclusion is, of course, of importance to general ethical theory, and will have to be defended more fully when it is related to the principle of the ultimacy of moral judgments. However, at this point I should like to call to the reader's attention one less sweeping implication that I consider it to have. This implication lies in the fact that even if one could establish that there is, in one sense, "invariance" among all moral judgments, regardless of by whom these judgments were made, one would not have thereby established a universally acceptable standard for conduct. For it might be the case (and I believe that it often is the case) that a common acknowledgment of the same "values" is compatible with differences in the rank-order assigned to these "values." For differing individuals, or for individuals in different cultures, judgments of comparative worth may vary even when there is a common acknowledgment of the rightness of certain forms of actions or of the moral worth of certain traits of character. Common allegiance to the ideal of loyalty-to-the-family and to the ideal of loyalty-to-the-state does not guarantee that the relative stringency of these obligations will be invariantly judged; nor does common acknowledgment of the virtues of prudence and of courage entail that their rank-order for individuals of either the same or different cultures will itself be the same. Thus, if we are to hold to a theory of ethical invariance, and if we expect to derive a universally valid standard for conduct from it, we must hold with Hartmann that the rank-order of "values" is given with the intuition of these values, and is itself invariant; we cannot stop short with Duncker and merely hold the weaker form of the hypothesis of invariance. That the stronger form of invariance, which one finds in Hartmann, is capable of adequate *empirical* defense seems to me to be open to overwhelming doubt.[54]

Let us now turn to disagreements of the third type and see to what extent, if at all, the controversies which they engender may be satisfactorily resolved. Such disagreements are present when two persons who cognize all of the non-moral properties and relationships of an action in precisely the same way nonetheless fail, in a specific case, to judge its moral properties in the same way. While such disagreements cannot (by definition) be solved by any appeal to the principle of the primacy of the facts, it is by no means certain that they cannot be overcome. The fact that some such cases hinge upon the *degree* to which a person possesses a type of responsiveness to a moral situation suggests that the principle of universality may help to overcome them. Using the test of consistency which follows from this principle, it may be possible to hold that a person ought to feel demands which he does not feel. This can, of course, only be shown if it is clear that in other types of situation he acknowledges the presence of similar demands, and if it can then be shown that in these cases he has failed to do so because of the particular conditions obtaining at the time at which he cognized the act. For example, if it could be shown that a parent's failure to be sensitive to the needs of his child arose out of other pressures obtaining at the moment that the judgment was made, such a judgment would be considered invalid. The fact that it was made would still be attributable to the relative lack of strength of his sensitivity to these types of demand (for a person more susceptible to their influence might not have had them overpowered by the other pressures), but the moral disagreement which ensued would be corrigible, so long as the person were sensitive, to some degree, to such demands and based his other moral judgments upon their presence.

The situation would, of course, be entirely different if the moral disagreement rested upon a *total incapacity* of one person to feel the demands which were felt by another when they viewed an identical situation. I do not know whether any such cases exist,[55] but it should be clear that if they did exist they would be wholly irreconcilable. The person who failed to experience such demands could not be demonstrated to have been morally blind by means of any argument which he would accept, or which would be adequate to convince any one else who, on the basis of his own judgment, was not already confident that this was the case. In this respect the situation is not, I submit, in all respects like the situation which obtains when one seeks to convince a color-blind person that he cannot discriminate all that we can discriminate, or when a person born blind becomes convinced that the world as others experience it has properties which he cannot find within his own experience. In the latter cases the acceptance of assertions which are not verified within the individual's own experience follows from empirical tests which the person himself willingly allows to be decisive, or else it follows from an acknowledgement of one's limitations as compared with others. In moral disputes, however, there is no empirical test which does not presuppose an accepted moral standard, and there is no sense of moral inadequacy unless it be based upon a standard which the person himself already accepts. Thus, the puzzlement which naturally arises in the moral case is not resolved as it can be in the other two cases by an appeal to a standard which is not itself in dispute. In moral matters it is only authority which could resolve the perplexity, and for this reason there are those who will accept authority merely to escape a bewilderment. But the appeal to authority, I need not again point out, is theoretically indefensible no matter how much it may in fact be used.

Before relating these three types of disagreement to the principle of ultimacy, it will be well to note that we have now reached a point which permits us to understand the appeal which the psychological approach to ethics possesses. This appeal lies in the fact that there must be acknowledged to be an infrangible bond between what man values or feels obligated to do and what is characteristic of his psychological nature. If men were differently constituted, one from another, there would be no common standard to which they could appeal to settle any moral controversies which arose between them. And if they were all differently constituted from the way in which they are, there would be no reason to suppose that they would then have any moral standards whatsoever. Thus, the psychological approach and the metaphysical approach have some plausibility when they claim that one cannot reach a final conclusion concerning any normative problem without understanding what is, in fact, man's real nature.

Let us now see in what way the principle of ultimacy is related to the solution of these normative questions.

It has become clear that in each of the three types of moral disagreement, the principle of universality may in some cases enable us to resolve moral controversies by means of the test of consistency. Yet it is also possible that this test will not permit us to reach a resolution, since it is possible that two persons will consistently espouse alternative ways of structuring a moral situation, will consistently assign a higher degree of rightness or of moral worth to one object of judgment than to another, and will consistently hold that certain types of action do or do not possess moral goodness. When this occurs we have, I submit, reached the end of any justifiable moral argument: the principle of ultimacy demands that these judgments be taken as incorrigible so long as they represent direct responses to the non-moral aspects of that which is being judged (if the view of these aspects is not demonstrably mistaken), and so long as they are consistently adhered to. Here, then, we reach a limit to justifiable moral controversy. Whether, in fact, such a limit is ever actually reached cannot be decided with assurance. However that it is theoretically possible follows from our previous argument. And it therefore also follows that if anyone wishes to establish that there is a universally valid contentual standard for conduct, applicable to all persons and in all cultures, he must empirically show that this standard is implicit in every moral judgment which any person is willing to be consistent in affirming. The evidence that such is the case is not, I believe, available. And even were it to be established we should still have to admit that it would be theoretically possible that such should not always be the case. Therefore the belief that there is a standard for conduct the validity of which may be affirmed regardless of what now is, or ever may be, the nature of man is not a belief which can in my opinion be defended.

Now, there are moralists who doubtless would hold that such a conclusion demands that the previous argument be rejected. However, if it is to be rejected, the rejection must rest upon either, or both, of two grounds: first, that the phenomenological analysis of moral experience which has been given is either false in what it has asserted or inadequate because of what it has failed to take into account; or, second, that any such phenomenological analysis, even if it be granted to be on the whole adequate, must be supplemented by another method which is capable of establishing a more ultimate range of moral truths. If moralists should base their objections on the first count, I should consider myself to have been refuted. However, if they were to base their objections on the second, I should demand that they demonstrate by what method they can reach any more ultimate conclusion than has here been obtained, and that they then show how this conclusion relates to the moral experience with which, throughout this book, we have been concerned.

And I cannot forbear from noting that while our final conclusion is "sceptical," in the sense that it holds that there either are or that there may be moral controversies which cannot be resolved, this conclusion is not the only conclusion we have reached which is relevant to the traditional problems of a normative ethics. Before reaching that ultimate impasse, moral controversies were traced through a series of stages at any one of which it was in principle possible to reach an agreement. And if our first two principles of validity are accepted, it is possible to say something (at the least) concerning the actual obligations of men. Not only may we say that it is their obligation to act as their sense of moral obligation dictates, but also that their sense of moral obligation itself stands in need of a dogged exercise of self-criticism on their part. If their sense of obligation is to be able to withstand the critical scrutiny of others, it must be informed by a conscientious appraisal of the facts concerning which they judge, and be capable of being consistently espoused. That which stands in the way of our achieving such a sense of obligation is self-deception. It is self-deception which permits us to twist facts, to pretend to a consistency which we do not have; it is self-deception that, as Butler says, "is a corruption of the whole moral character in its principle."

But, as Butler warns us, "we are all of us influenced by it in some degree." And I am not unmindful that self-deception invades our intellectual no less than our moral life. For this reason I forebear from drawing any explicit conclusions concerning our duties, until what I have said may be tested by what others may have to say concerning its adequacy as an analysis of moral experience. In writing these pages I have felt as did Stendhal when he attempted to understand love:

"Je fais tous les efforts possible pour être *sec*. Je veux imposer silence à mon coeur qui croit avoir beaucoup à dire. Je tremble toujours de n'avoir écrit qu'un soupir, quand je crois avoir noté une vérité."

NOTES

Chapter 1

THE PROBLEM OF METHOD

1. The distinction between normative and descriptive sciences is generally attributed to Wundt's *Ethik,* published in 1885. (Cf. "normatif" in Lalande: *Vocabulaire de la philosophie.*) However, the distinction which is involved (although not the terms "descriptive" and "normative") is clearly stated by Sidgwick in the first edition of his *Methods of Ethics* (1874). After stating the distinction in Sect. 1 of his first chapter he goes on to discuss it further in Sect. 3, utilizing Dugald Stewart's distinction between "the nature of the moral faculty" and "the proper object of moral approbation." In this section Sidgwick attempts to show that it is the second and not the first which is the basic question for ethics. This passage is at best inconclusive, and it is noteworthy that it was dropped (but the same position retained) in the second edition of the work (1877).

2. It is worth noting that Sidgwick was actually unable to carry through his attempt to separate the question of the moral faculty from the question of the proper object of moral approbation. For example, even his contention that "right" is an unanalyzable notion depended upon the acceptance of certain matters of psychological fact (*Methods,* Bk. I, Ch. 3, Sect. 1-3 of the 6th edition). Moore, on the other hand, attempted to treat the problem of analyzability in a purely linguistic manner.

(It is interesting to follow through successive editions those changes which Sidgwick made in the sections cited. Even the title of the chapter is changed from "Reason and Feeling" to "Ethical Judgments." However, my point is, I believe, unaffected thereby.)

3. More recently, those who have been influenced by the analytic method have sometimes been concerned with descriptive problems, and have dealt with questions of psychological fact. (Cf. Frankena's masterful taxonomic study: "Moral Philosophy at Mid-Century," in *The Philosophical Review,* vol. LX [1951], pp. 44-55.) However, they are still generally concerned with problems of moral language, having shifted attention from the analysis of what terms are to be used in constructing an ethical theory to the analysis of the language used in moral controversies. For example, Stevenson (*Ethics and Language,* 1944) clearly represents this shift, while Toulmin (*Examination of the Place of Reason in Ethics,* 1950) is concerned with both problems; neither, however, seeks to analyze moral experience except through its reflection in language.

4. Cf. Green: *Prolegomena to Ethics* (5th ed.), p. 58; Bradley: *Ethical Studies* (2nd ed.), p. 65.

5. Cf. pp. 33-35, 36 f., et pass.

6. For example, in so far as Westermarck represents a psychological approach to ethics, his theory is a clear example of one which places emphasis upon the first question. Mandeville, on the other hand, is almost exclusively concerned with the second. Freudian theory stresses both in approximately equal measure.

7. It is often assumed that one who employs the psychological approach must deny that there is any

valid standard for conduct. The extent to which Bentham and Mill approached ethics from this point of view suggests, though it does not prove (for there may have been mistakes in their arguments), that this generalization is erroneous. (For a partial defense of Mill's "proof" of hedonism, cf. p. 23 f.)

8. However, it is perhaps worth noting that in earlier times, before the rise of a separate empirical science of psychology, the metaphysical approach saw fit to incorporate within itself a discussion of many problems concerning psychological matters of fact which are now being investigated by psychology. If solutions of these problems were relevant to ethics when they were dealt with by Plato, Aristotle, Aquinas, or Spinoza, one might expect them still to be. The rejection of the relevance of an empirical science of psychology ought not then to be based upon the problems with which it deals. Nor ought it to be based (as is often the case) on a rejection of its "method." Rather, the claim must be made that it has not solved (and, because of its method, cannot solve) these problems. And it must furthermore be contended that the metaphysical approach (whether of a theological or a non-theological stamp) is itself better able to solve them. Such a claim is not, in my opinion, one which it is easy to establish. I am therefore inclined to think that an attack on the psychological approach from those who would themselves hold to a metaphysical approach is not a serious threat to the former.

9. For example, note Scheler's emotional apriori.

10. As classical examples of the ways in which psychological inquiry is relevant to the problem of error in moral judgment, I should cite Butler's analysis of self-deception and Scheler's analysis of the influence of *ressentiment*.

11. *Utilitarianism* (Longmans, Green, London, 1885), p. 52 f.

12. It is often contended that we should not even hold that a given man has an obligation to act from a certain motive (or to have a certain sentiment), since it is not within his power to choose to act (or to feel) in this fashion. Here what lies well within the power of man, *qua* man, is not held to be obligatory because it does not lie within the power of *this* man. This may be taken as an *afortiori* proof of our point.

13. Cf. the author's "A Note on 'Anthropomorphism' in Psychology," *Journal of Philosophy*, v. 40 (1943), pp. 246-248.

14. Obvious exceptions are to be found in the Freudian psychology, in a social psychology of "attitudes," and in Gestalt psychology. It is characteristic of all three approaches that their methodologies (though dissimilar in other respects) demand that they take as their point of theoretical departure the data of specifically human experience.

15. One of the clearest examples of this dependence is to be found in Sumner. In my opinion, some of the vagueness in the moral theories of Marx and of Durkheim stems from their failure to link the sociological and the moral by means of an explicit psychological hypothesis. (In popular criticisms of Marx, to be sure, it is often assumed that the psychological mechanism which he postulates is "the economic motive"; this interpretation seems to me to be without foundation.)

16. Cf. the investigations of Duncker: "Ethical Relativity?", in *Mind*, v. 48 (1939), pp. 39-57.

17. It might, of course, also be claimed that any sociological the-

ory presupposes a metaphysical theory, and therefore that a sociological approach to ethics cannot be indendent of the metaphysical approach. However, this claim would seem to me to be more dubious.

18. In using the term "phenomenological" I do not refer to the specific methods of the phenomenological school. I use "phenomenology" to connote any examination of experience or of experienced objects which aims at describing their nature rather than seeking to give an "explanation" of them. The origin of an experience or object, a physiological or physical theory of its characteristics, or a discussion of its ontological status, are thus excluded from phenomenology. What is included is every descriptive investigation of "the phenomenal world," that is, of whatever is directly experienced by me or by others.

19. This is, for example, Sidgwick's definition of ethics. (Cf. *Methods*, 6th ed., p. 1-2.)

20. Bk. VII, 1 (1145b2-7). [Quoted by permission of Oxford Univ. Press.] Cf. Ross: *Foundations of Ethics*, pp. 1-3.

21. Nonetheless it has been suggested by Duncker (*loc. cit.*) that when certain confusions are removed the attempt appears feasible. However, I am by no means convinced that his suggestions are adequate for this purpose. (Cf. Ch. 5.)

22. As examples of a generic approach to value I should cite Spinoza and Perry, though, to be sure, neither follows a strictly phenomenological method in attempting to set up and to validate his theory.

23. Such an examination is also indispensable for those who would attempt to hold that there really are no ultimate disagreements among apparently inconsistent moral judgments. Their thesis of invariance presupposes that they distinguish between "moral judgments" (or "judgments of value") and derivative "objectifications" of these judgments (for example, what Scheler and Hartmann would term "judgments of goods").

24. A noteworthy exception is von Hildebrand's "Sittlichkeit und ethische Werterkenntnis" (*Jahrbuch fuer Philosophie u. Phaenomenologische Forschung*, v. 5), even though his study does not consistently adhere to what I have termed a generic approach.

25. *Ethics*, p. 185 ff.

26. Cf. Broad: "Some of the Main Problems of Ethics" in *Philosophy*, v. 21 (1946), p. 99.

27. Note the still prevalent use of the inadequate twin dichotomies of instrumental-intrinsic and hypothetical-categorical as a means of separating non-moral from moral uses of "good" and of "right" or "ought." (There are many cases in which we use the term "good" in a non-instrumental sense, and "right" or "ought" in a non-hypothetical sense, and yet do not hold that a moral judgment has been made: for example, "it feels good to relax after exercise"; "she owns a good French poodle"; "that is the right answer"; "that picture ought to have another frame.")

28. If one is willing to hold that the common content is merely that both are instances of intrinsic value, and that intrinsic value is in all senses indefinable, this objection would not hold. However, there seems to be considerable dissatisfaction with holding that the common content is merely of this type. There are those who would hold that both propositions contain an implicit assertion that something is "worthy of approval" (Ewing) or that something "ought-to-be" (Urban; Hartmann). However, what is

thereby meant seems always to involve some reference to attitudinal factors; indeed, in the former phrase this reference is explicit, just as it is in those cases in which the common content is identified with the "praiseworthy-blameworthy" dichotomy.

29. This approach might also be termed "situational" or "contextual." However, each of these terms may have connotations for the reader which are not wholly consonant with some of the views which are to follow. I therefore prefer to use the less common designation "a structural approach."

30. The secondary data of a normative study need not, of course, also be normative in character.

31. It will be noted that I do not assume that ethics deals with all normative judgments; what distinguishes moral from non-moral (e.g. aesthetic) normative judgments will occupy us later.

32. It may, however, have often been tacitly assumed that ethics could do something like this. It is, in fact, commonly so supposed by "the man in the street," which accounts (in part) for the contempt in which ethical inquiry is currently held. (It is also interesting to note that definitions of ethics frequently state that it is the aim of ethics to "determine" the valid standard for conduct [cf. Sidgwick: *Methods,* p. 1 and p. 2]. The word "determine" if not ambiguous, is at least ambivalent when used in this connection.)

33. In order not to suggest that I shall attempt to do what I feel cannot be done, I must state that the possibility of such a discrimination does not necessarily imply that there is a single universally valid standard for conduct. As we shall in the end see, the validity of a moral judgment is to be distinguished from its truth.

Chapter 2

DIRECT MORAL JUDGMENTS

1. For the sake of convenience I use the terms "direct moral judgments" and "removed moral judgments" as equivalent to "direct (and removed) judgments of moral rightness and wrongness."

2. One notable exception to this stricture is to be found in von Hildebrand's too little known work, *Die Idee der sittlichen Handlung* (*Jahrbuch fuer Philosophie und Phaenomenologie,* v. 3). Those acquainted with that work will recognize how much the immediately ensuing pages owe to it, even though von Hildebrand does not distinguish between direct and removed moral judgments, and even though his axiological presuppositions are foreign to the method of this work.

3. The distinctions which may be drawn between what is right, what one ought to do, and what is one's duty, seem to me, as they seem to Ross and to Ewing, relatively unimportant (Cf. Ross: *Right and Good,* pp. 3-4; *Foundations,* p. 44; Ewing: *Definition of Good,* pp. 123-125). This is, I believe, especially true when one is dealing with direct moral judgments.

4. It is to be noted that in such cases we are inclined to reject moral praise for our action, often deflecting it by holding that "anyone else would have done the same." When it is pointed out that this is not in fact true (since such reactions depend, in large part, upon the character of the person), we feel that our reaction was "fortunate" rather

than praiseworthy, for the feeling of responsibility was lacking in it. However, we are willing to accept blame when we judge a spontaneous reaction to have been wrong.

5. I exclude a physiological explanation (which, incidentally, is the only appropriate means of explaining reflex action) since we are here solely concerned with what is given in direct experience.

6. This does not imply that the reason need lie in a specific "value-quality"; as we shall see, in a direct moral judgment that which appears as irreducibly "right" also appears as valuable.

7. That this is the case is one of the most universally accepted propositions in ethical theory. Whatever dissenting opinions one may find are explicable by the fact that those who deny it have been concerned with instances in which spontaneous actions are the objects of either removed moral judgments or judgments of moral worth.

8. Those who would claim that every willed action can be denominated as being either morally right or morally wrong are obviously not concerned with our present problem: the phenomenology of direct moral judgments. Rather, their interest lies in holding that there is some moral standard applicable to all voluntary human actions; they would not even be forced to say (and I should assume that it would be implausible to say) that every willed action *should be* accompanied by a direct moral judgment.

9. If this were not the case, the distinction between the categorical (moral) "ought" and the hypothetical (prudential) "ought" would be coterminous with a distinction between actions which have important consequences and actions which do not. Such, I take it, is not the case.

10. E.g., pp. 92-3. I shall not deal with the matter at length since it appears to me that the role played by general rules in direct moral judgments varies widely from individual to individual, as well as from case to case.

11. This has been one of the major factors responsible for the contumely which is evinced by psychologists when the feeling of moral obligation is discussed. If our sense of obligation were indeed a unique type of fact, unrelated to the rest of our behavior, it would be difficult to understand either its origin or its efficacy in psychological terms.

12. The point need not be labored; a few references will suffice to show how widely it is acknowledged. Cf. Kant on duty vs. the holy will; E. von Hartmann: *Die sittliche Bewusstsein*, p. 247 f., on the phenomenon of duty in his discussion of innocence, duty, and virtue; Sidgwick: *Methods*, pp. 34, 35, 217; Scheler: *Der Formalismus*, p. 194; Broad: *Five Types of Ethical Theory*, p. 164; Stoker: *Das Gewissen*, p. 197 f.; and, by implication, Ross: *Foundations*, p. 48 f. (Cf. also James' dictum that duty consists in following the line of greatest resistance (*Principles of Psychology*, v. II, pp. 548-549).

13. If this were not the case, it would seem to me unlikely that Lewin's "topological" psychology, or the use of concepts such as homeostasis to explain behavior, would have even the degree of plausibility which they do have.

14. To appeal to the concept of "introjection," and thus explain the apparent objectivity in genetic terms, is (it appears to me) invalid. The problem is then merely pushed back to the past, and the question of why "introjection" operates in one case and not in another (for

we do not store up all the demands made upon us) becomes, if not insoluble, at least more difficult to handle.

15. If phenomenology is narrowly conceived, the foregoing statement would mark a departure from a phenomenological approach. However, I see no reason why a comparison of cases must be excluded from the phenomenological method. All that is excluded is the attempt to account for what we experience in terms of some factor which cannot be identified as one of the components within that experience. A comparison of instances is one of the most favorable means which we can use to uncover the presence of factors which might otherwise be overlooked. (On what I should exclude from the phenomenological approach, cf. note 18, Ch. 1.)

16. The chief place at which this is to be noted will be found in Ch. 4, in our discussions of the virtues and vices.

17. This is, I believe, assumed by each of them, although in their discussions it is only *moral* fittingness which is explicitly held to be indefinable.

18. *Definition of Good*, p. 133.

19. In this opinion I share the view of Ross (*Foundations*, p. 81 f.) as against Broad (*Five Types*, pp. 218-220).

20. Many strict deontologists have included the envisioned consequences as part of the action itself (cf. Butler's most deontological work: *Dissertation on the Nature of Virtue and Vice*, Sect. 4; also, Whewell: *Elements of Morality*, v. I, Sect. 336, 337, and 447, and Ross: *Right and Good*, p. 21).

21. To the extent to which Ross neglects the future in his disagreement with Broad, I am forced to diverge from his contention. (Cf. note 19.)

22. Broad's neglect of this phenomenological fact is doubtless, in part, what led Ross to reject his analysis.

23. I use the term "quasi-aesthetic experiences" to denote such cases as finding it perceptually bad that a picture hangs crookedly or that a simple figure, such as a circle, contains an irregularity. It appears to me that there are marked phenomenological differences between such experiences and the aesthetic experience proper (cf. note 26 below), though the two types are without doubt analyzable in the same terms.

24. Often in such cases (and sometimes in the case of an incomplete figure) we feel a demand placed *upon us* to correct what is "wrong"; but this reflexive demand depends upon our experiencing a demand *within* the perceived situation.

25. If the parts of the object (or objects in relation to their contexts) set up no demands we do not experience a lack of fittingness; with respect to fittingness these parts appear as indifferent. Thus, on the analogy of other terms, we may distinguish between *un*fittingness and *non*-fittingness: the former is a case of being "misfitting," the latter of being indifferent with respect to fittingness. It is, of course, only with fittingness and unfittingness that we are here concerned.

26. This is the most striking phenomenological distinction between aesthetically good objects and quasi-aesthetic objects which are not "bad." (Cf. note 23.)

27. The type of apparent exception which has just been noted is, however, of importance to a general theory of value if (as I believe) fittingness is also the basis of experienced value.

28. Cf. pp. 50, 53 ff.

29. Cf. Ross' analysis of the cases given by Pickard-Cambridge (*Foundations*, pp. 94-98). It seems to me, however, that in some of these cases we would feel a demand to make some gesture to the promisee in lieu of the fulfilment of the explicit promise. Such a gesture would seem to us to be demanded by the situation which we face. For example, if I have promised to do something with a friend and he becomes ill, I might feel that his illness did not wholly release me from my promise, and might feel that I ought to spend that particular evening with him; or if I became ill and were obviously incapable of fulfilling my promise (for example playing tennis with him), I would feel that I should make restitution to him at some appropriate time. That such other demands should arise out of the fact that I have made a promise which is no longer binding does not, of course, alter Ross' reply to Pickard-Cambridge. It does, however, add to the accuracy of Ross' phenomenological analysis, and does also suggest that moral demands are not to be as atomistically conceived as is the case in Ross' positive theory. (On the last point, cf. pp. 73-78.) (Where Ross cites such other demands—e.g., *Right and Good*, p. 28—he seems to me to interpret them too rigoristically.)

30. On the phenomenon of self-deception, cf. Butler and Scheler.

31. Cf. *Five Types*, pp. 218 ff.

32. Ross, in disagreeing with Broad, approaches this position, holding that the tendency of an act to promote good consequences is "something in virtue of which that act tends to be fitting to the situation" (*Foundations*, p. 81). However, he fails to absorb "utility" wholly within fittingness, for he distinguishes between "fittingness arising from utility and fittingness arising from other sources" presumably from other "*prima facie* obligations"). So far as direct moral judgments are concerned (and, as we shall see, in other cases as well) even this distinction is unnecessary.

33. For their statements, cf. *Five Types*, p. 165, and *Foundations*, p. 53 f. It may also be noted that Ewing's three arguments concerning the distinction between moral obligatoriness and fittingness (*Definition of Good*, p. 133) presuppose that we should only speak of the morally obligatory when dealing with direct moral judgments and only speak of fittingness when speaking of removed moral judgments.

34. Cf. Broad on "optimizing" *vs.* "optimific" acts ("Certain Features in Moore's Ethical Doctrines," in *The Philosophy of G. E. Moore*, ed. by Schilpp, pp. 48 ff.)

35. Cf. Ross: *Foundations*, p. 81, et pass.

36. It is however amusing to note that if the first form of this revised teleological theory were true—i.e. if the relevant value of an action included both the value of its consequences and the value of the motive from which it was done—a peculiar paradox would arise. Unless we were willing to hold that an agent ought to be moved by the value of his own motives (which, I submit, we do not say), an act which an observer might judge to be right (because he *does* set store by the value of the agent's motive) ought to be judged wrong by the agent himself.

The second form of this revised teleology is apparently not open to this objection, although I am inclined to believe that unless it too makes references to motives, the "direct" value of an act is not part of the ground of that act's rightness, but *is* its rightness.

37. Cf. note 20.

38. It appears to me that in *The Right and the Good* Ross' view of the *prima facie* obligations of beneficence and non-maleficence was not really equivalent to his later view, and that these two *prima facie* obligations could be interpreted in such a way as not to be open to my objection.

39. If the promotion of good consequences is taken to be a *prima facie* obligation, as it is by Ross, the second type of case reduces, of course, to the first. We shall, however, deal with it separately, since Broad, among others, maintains that the promotion of good consequences is not an example of the immediate fittingness which underlies *prima facie* obligations.

40. Cf. Ross' summary statement in *Foundations*, p. 320 f.

41. The analogy which Ross draws between physical laws and *prima facie* obligations (both being tendencies which will manifest themselves if nothing intervenes) shows that he is primarily interested in normative generalizations, and has not put forward his theory of *prima facie* obligations in an attempt to give an adequate phenomenological account of our moral judgments. If one were to ask how we cognize the two "tendencies" it would become clear that there is no analogy between them, so far as direct experience is concerned. As we shall later see (pp. 79-80), there is also no analogy between them with respect to their status as constant "tendencies."

42. *Foundations*, p. 321.

43. Cf. *Foundations*, p. 101, and many of his illustrations.

44. Cf. *Right and Good*, p. 46; *Foundations*, p. 85.

45. *Foundations*, p. 84; cf. *Right and Good*, p. 20, p. 28. [Quotation with permission of Oxford Univ. Press.]

46. Ross seems to me to have been led to his atomization of real obligation by his concern to show that the *prima facie* obligations do not merely "appear" to be binding, but are intrinsic non-natural properties of the acts in which they are cognized. (Cf. *Right and Good*, p. 20.)

47. It is by no means certain that this interpretation (and therefore the following criticism) of Ross is correct. In the most explicit passage concerning the problem he says that when we feel justified in acting counter to a *prima facie* obligation we are led to feel "not indeed shame or repentance, but certainly compunction, for acting as we do" (*Right and Good*, p. 28. Quoted by permission of Oxford Univ. Press.) If "compunction" be interpreted as *moral* regret my criticism holds. If it is not so interpreted it is difficult to see the meaning of the analogy which Ross draws between *prima facie* obligations and natural laws (*Right and Good*, p. 28 f.; *Foundations*, p. 86). The matter is certainly one that should not have been neglected, and cannot be neglected by any one who is willing to speak of *prima facie* obligations. (Other relevant passages, not including those which deal with the related problem of "stringency," are: *Right and Good*, p. 33, p. 41, and, perhaps, p. 64; *Foundations*, p. 315.)

48. Cf. note 47.

It will be noted that in dealing with this problem I have been compelled to go beyond our direct moral judgments and discuss removed moral judgments on our own conduct. This has been made necessary by Ross' view that a *prima facie* obligation contains within itself a "tendency" to be binding even after it has been overridden. If we consistently maintain the point of view of a direct moral judgment, it seems to me to be even more clear that the initial claim which we ultimately do not find to be binding does not, at the time at which we make our decision, continue to be felt as placing a moral demand upon us (though we may then *wish* to help the person who would have benefitted from a contrary action).

49. Cf. the preceding analyses. If it were to be insisted that all such cases can be explained in teleological terms, one would have to depart from a phenomenological analysis, and explain them by a genetic psychological theory. Such attempts have been made, but I consider them inadequate.

50. Cf. pp. 54 f., et pass.

51. But when we are confronted by the grief of a stranger we often feel a demand to act for his welfare which is comparable to the demand which we feel to act for the welfare of our own child. In such cases we often cannot push the vision of his suffering out of our minds, and its persistence makes it part of the situation which we confront.

Individuals obviously vary with respect to what they consider to be the scope of the situations which they confront. It may, perhaps, be argued that we *ought* to enlarge our horizons until the promotion of all good consequences is our concern. This is not a point which is here at issue, for my claim merely is that unless we see a good state of affairs as relevant to the situation which we confront we do not feel obliged to act for it.

52. It can, I believe, be explained on the basis of a single assumption, which I shall not attempt to justify within the present book. This assumption is that the experienced value of an entity rests upon its serving as a fitting answer to a demand. If this be true, then a person who apprehends the consequences of an action as good, is aware of this action as providing a fitting answer to demands. In so far as he sees these demands as present in the situation which he himself confronts, an envisioned action which will answer to these demands will not only be an action which promotes good consequences, it will also be felt to be obligatory.

53. For a criticism of the teleological position, cf. pp. 85-87.

54. Those Ideal Utilitarians who have held that the direct as well as the consequential value of an act must be considered in assessing its total value, have in my opinion approached such a position. However, I do not think it legitimate to exclude all causal consequences from the nature of an act. I am therefore not forced to hold that we must consider what they term the "optimific" character of an act in assessing its rightness, and I can hold that no distinction need be drawn between the direct value of an act and its rightness. (Cf. notes 34 and 36, and p. 107 f.)

55. I assume that the reader will not equate the value of an action with the sum of the value of its consequences. If the so-called "direct" value of an action is excluded from consideration, then the translatability proceeds in only one direction: while all moral actions which could be described in value-terms could also be adequately described in the language of obligation, some obligations could not equally well be described in the language of value.

56. Cf. p. 63 ff., on internality of relationship and the phenomenon of demand.

57. E.g., pp. 107-109. The reason for this equivalence has been suggested in note 52.

58. Cf. notes 52 and 49.

59. We may of course also pass judgments of moral worth on our own character, and then use these judgments as the basis for guidance in action.

60. That is to say, we must neither introduce removed judgments of rightness or wrongness, nor distort our direct judgments in the interests of upholding a theory as the traditional teleological position is inclined to do.

61. Cf. note 10 on individual variations regarding the apprehension of general rules.

62. Cf. p. 48 ff., et pass.

63. Cf. p. 82 f.

64. Cf. Sidgwick's classification of the types of "intuitionism" (*Methods*, Bk. I, Ch. 8). He, of course uses "intuitionism" to refer to deontological theories.

Chapter 3

REMOVED MORAL JUDGMENTS

1. As has already been suggested, the deontological tradition draws its chief support from direct moral judgments, while the teleological tradition has been primarily concerned with the interpretation of removed moral judgments. (Cf. p. 51 and p. 72.)

2. If on metaphysical or psychological grounds we hold to a traditional deterministic view, the actions of others should be interpreted to be good or bad, not morally right or morally wrong. In this respect removed moral judgments differ from direct moral judgments, for the feeling of responsibility for one's own action does not seem to disappear for even the most convinced determinist.

3. Conversely, an agent may make a direct moral judgment in cases where no observer makes a removed moral judgment. On the problems which thus arise, cf. p. 189 ff.

4. Cf. pp. 62 f.

5. For example, Prichard: *Duty and Ignorance of Fact*, and Ross: *Foundations*, Ch. 7.

6. This mistake is in part explicable by the fact that teleological theories, since the time of Bentham, have been concerned to find a standard which would be "universal" in its applicability.

7. Cf. p. 100 f.

8. Cf. p. 72 f.

9. "Other things being equal" here refers to the amount of self-sacrifice, effort, generosity, sensitivity to needs, etc. which are involved.

10. In such cases we are not solely involved in judgments of moral worth; we also deem the action to be morally right.

11. Cf. Alexander: *Beauty and Other Forms of Value*, p. 137.

12. On "willed action" cf. pp. 47-50.

13. Of course it may become so *indirectly* by virtue of the fact that we judge that a particular goal-directed act should have been performed.

14. The clearest and most general statement of this type of view is to be found in Broad's discussion of the difference between the optimific and the optimizing act. (Cf. note 34, Ch. 2.)

15. Even Moore, in spite of his doctrine of "organic wholes," treats the value of an act as the sum of isolable elements: there is in such a whole not merely the value which it possesses as a whole, but "the

part of a valuable whole retains exactly the same value when it is, as when it is not, a part of that whole." (*Principia Ethica*, Cambridge Univ. Press, p. 30.)

16. For a fuller justification of this view of specific "intrinsic values," cf. Ch. 4.

17. If this were the case there would be a very significant difference between direct and removed moral judgments.

18. Cf. Joseph's interesting footnote in *Some Problems in Ethics*, p. 50.

19. In my opinion, all that keeps the Ideal Utilitarian from recognizing this fact is that he wishes to keep the actual consequences of an action as part of the ground of its rightness. But this, I have also argued, is a mistake.

20. Overt behavior can also be seen as valuable or disvaluable, fitting or unfitting, from a biological point of view, but with that we are not here concerned.

21. Cf. pp. 100 ff.

22. The reader will recall that I am not here concerned with the problem of why we should feel the situation as incomplete, nor whether all individuals, regardless of their "cultural conditioning," will do so. If any individual failed to find an incompleteness in such a situation he would also fail to see any element of intrinsic value in the performance of a benevolent act: its sole value would lie in its consequences, and no moral judgment would be made.

23. Cf. Ch. 2, p. 63 f.

24. The fact that we feel this situation to be incomplete obviously presupposes some altruistic impulse. The existence or nature of this impulse, or whether it is a universal human impulse, is not our concern. (Cf. note 22.)

25. The question of what would happen to our estimate of value if the agent were not aware of the other's intentions, or were not aware of their wrongness, will be discussed in sect. 4 (Cf. pp. 129, 131.)

26. Cf. pp. 104-105.

27. This would be as true of an Ideal Utilitarian view as it would be of the older view.

28. Cf. the similar finding regarding direct moral judgments, Ch. 2, pp. 90-91.

29. Cf. for example Brandt's two papers in *Ethics*, v. 52 (1941), pp. 41-79, and v. 56 (1946), pp. 106-121.

30. The assumption that if moral judgments are based upon feeling they will differ from person to person, and that if they do not so differ they are based upon reason rather than feeling, is an assumption which I do not believe to be warranted.

31. For a discussion of the indirect and variable influence of affective states on moral judgments, cf. Ch. 5, pp. 207-218.

32. Cf. Pfänder: "Zur Psychologie der Gesinnungen" (*Jahrbuch für Philosophie u. Phaenomenologische Forschung*, v. VI, pt. I, pp. 333-334).

33. I do not of course wish to suggest that all attitudes are purely "for" or purely "against." For example, in the sphere of sexual attraction we may find mixtures of desire and contempt, or desire and hate. It is also widely recognized that two moments may be present in the attitude of awe, and many other examples of such "mixed" attitudes might be given.

34. Cf. Perry: *General Theory of Value*, p. 115, et pass.

35. It is not unusual to contrast "objectless" and "objectified" emotions (cf. Ruckmick: *Psychology of Feeling and Emotion*, p. 66); others speak of this contrast as one of "differentiated" and "undiffer-

entiated" emotion (cf. Stratton in *Feelings and Emotions*: The Wittenberg Symposium [1928], p. 219.)

36. The same point may be made by calling attention to the difference there is between being "seized" by a feeling and responding to something in our feeling. In both cases, of course, the feeling is "ours," but the difference between experiencing irritation when we see a friend being obtuse in grasping a problem and experiencing irritation because we ourselves are thwarted should not be overlooked. Similarly, there is a difference between the satisfaction which I feel because I have achieved a particular goal, and the satisfaction which comes because a chance acquaintance has been heard to state that he admires me.

37. *Treatise*, Bk. III, Pt. I, sec. 2.

38. The concept of the "impartial spectator" is suggestive for an analysis of removed moral judgments, for it calls attention to the fact that some of the affective states which may accompany our judgments are not essential constituents of them. For example, the satisfaction which I may feel in witnessing an enemy perform a wrong act, or in observing my own child perform a right one, is a satisfaction which springs from my relation to the agent, and not from the rightness or wrongness of the act; as such it does not properly belong to my moral judgment. To this fact the concept of "the impartial spectator" calls attention.

39. Cf. Brandt: "Moral Valuation" in *Ethics*, v. 56, pp. 113 ff.

40. I use the term "original" to denote those judgments which reflect our own present experience of objects, rather than those which are based upon the authority of others or upon what our past experience with the same or similar objects has been. (Cf. Westermarck: *Ethical Relativity*, p. 115; Brandt, *op. cit.*, *Ethics*, v. 52, p. 44.)

41. I use this illustration because the adjective "boring" is frequently cited in discussions of our problem (e.g. Perry: *General Theory of Value*, p. 31) and because it can be classed in either of the two groups of evaluative adjectives which Brandt finds to be of most importance in moral judgments (cf. "Moral Valuation," in *Ethics*, v. 56, pp. 106-121.)

42. It is sometimes possible that we are bored without characterizing the lecture as boring: for example, when we know that our boredom arises from "within," that is from subjective factors such as a desire to be elsewhere.

43. It is of course often true that what we take to be the causal ground of our fear is not its actual cause. And it may be that a prior fear may predispose us to see objects as fearful or malignant, as Murray claims (*Journ. of Social Psych.*, v. 4, 1933, pp. 310-329). However, it should be recognized that Murray's experiment dealt with a special type of situation, in which reactions to highly ambiguous materials were called for. Whether his conclusion also holds in real-life situations may be open to question. (It would, of course, seem to hold of psychotic patients, though here again what the patient apprehends in a given situation may possibly (quite apart from fear) be so structured that the materials to which he reacts, like those in Murray's experiment, are isolated from a wider context and are therefore ambiguous.)

Cf. pp. 208-11 for a discussion of the *indirect* effects of emotions on perception.

44. Cf. pp. 212-18.

45. However, as we have noted, the observer views the action as

one which did have an alternative. (Cf. p. 96 f.)

46. Cf. p. 121.

47. In a few cases it may be one of the other selfless attitudes (for example disgust) but it is usually the case that these attitudes are directed toward ourselves, not toward the action which we have done.

48. It is interesting to note that pride and shame only accompany our judgments concerning the actions of other persons if we are closely bound to the person through a sentiment, for example in the case of the actions of our children. (Naturally, remorse is only aroused when we contemplate our own actions.)

49. Cf. Sidgwick's use of the "cool hour" in seeking to determine what is ultimately good (*Methods*, p. 401).

50. That this motive has been operative can be seen in such writers as Samuel Clarke (*Works* [London, 1758], v. 3, p. 616) and E. von Hartmann (*Das sittliche Bewusstsein,* p. 146) who are among the few who make reference to, and utilize, the distinction between direct and removed moral judgments. (Adam Smith's concern with the problem was of course dictated by a quite different approach.)

51. This is not of course true of those traditional theories which have had strong religious orientations, for the problem of choice in relation to conscience and sin have focussed their attention upon motives.

52. Cf. Hutcheson's example: "A slothful, profuse man cannot now discharge his debts, yet as a prior course of prudent economy would have prevented this injury to his creditors, the non-payment is imputable. In these cases, indeed, the unavoidable event or omission . . . shows no present evil affection. But the former negligence . . . argues a prior culpable defect of good inclinations. And 'tis here that the guilt properly lies." (*System of Moral Philosophy*, v. I, p. 230.)

53. Cf. Sidgwick: "No doubt we hold a man responsible for unintended bad consequences of his acts or omissions, when they are such as he might with ordinary care have foreseen; still . . . we admit on reflection that moral blame only attaches to such careless acts or omissions indirectly, in so far as the carelessness is the result of some previous wilful neglect of duty." (*Methods*, p. 201, n. 2.) [Quoted by permission of Macmillan and Co., Ltd.]

54. It is worth noting in this connection that if our judgments of moral worth regarding a specific agent are high, we are less likely to hold fast to any judgment of specific rightness or wrongness which runs counter to the direct judgments which he makes.

(For further discussion of the problems of precedence among the three types of judgment, cf. pp. 169-174, 180 f., 189, 287.)

55. "Repentance does not properly concern what is not in our power; sorrow does." (Montaigne: "Of Repentance," *Essays* [Oxford Univ. Press, 1927] v. II, p. 267.)

56. For want of a better term I use this in the wide sense in which Spinoza used it.

Chapter 4

JUDGMENTS OF MORAL WORTH

1. Cf. p. 92.

2. It is not intended that this criticism should apply to the Aristotelian analysis of the virtues and vices (cf. the following footnote)

nor to traditional hedonistic aretaics.

3. Aristotle's aretaics does not, of course, represent the direct approach which is under discussion. Nor does his approach represent the method which is here to be adopted. Rather, it is a psychological approach which assumes from the outset the materials with which I shall be concerned: it assumes that we already understand and grant that a judgment concerning a virtue or a vice is relative to the situation and to the character of the agent (cf. *Nichomachean Ethics*, 1104b26, et pass.).

4. The justification for treating these two types of judgment separately lies in the fact that we may acknowledge that someone who appears to us to be evil has certain virtues, and that someone who appears to us to be virtuous has certain vices. This fact need not entail that the two types of judgment are unrelated, but it suggests that one is not merely a special case of the other.

5. Other elements of his personality may, of course, have an indirect bearing upon these judgments, since they may influence the forms which his motivation takes. The point is that interests, endowments, sentiments, and temperamental characteristics are not themselves virtues or vices.

6. Any trait of character is, of course, a "dispositional trait" in the philosophic sense in which the term "disposition" is currently used. However, in default of a better term ("attitudes" being even more misleading), I shall use "dispositions" to refer to certain aspects of feeling, contrasting them with actional traits.

7. "Fear even when morbid is not cowardice. That is a label we reserve for something a man does. What passes through his mind is his own affair." C. M. W. Moran: *Anatomy of Courage*, p. 19.

8. It is to be noted that what is sometimes termed "gratitude" is not a character attribute, and therefore not a disposition. For example, a person may be "grateful" toward one person only, and fail to show gratitude in any other instance. Such cases, when they are not confined to a passing, momentary attitude of benevolent affection, are the by-products of a sentiment. Unless a person has a particular attitude toward the fact that a favor has been bestowed, gratitude is not an attribute of his character.

9. Though we may also, and perhaps more effectively, foster this trait by changing his dispositional attitudes, for, as we shall see, there is a relation between dispositions and actional traits.

10. It might be thought that only those actional traits which are grounded in a morally worthy disposition represent traits which themselves have moral worth. (For example, it might be thought that courage is only judged a virtue when it is connected with a particular type of disposition, and does not spring from combativeness or self-interest, or the like.) However, as we shall see, such is not the case.

11. Cf. pp. 158 f., 161 f.

12. Cf. Ch. 3, Sect. ii.

13. Cf. Julien Sorel's duel; also Browning: *The Glove*.

14. Hartmann in his otherwise unexceptionable and eloquent pages on courage fails to see this point. In distinguishing between courage and foolhardiness he says: "We may therefore morally condemn the object and still morally admire the high spirit which is devoted to it. This independence of its object has no connection with that caricature of bravery, impetuous fool-

hardiness, the gambling with danger (which can become mere delight in excitement). On the one hand, there is genuine bravery; and, although the object be a bad one, yet subjectively, faith in it is the presupposition of the commitment. On the other hand, foolhardiness has only an outward resemblance to it. In it the principal thing is lacking, the felt seriousness of the commitment and the seriousness, although only presumed, of the object in view. Nothing but the deliberate entering into the danger of the project, a staking one's life upon it—which is reasonable only if the value of the project is more precious than one's own life—is genuine fortitude." (*Ethics,* v. II, p. 245 f.) [Quoted by permission of Macmillan and Co., Ltd.] To this the answer is: A courageous act need not be reasonable (nor need it be morally justifiable) in order to be an example of courage.

15. Cf. Sharp's illustrations, *Ethics,* pp. 155-161, and p. 325.

16. It will be noted that the deficiency of courage is cowardice, but the excess of prudence is timorousness. Cowardice and timorousness are not identical, in spite of the part which "fear" plays in both, for the structure of the fear is different.

17. On personality and character, cf. p. 141.

18. What is here said is of course true of the dispositional as well as the actional virtues and vices—and for the same reasons.

19. Cf. Augustine: *The City of God,* X, 30.

20. For a criticism of Ideal Utilitarianism based upon this point, cf. p. 72 f.

21. Cf. pp. 287 ff.

22. Due to the fact that any dispositional attribute will be the source of certain types of action, to each of the dispositional virtues and vices there will correspond an actional trait which will also be designated as a virtue or vice. (Cf. the case of generosity, cited on p. 143.)

23. Cf. pp. 161 ff.

24. Cf. pp. 142 f.

25. In dealing with the actional virtues and vices it was essential to avoid relying upon a dirct approach. Now, having attempted to establish my general position, I shall for the sake of brevity in this section forego a general discussion and deal with the problem by analyzing specific examples.

26. Cf. Adam Smith: *Theory of Moral Sentiments,* Pt. II, Sec. II, Ch. 3 (Bohn Ed. pp. 129-130).

27. On the difference between cruelty and callousness, cf. p. 164 f.

28. Cf. the analyses given in Ch. 3, Sec. 2.

29. If it be objected that gratitude may be purely "impulsive," I should admit this fact, but would claim that virtues and vices may in some cases be admitted to be purely impulsive and yet be acknowledged to be the objects of judgments of moral worth.

30. Hartmann rightly points out that the disposition connected with one's relation to other persons is modesty, although in common language we also speak of this as an example of humility. (Cf. *Ethics,* v. II, p. 300 and p. 298 f.)

31. As we have seen, the actional trait of "generosity," when it is not based upon this disposition, may be based upon a tendency toward self-aggrandizement.

32. This is a phrase used in a wholly different context by Ducasse. (Cf. *Philosophy of Art,* pp. 139 ff.)

33. The limitations of sympathy are well-known: sympathy, of itself, does not fully answer the demands which the suffering of an-

other involves; we must also act to relieve his suffering. However, unless we feel sympathy we will not feel the need for such action.

34. I borrow this term from Laird: *The Idea of Value*, pp. 234 ff.

35. What is here said is not applicable to Hume, but is applicable to the hedonism of, say, Bentham or Mill.

36. Cf. Kant: *Fundamental Principles of the Metaphysic of Morals*, Sect. I.

37. At best, action consistently in accord with what we take to be objective moral demands is a convenient sign that a man is virtuous: it would be rare chance that a man should always act rightly unless he either felt these demands and acted in accordance with them, or possessed such excellences of character that he could act rightly without feeling bound by duty. But even this is merely a convenient sign, and not infallible. A man lacking in virtue might out of self-interest always act as our moral judgments demand that he should. (It is no accident that Bentham, who represents a complete denial of significance to virtue, should have laid the stress which he did upon sanctions.)

38. A clear statement of the additive conception is given by Ross when he says: "A character is a larger and grander bearer of moral goodness than any single manifestation of character—whether it be an action, a desire, or an emotion—can be. But if character is the grandest bearer of moral value, it is also true that we can build up our conception of an ideal character only by considering first the various elements, the various interests that would compose it, and by adding that in the ideal character these various interests would be present with intensities proportioned to their goodness." *Foundations*, p. 293. [Quoted by permission of Oxford Univ. Press.] (It must be noted that in his subsequent consideration of morally good elements of character Ross includes "conscientiousness" as one among others.)

39. Cf. pp. 177 ff.

40. Cf. Ross: *Right and Good*, pp. 121-123.

41. Cf. Ch. 3, pp. 130-132.

42. Cf. above, p. 141.

43. Ch. 5, Sect. i.

CHAPTER 5

THE SOURCES OF MORAL CONTROVERSIES

1. It is here that I believe Stevenson's otherwise painstaking efforts to elucidate moral disputes may be said to fail: his original starting point precludes any solution of the normative issue other than that which he finally gives. His reasons for adopting this starting point are, I believe, insufficient, unless one includes among them the conviction that this solution of the normative issue is the only tenable one.

2. Cf. Duncker's use of Alec Waugh's statement: "the ethics of cribbing . . . are based entirely on the assumption that a success in form is of inconsiderable importance, it is permissible for a boy to crib in order to save his energies for worthier causes." (Duncker: "Ethical Relativity?" in *Mind*, v. 48 [1939], p. 45 f.)

3. Cf. Ch. 6, p. 295 f.

4. Cf. pp. 180-181.

5. Cf. note 40, below.

6. Cf. the distinction between disparities and disagreements, pp. 186-188.

7. Cf. pp. 295 ff.

8. Therefore, if one accepted the

more obvious definition of the difference between disparities and disagreements (cf. p. 186 f.), one could not conclusively say that any disagreements in fact exist (cf. p. 296).

9. Cf. Waugh, as cited by Duncker. (Note 2, above.)

10. This is analogous to the transformation of a divergence in moral judgment into a disagreement between moral judgments (cf. pp. 191 f. and 231 f.)

11. In my opinion, many of the disparities between moral judgments made in differing societies actually turn upon the question of what remote consequences a given act is believed to have.

12. Cf. note 36, Ch. 2.

13. Cf. Chapter 6.

14. E.g., *Ethical Relativity*, pp. 184 ff.

15. "Ethical Relativity?" in *Mind*, v. 48 (1939), pp. 39-57.

16. Therefore, if such disagreements exist, they differ from the disagreements thus far noted, and represent those disagreements which I have admitted (p. 192 f.) to be difficult to demonstrate. It will be easier to show that they do in all likelihood exist after we have examined the role played by emotions, sentiments, and "personality" in moral controversies.

17. Cf. above, p. 119 f.

18. If one accepted the more obvious distinction between disparities and disagreements instead of the distinction I have given, all three types of case would, by definition, be instances of disparities.

19. I believe that this will be universally acknowledged by moralists. *Why* it is acknowledged will only become clear when, in the next Chapter, I deal with the principles of validity for moral judgments.

20. I say "presumably" since a demonstration that this occurs, and that it is not simply a form of the first type, would probably involve psychological hypotheses as well as phenomenological description. I consider it here as a distinct type (which I am inclined to believe it is), because it has had an influence upon ethical theorizing, and has often been held to give rise to moral disagreements, rather than only being a source of disparities between moral judgments.

21. It might be denied that it is possible to settle the question of what is the "real" nature of a situation when two people are emotionally affected by it in different ways. However, this would merely be to say that some disparities between moral judgments cannot be resolved; it would not prove that these cases exemplify moral disagreements.

22. I am not here concerned with the problem of empathy in relation to the apprehension of anything other than human feelings; nor do I wish to be understood as subscribing to any of the supposed explanations of how empathy takes place. I am using the term to refer to a genuine phenomenon in human experience, and not as an explanatory concept.

23. I do not myself assume that prior experience of an emotion is a necessary condition for empathizing it, though this is a view often held.

24. Cf. Ch. 4, p. 168.

25. I wish to repeat (cf. note 20 above) that the second type of case may actually be reducible to the first. However, I am inclined to believe, on both phenomenological and psychological grounds, that a restructuring of a situation because of emotional valences is not identical with the confusing or the distracting roles which emotions can play.

26. I find particular difficulty in the relation which is assumed to exist between perception and the

emotions. In the first place, the theory demands that we "project" our feelings into objects in all of those cases in which an emotional quality really appears as localized in an object. The epistemological arguments which have been held to prove that this *must* occur do not seem to me to be sound; the psychological experiments which are usually held to prove that it *does* occur seem to me to be ambiguous; and no theory has ever adequately explained *how* it can occur. In the second place, the theory, having stripped the object of precisely those qualities which seem to be connected with the emotions, has difficulty in explaining the origin of these emotions. If consistently carried through, it would be forced to deny that there are perceptual factors which (in some cases at least) are responsible for arousing the emotions felt. All emotional experience would then have to be explained in terms of, say, pleasure-pain conditioning. On such a view it seems to me to be impossible adequately to interpret, or to explain, emotional experiences.

That my doubts are warranted cannot be demonstrated here. My objections to this theory are only relevant in so far as they serve to suggest that in interpreting the nature of the emotions one cannot in my opinion neglect qualities which an object is apprehended as having.

27. For the sake of simplicity in exposition I shall hereafter mention merely those cases in which judgments of rightness or wrongness are made. However, what is said will also be applicable to judgments of moral worth.

28. It is doubtful whether *all* tied emotions provide instances of states which become commingled with moral judgments. For example, fear may never be of this sort. However, such questions (along with questions such as why more of these emotions represent "negative" rather than "positive" attitudes) belong to the detailed analyses which we must here forego.

29. The only point at which we can assume a necessary connection between the respective judgments and the respective emotions of two persons is that when they make diametrically opposed moral judgments their emotions will not be the same. This follows from the fact that one of the opposed moral judgments will involve a pro-attitude and the other will not; since emotions always contain a similar vectorial factor, the emotions aroused will not be the same.

30. A secondary reason is surely to be found in the fact that the term "emotion" is—as I have pointed out—so frequently used in an extremely wide and loose sense.

31. The most comprehensive and suggestive attempt to treat of these problems is surely the now neglected work of Alexander F. Shand: *The Foundations of Character.*

32. Cf. Stendhal's analysis of "crystallization" in the growth of love (*De l'amour*).

33. Cf. Duncker, "Experimental Modification of Children's Food Preferences Through Social Suggestion," in *Journal of Abnormal and Social Psychology*, v. 33 (1938), pp. 489-507. Cf. also radio advertising of breakfast foods.

34. Whether the first object of our sentiments is a father-image, as some would hold, is a matter of indifference: we are here dealing with the phenomenology of sentiments, not with hypotheses (genuine or fanciful) designed to explain them.

35. There is, so far as I can see, no reason to deny that the object of a sentiment can be one's self.

However, it is almost certain that such a sentiment manifests forms which are in some ways different from those manifested by other sentiments.

36. Cf. p. 141.

37. On the direct influence which does not affect content, cf. p. 230 f.

38. This type of theory is usually based upon hypotheses drawn from surveys of other areas of experience. It seems to me doubtful whether these hypotheses have been adequately demonstrated in those other areas, and therefore doubtful that one should attempt to transfer them to the moral field.

39. The fact that they *ever* converge would itself demand supplementary explanation—probably in cultural terms. However, the cultural explanations which are usually given frequently tend to conflict with the psychological explanations which they are designed to support.

40. It is in such factors that we may perhaps seek for the explanation of the differences in emphasis on judgments of rightness and wrongness and judgments of moral worth, which were referred to above (p. 189).

41. The existence of *some* disagreements of this sort would not prove an ultimate heterogeneity of moral experience if one could show that these disagreements arose out of the influence of emotions, sentiments, or the like, upon these particular judgments. Upon reflection, we recognize such influences as operative upon some of our own judgments, and their presence in the judgments of others suggests that our moral experience is similar to theirs, rather than supporting the thesis that there is a difference between what we and they take to be the nature of right and wrong, praiseworthy and blameworthy.

Chapter 6

THE RESOLUTION OF MORAL CONTROVERSIES

1. However, it appears to me that there is at the present time a growing interest in the subject, and that this interest springs in large measure from a concern with the problems which Stevenson's theory has raised.

2. Cf. pp. 187, 193, et pass.

3. Cf. below, p. 243. It may also be pointed out that an actual agreement emerging from a controversy does not prove that the original point of controversy has been solved: it is as relevant to ask in the case of a moral controversy as it is in the case of a mathematical or theoretical controversy by what means one or the other party was led to accept the agreement which emerged. Cf. Tomas' discussion of Stevenson ("Ethical Disagreements and the Emotive Theory of Values," in *Mind*, v. 60 [1951] pp. 205-222.)

4. Cf. below, p. 247 f.

5. Sharp is among the few moralists who explicitly raise the problem of validity regarding moral judgments (though he does so in an exceedingly brief form); it is worth noting that his view of what constitutes an invalid, as distinct from a valid, moral judgment also seems ultimately to turn on the real source of the judgment which is made. (Cf. *Ethics*, p. 111.)

6. Cf. p. 240 f.

7. I in fact believe that the principles of moral judgment which I shall state parallel some of the principles of factual judgments. However, as I shall state them, the principles specifically applicable to moral judgments are not to be con-

sidered as identical with the principles of factual judgments.

8. Some uses to which C. L. Stevenson's theory of "persuasive definitions" might be put, when applied to matters of fact, seem to me to constitute possible exceptions.

9. As we have seen, not every non-moral aspect of an action—e.g., its ultimate causal consequences—is relevant to the moral judgments which are made concerning this action. With this problem we have already dealt (cf. pp. 62 ff., 98 100 ff.); it will therefore be understood that only a true cognition of the morally relevant aspects of an action are necessary if a moral judgment is to be valid.

10. Cf. Mandeville's analysis of the origin of moral terms.

11. Note, for example, Sharp's discussion of the meaning of "right." (*Ethics*, Ch. 7.)

12. For the discussion of the element of universality, cf. Sect. ii, especially pp. 271, 275 ff.

13. To be sure, when we find that considerations of self have been unduly neglected we do not censure the person to the same degree as when an interest in self is the distorting factor: the attribute of character which leads to the first we consider a virtue, that which leads to the second a vice. However, we do not consider either judgment to be valid, and would equally reject both in attempting to answer what it would be right for a person in this situation to do.

14. The same analysis applies, of course, to other emotions.

15. In fact it is probably no accident that those theories which place most emphasis on this ideal are the theories which hold that moral judgments rest on an emotional rather than a cognitive basis. Not only Adam Smith but Westermarck comes immediately to mind in this connection. (Cf. *Origin and Development of Moral Ideas*, v. I, pp. 101-104; *Ethical Relativity*, Ch. IV.)

16. "Ethical Absolutism and the Ideal Observer," in *Philosophy and Phenomenological Research*, v. 12, pp. 317-345. I cannot agree with Firth that his formulation constitutes a definition of the meaning of "right," though it is extensionally equivalent to "right." The root of my difficulty is (I believe) that Firth is concerned to formulate a definition of what "really" is right, as contrasted with what is only "apparently" right, and I do not think it legitimate to provide a definition of one of these concepts which is not also relevant to the other. Now, if "real" rightness is that which would be approved by the ideal observer, what becomes of "apparent" rightness? Is it that which would be *thought to be* something which would be approved by the ideal observer, or is it that which would be (or is) approved by some observer other than the ideal observer? The first interpretation, depending as it does upon "independent-of-fact conditionals" (p. 323), would leave us as far as ever from saying anything significant about the specific characteristics possessed in common by all things which we in fact denominate as "right"; the second interpretation would seem to me to be inconsistent with our meaning when we denominate anything as right. Thus, while I should not deny that when we hold something to be right we do think that "an ideal observer" would approve of it, this formulation is not, I believe, an adequate definition of rightness. (And I also believe that the sole reason why Firth's formulation and our idea of what "really" is right are extensionally equivalent is that the char-

acteristics of the ideal observer which Firth specifies represent the principles of validity which we use in assessing moral judgments.)

17. Cf. the first two of Firth's criteria of the ideal observer: omniscience and omnipercipience.

18. The attribute of consistency, which Firth rightly includes, pertains to the second of our principles of moral judgment: universality.

19. *The Right and the Good*, p. 121 f.

20. Ross, *loc cit.* [Quoted by permission of Oxford Univ. Press.]

21. In the case of Ross no qualification of this statement is needed, since he holds that moral predicates are not only "consequential," but are "toti-resultant" properties—i.e. depend upon the whole nature of that which possesses them (*loc. cit.* p. 122). For those who would reject this view we need only qualify the statement to say that a moral judgment will only be valid if he who makes it has truly apprehended those particular non-moral characteristics of an object upon which its moral characteristics rests. (This qualification does not fail to conform to the principle of the primacy of the facts since that principle is so stated as to apply only to non-moral characteristics which are morally relevant.)

22. The cognitive theorists here referred to are, of course, those who hold a *non-naturalistic* cognitive theory. The sense attached to "valid" and "invalid" in the debates between these two non-naturalistic schools seems to me always to involve the question of whether moral propositions may be claimed to be either *true* or *false*: the question of their validity is not generally raised.

23. Even if it is true that affective or attitudinal factors may causally affect our beliefs, our attempts at a justification of a moral judgment proceed on the basis of what we experience the nature of the object to be.

24. I am here, of course, speaking from a strictly phenomenological point of view. Moore's similar argument (e.g., *Ethics*, pp. 100 ff.) was designed to prove that moral assertions must be interpreted as being either "really" true or "really" false. That argument lacked cogency. However, the relativist's answer to Moore would not touch the point which I am here making. So far as I can see, even the relativist has no escape from admitting that the existence of moral controversies presupposes the fact that individuals believe that their moral assertions are true, and are not to be interpreted as being merely expressions of what appears to be true when an action is regarded from a particular point of view. (It cannot, for example, be said that moral controversies would still arise since there would still be a conflict in attitudes: a conflict in attitudes is not a moral controversy, but only becomes one when we argue which attitude ought to be adopted.)

25. Cf. Firth's definition of ethical relativism: "Ethical Absolutism and the Ideal Observer," in *Philosophy and Phenomenological Research*, vol. XII (1952), pp. 318 f.

26. I am here of course dealing only with what I have previously termed "genuine" moral judgments, excluding lies and other statements which appear to express moral judgments but which are made for other purposes. (Cf. p. 247 f.)

27. Other examples would be changes in judgment concerning the praiseworthiness of a trait of character or of a person, or shifts in

the relative praiseworthiness of specific traits of character.

28. That is, one which concerns not mere matters of fact, but the question of which of two ways of structuralizing the situation is morally more adequate (cf. above, pp. 187, 193, et pass.).

29. I probably need not point out again that the acceptance of the principle of the primacy of the facts is sufficient to solve the moral issues which are involved in a simple disparity.

30. To use the criterion of consistency with other moral assertions concerning the same action would obviously be question-begging. It would be tantamount to deciding in terms of the frequency with which we had formed the same judgment on this particular action or else in terms of the number of persons who had made the same judgment. I do not doubt that both appeals (and especially the latter) may be psychologically compelling, but they are a methodologically indefensible means of reaching a normative conclusion.

31. Cf. Firth, *loc. cit.*, p. 342. As will be seen, some of what follows is very close to Firth's analysis of consistency, and to parts of his analysis of impartiality. However, the point which our analysis reaches is not mentioned by Firth.

32. The confidence with which most hedonistic utilitarians dismiss those judgments which seem to support a deontological position springs from a failure to see the question-begging character of this form of the appeal to consistency. Their failure in this respect was, I believe, in large measure due to their view that the function of ethical theory was to legislate for the moral consciousness.

33. Similarly, I would have to introduce further premises in order to deduce whether or not I was morally blameworthy for having made the judgment which I did.

34. So far as my own experience goes, I also find that I always have a tendency to sympathize with my own past moral judgments, no matter how mistaken I now take them to have been. Whether this would also be the case with those who are among "the twice-born" is certainly open to doubt.

35. I venture to suggest that in *non*-moral judgments a similar situation obtains. The grounds on which we can justify a rejection of a specific empirical judgment must concern the principles through which we attempt to establish veridical assertions, not the specific content of these assertions. That "coherence" (in some sense of that term) is one aspect of such principles explains, I believe, why the coherence theory of truth is (in various forms) so frequently maintained; that there are, however, other aspects to these principles would explain why a pure coherence theory (even as the test of truth) has rarely appeared to be wholly satisfactory.

36. It is for this reason that when Descartes gives us his second maxim for conduct (*Discours,* III) we feel that he fails to describe a real moral judgment. His failure in this respect follows, of course, from the nature of his first maxim. It is only when we reach the third maxim that we find (I should say) that he is speaking in terms of his own moral consciousness.

37. On the *indirect* influence of preference upon moral judgments, cf. the discussions of emotions in Chap. 5.

38. In those cases in which it seems to do so, what we actually do is to shift our attention so that we are not focussing on the same

aspect of the object which we had previously seen. Thus we can in some cases at least reduce the discrepancy in the Muller-Lyer illusion by trying to neglect the arrows in order to fixate merely the lengths of the connecting lines, or we can in induced movement (or other cases of movement) look for alternative perceptual cues. But such cases act on our perception "indirectly" in the sense that they undermine our conviction by shifting our attention to a new appearance.

39. Cf. above, p. 190 f.

40. It will be noted that, using the terms in this sense, second-order judgments do not ever presuppose judgments of moral worth. However, there are some analogues to these two orders of judgment among our judgments of moral worth. With their nature I feel it unnecessary to deal.

41. I see no evidence which would lead us to assume that it would rest upon a denial of the principle of the primacy of the facts.

42. Cf. the cases of simple disparities given in Sect. ii of Ch. 5.

43. For examples of disparities arising in this way, cf. pp. 208 ff. and pp. 219 ff.

44. However, I am more inclined to believe that each rests upon complementary aspects of a single more basic characteristic of human experience, and that this more basic characteristic is also the source of analogous principles in the field of non-moral cognition.

45. It is, I believe, often the case that when we suspect that a distortion of facts has been introduced by the presence of an emotion or a sentiment we do not appeal to the principle of universality but to its non-moral analogue: i.e., we attempt to establish the distorting effect of the emotion or sentiment upon the person's apprehension of the facts in the case. An examination of such cases would, of course, lead us into further problems, which I wish to avoid. I have only wished to claim that it is *sometimes* the case that we use the principle of the universality of valid moral judgments to undercut a person's confidence that his judgment was actually based upon a correct appraisal of the facts being judged.

46. I see no reason why there should not be this difference between removed moral judgments and other moral judgments. Even from a strictly phenomenological point of view, the role of "responsiveness" is different in direct and in removed moral judgments: in the one case the vectors issue from the contemplated object against me; in the other they are wholly embedded within the phenomenal properties of that which is judged. And, if I am not mistaken, it is also true that even from a phenomenological point of view an element of "responsiveness" is present in our experience when we make judgments of moral worth.

47. On these two points, cf. pp. 198 f., 202 f., et pass.

48. And it may become doubly apparent when we witness the person protesting too much concerning the truth of his assertion, and then find that in future cases he carefully avoids judging in the same manner (and may even "overcompensate").

49. Cf. pp. 230 f.

50. In other cases these principles are used in a complementary fashion; I believe that it is only in this type of case that we use them jointly.

51. This conviction is, I believe, generally held. It seems to me to be undeniable unless one can satisfactorily show that "the moral emotions" constitute a species of

emotion distinct from non-moral emotions. (Cf. pp. 214 ff.) If that were the case, then one might hold that the former serve as the exclusive basis for moral "cognition," and there would then be no reason for denying that strength of emotion is concomitant with degree of moral value. However, I know of no moralist who has ever wished to maintain this position without qualification.

52. Cf. above, p. 302.

53. Cf. p. 300.

54. If it be answered that the defense need not be empirical (and it is not for Hartmann) our same old methodological problems recur.

55. It is possible that they do, but difficult to establish, for any such ultimate difference between persons may well be correlated with differences in their cognition of the non-moral aspects of that which they judge, and thus be a case of a moral disparity. (Cf. p. 193 and p. 296.)

INDEX OF NAMES

INDEX OF SUBJECTS